The Truth about Nature

The publisher and the University of California Press Foundation gratefully acknowledge the generous support of the Ralph and Shirley Shapiro Endowment Fund in Environmental Studies.

The Truth about Nature

*Environmentalism in the Era of Post-truth
Politics and Platform Capitalism*

Bram Büscher

UNIVERSITY OF CALIFORNIA PRESS

The publication of this book was supported through a
financial contribution by the Netherlands Organisation
for Scientific Research, NWO (Veni grant, Dossier
number 451-11-010).

University of California Press
Oakland, California

Library of Congress Cataloging-in-Publication Data

Names: Büscher, Bram, 1977– author.
Title: The truth about nature : environmentalism in the
   era of post-truth politics and platform capitalism /
   Bram Büscher.
Description: Oakland, California : University of
   California Press, [2021] | Includes bibliographical
   references and index.
Identifiers: LCCN 2020021307 (print) |
   LCCN 2020021308 (ebook) | ISBN 9780520371446
   (cloth) | ISBN 9780520371453 (paperback) |
   ISBN 9780520976153 (epub)
Subjects: LCSH: Environmentalism—Political
   aspects. | Wildlife conservation—Africa, Southern. |
   Conservation of natural resources—Political aspects. |
   Environmental protection—Political aspects.
Classification: LCC JA75.8 .B83 2021 (print) |
   LCC JA75.8 (ebook) | DDC 363.7—dc23
LC record available at https://lccn.loc.gov/2020021307
LC ebook record available at https://lccn.loc.gov/2020021308

Manufactured in the United States of America

30 29 28 27 26 25 24 23 22 21
10 9 8 7 6 5 4 3 2 1

To Arana and her generation

Contents

Preface and Acknowledgments   *ix*

Introduction: The Truth about Nature?   *1*

PART ONE. (META)THEORETICAL BEARINGS

1. Truth Tensions   *13*

PART TWO. THE POLITICAL ECONOMY
OF PLATFORMS, POST-TRUTH, AND POWER

2. Sharing Truths and Natures   *35*

3. Between Platforms, Post-truth, and Power   *57*

PART THREE. ENVIRONMENTALISM 2.0

4. Conservation 2.0: The Politics of Cocreation   *81*

5. Elephant 2.0: The Politics of Platforms   *105*

6. Kruger 2.0: The Politics of Distinction   *123*

7. Rhino 2.0: The Politics of Hysteria   *146*

Conclusion: Speaking Truth to Power   *167*

Notes   *183*

Bibliography   *215*

Index   *231*

Preface and Acknowledgments

How to search for something as elusive as "truth" in an age of deeply troubling forms of post-truth politics? And how to do so in relation to an equally troubling ecological crisis? Is this at all relevant or possible in this day and age? With hindsight I can say that a large part of the journey that led to this book was spent mulling over these questions. At first this did not concern post-truth or platform capitalism. The beginning of the journey in 2010 simply involved a curiosity about new online media and how these might influence environmentalism and human-nature relations. The rather straightforward hunch that led to a grant supporting the research was that these new trends were likely to affect environmentalism quite a bit. Little did I realize how big an understatement this proved to be.

As I dug into the research and started spending (even) more time online, my attention gradually shifted from online environmental discourses and images to the power dynamics behind new media platforms. The larger truth was that these different sides could (and should) not be separated. Yet it also meant that the challenges of the research multiplied rapidly. No longer content to limit the study to how online natures related to offline natures, I now also wanted to tie these into the power structures behind online platforms. And as these were changing extremely rapidly, it was hard to keep the project together. Let alone to work it into a larger storyline and argumentation that could intervene productively into contemporary debates on swiftly escalating environmental crises.

Basically, this new and expanded aim of the research meant working on and connecting three levels: the level of everyday environmental politics, the more structural level of political economy and the level of (meta)theory or epistemology, and how all these and their relations are changing due to the rise of new media and online platforms. I was and am still convinced that connecting these levels is necessary to come to a holistic understanding of contemporary socio-environmental realities. At the same time, this was clearly a lot to handle. Around 2015–2016, it even felt as though the project was starting to succumb to the centrifugal forces unleashed by the empirical and intellectual demands of these various levels. Two developments hindered the project from collapsing altogether.

The first was the emergence of "platform capitalism"—and later "surveillance capitalism"—to illuminate the workings of the political economy of online platforms. The thinkers that blazed this trail to a theoretical breakthrough, especially Nick Srnicek and Shoshana Zuboff, provided conceptual clarity to this emerging political economy and so enabled me to organize the crucial intermediate level in my developing intellectual edifice. The present work, therefore, quite literally stands on their (and others') earlier, pioneering efforts, showing once again how the possibility for academic insight is innately tied to the common and the collective.

The second was the emergence of the concept of post-truth to designate the troubling political earthquakes of 2016, in combination with a realization that contemporary social theory had few explanations for, let alone defenses against, this development. It started dawning on me that my project could contribute to both: to help understand the emergence of post-truth (in general and specifically in relation to the environmental crisis) and to aid the collective intellectual endeavor to build defenses against it. To do so, I needed to not only develop a novel understanding of post-truth, but also to start searching for truth itself. Against dominant theoretical currents, I came to the conclusion that a genuine and meaningful search for truth—which is different from any expectation of its ultimate attainment—is *the* critical intellectual defense line against debilitating post-truth politics. I also became convinced that it is the basis for any effective environmental politics going forward.

The details of what all this entails are explained in ensuing chapters and start making sense through the narrative that binds them. By definition, this cannot be a settled or completed narrative. It is, rather, a journey where beginning and end are but a pretense of overcoming what this book ultimately is: a static snapshot of the dynamic current moment in which we live. It is therefore fitting to conclude this preface by emphasizing that the book itself should be approached as a journey: crossing diverse epistemological, theoretical, empirical, and thematic terrains that together form an open-ended whole that must necessarily trigger further journeys. Only this (pace Hannah Arendt) leads to *understanding*, the opposite of post-truth. It is my hope and conviction that this type of understanding can help build the post-capitalist platforms we need to confront the troubling socio-ecological crises that beset our common world.

Along the path of researching and writing this book, I accumulated many intellectual, inspirational, and material debts, both to the common and the collective and to many specific individuals and communities that nourished and supported me along the way. Many thanks to: David Bunn, Xolani Tembu, Wayne Twine, and all at Wits Rural Facility, which I was fortunate to call home for many months during the research; Louise Swemmer, Nedret Saidova, Rina and Harry Biggs, Marna Herbst, Markus Hofmeyr, Xolani Nicholas Funda, Sam Ferreira, and all at South African National Parks; Freddy Mathabela, Risimati Chauke, and Velly Victoria Ndlovu, who helped implement a large survey at three Kruger National Parks gates in April 2014, and all at Ploughback to the Communities; Malcolm and Eideen Draper, Jenny Renne, Monique and Heidi, and all my friends and colleagues in KwaZulu Natal; Mokganedi Ntana and colleagues in Kasane; my dear friends in Gauteng, including Thea, Sean, Rob, Pam, Sonja, Neels, Gerhard, Marina, Bafana, Marloes, and Shane; and all others who supported field research in South Africa, the Netherlands, and the United States.

I am grateful for institutional support from the Institute of Social Studies, Erasmus University, where I started the project. I was relieved of most of my teaching duties in the last years of my tenure there, which allowed me to think, reflect, do research and write. Many thanks to my former colleagues Murat Arsel, Sharmini Bisessar-Selvarajah, Max Spoor, Lorenzo Pellegrini, Wendy Harcourt, Jun Borras, Andrew Fischer, Julien-François Gerber, Wil Hout, Roy Huijsmans, Paul Huber, and others for their collegiality and friendship.

I hugely benefitted from a two-month appointment as a Van Zyl Slabbert visiting professor at the Department of Politics and the Department of Sociology at the University of Cape Town from April to June 2017. This appointment came at a crucial time in the development of the manuscript, during which I was able to (re)write large parts of it and steer the whole endeavor in the direction of what is was ultimately to become. Special thanks to my good friends Frank Matose and Maano Ramutsindela for making this possible and the in-depth discussions.

I am also most grateful for the long-standing and continuing institutional support from the University of Johannesburg (UJ) and Stellenbosch University. At UJ, I have been connected to the Department of Geography, Environmental Management, and Energy Studies for over a decade now, and I thank Clare Kelso, Gijsbert Hoogendoorn, and other colleagues for their support, hospitality, and enduring friendship. At Stellenbosch University, I thank Cherryl Walker, Michela Marcatelli, and colleagues at the Department of Sociology and Social Anthropology for support, friendship, and hosting fantastic Forum sessions.

My current institutional home, the Sociology of Development and Change (SDC) group at Wageningen University, was the right intellectual home to bring the project to its conclusion. Even though I often struggled to find time for writing and reflection next to my responsibilities as department chair, I have always felt supported and encouraged by colleagues and (PhD) students in and around the SDC group, and those we closely collaborate with in the Rural Sociology, Health and Society, and Cultural Geography groups. Your collegiality and what we are building together through the Centre for Space, Place, and Society (CSPS) means the world to me. Sincere gratitude also to colleagues in the Water Resources Management group, the Forest and Nature Conservation Policy group, and the Social Science Department and beyond. Special thanks to CSPS visiting professors Erik Swyngedouw, Mike Goodman, and Scott Prudham for the inspiring discussions (and bike rides, Scott!).

I feel fortunate to be part of a large and diverse collective of scholars and practitioners, including those in the Political Ecology Network, POLLEN, who enjoy debating and thinking about socio-environmental change as much as I do, and who share a desire for understanding and how this can contribute to political change. Some of these have been close collaborators for many years and have taken the time to read (parts of) the manuscript and give extensive comments and suggestions: Wolfram Dressler, Robert Fletcher, Rosaleen Duffy, Francis Massé, Dan Brockington, and Jim Igoe. Many thanks to Ingrid Nelson and Stasja Koot for being associated with the project and thinking through Nature 2.0 together with me.

Over the course of almost a decade, I have had many other fruitful discussions and exchanges on this topic with inspiring scholars. Thanks to

Joel Wainwright, Jarkko Saarinen, Payal Arora, Koen Arts, Bill Adams, Chris Sandbrook, Sian Sullivan, René van der Wal, Emile Smidt, Jennifer Dodsworth, Audrey Verma, Glenn Banks, Nitin Rai, Karen Bakker, Max Ritts, the participants of the Nature 2.0 Aosta Valley workshop in 2015, Melissa Checker, Elizabeth Lunstrum, James Stinson, Eli Typhina, Roberta Hawkins, Jennifer Silver, Brett Matulis, Rob Fletcher, Stasja Koot, Jim Igoe, and Ingrid Nelson, and all participants and lecturers at the Wageningen Political Ecology summer schools in 2018 and 2019, where some of the ideas in the manuscript were presented and debated. I have given seminars on (parts of) the book at the University of Johannesburg, Stellenbosch University, the Ashoka Trust for Research in Ecology and the Environment, Oxford University, Cambridge University, University of Sheffield, the Swedish Agricultural University, the University of Gent, Aberdeen University, the University of Olou, the Africa Studies Centre, Leiden University, the University of KwaZulu Natal, University of Edinburgh, University of the Western Cape, and the University of Witwatersrand. I am grateful to all those who made these sessions possible: academic and intellectual growth depends on opportunities for genuine scholarly engagement like these and they were very important to help think through the arguments and interventions of the book.

The research for this book was made possible by a Netherlands Organisation for Scientific Research (NWO) Veni grant, Dossier number 451-11-010. I am deeply grateful not only for the trust the NWO gave me by offering me this opportunity, but also the efficient and flexible handling of the grant. This book is the final "output" of the grant, five years after it ended, which goes to show how transformative such an opportunity can be(come).

I can think of no better home for this book than the University of California Press and I thank Pete Alagona for making the connection. To Stacy Eisenstark, my amazing editor: thank you for your faith in the project right from the start and your enthusiastic championing of the manuscript. Your astute content and process guidance has been crucial to bring the book to the next level. I also thank Robin Manley and all others at the press for their professional handling of the production process and their hard work in ensuring academic and intellectual quality.

Writing this book has made me appreciate friends and family even more than I think I already did. But at the same time, there is a stark contradiction, as the intensive writing that goes into a book has the consequence of leading to much less time and attention for friends and family. This acknowledgment does not make up for lost time together, but I hope it indicates that it has no relation to how much I appreciate and depend on their love and support. This goes for all friends and family, but in particular for my brothers and sisters (in law) and their families; my parents, Henk and Lenny; my mom-in-law, Tina; and our neighbors-extraordinaire, Jan and Monika. It also and especially goes for the love of my life, Stacey Büscher-Brown, without whom—again and always—none of this would be possible or meaningful.

Last but not least: our daughter, Arana, was born during the early stages of the research for this book. The grant that enabled this research also enabled me to spend a lot of time with her during her early years, and this has been a true gift. Since then, it has been amazing seeing her grow and develop. Like many others, I worry about what the future will hold for her and other young people. The analysis in this book presents a rather gloomy picture above and beyond the problems that already beset our world. I remain convinced, however, that we need to critically *understand* challenges in order to face them. This text has therefore also been written with the hope that my generation can help pave the way for my daughter and her generation to do better. I do not wish to lay all responsibility for dealing with past mistakes and wrong political-economic turns on their shoulders, but rather to join them in combined intellectual and practical struggle for a better world. It is for this reason that the book is dedicated to Arana and her generation.

PUBLISHED MATERIAL

I am grateful to various publishers to allow me to use (parts of) the following published papers in (substantially) revised form in this book:

Büscher, Bram. "Conservation and Development 2.0: Intensifications and Disjunctures in the Politics of Online 'Do-Good' Platforms." *Geoforum* 79 (2017): 163–173.

Büscher, Bram. "'Rhino Poaching Is out of Control!' Violence, Race and the Politics of Hysteria in Online Conservation." *Environment and Planning A* 48, no. 5 (2016): 979–998.

Büscher, Bram. "Nature 2.0: Exploring and Theorizing the Links between New Media and Nature Conservation." *New Media and Society* 18, no. 5 (2016): 726–743.

Büscher, Bram. "Reassessing Fortress Conservation: New Media and the Politics of Distinction in Kruger National Park." *Annals of the Association of American Geographers* 106, no. 1 (2016): 114–129.

Introduction

The Truth about Nature?

#ClimateTruth
#FactsOfWildlife

The two popular hashtags above are meant to communicate the "correct" status of the environment and to push for its conservation. Recently, it seems that promoting environmental facts and truths has become increasingly necessary. On its website about wildlife trafficking, for example, Conservation International argues that this trafficking "is a global problem. One of the best ways to counteract the illicit trade and profit is through education. Share these facts about wildlife trafficking and help make a difference" (figure 1). Below this statement, the site offers several videos, accompanied by short texts that convey the facts about different aspects of wildlife crime. They include the plight of rhinos, pangolins, and tigers, but also the threat that wildlife trafficking poses to international security. If you click on the Facebook or Twitter buttons below them, you can immediately share these facts, along with the hashtag #FactsOfWildlife.

Communicating environmental predicaments is not easy. "Doom and gloom," a favorite mode of conveying environmental crises, can lead to apathy rather than action. On the other side, being optimistic about where things are heading and focusing on positive success stories seems naive in the face of current environmental realities.[1] And while both styles remain popular it might be better, many seem to think, to concentrate on facts and truths. After all, conservation is supposed to be based on facts and truths about nature, which are revealed through science. And as science continues to show that many environmental indicators

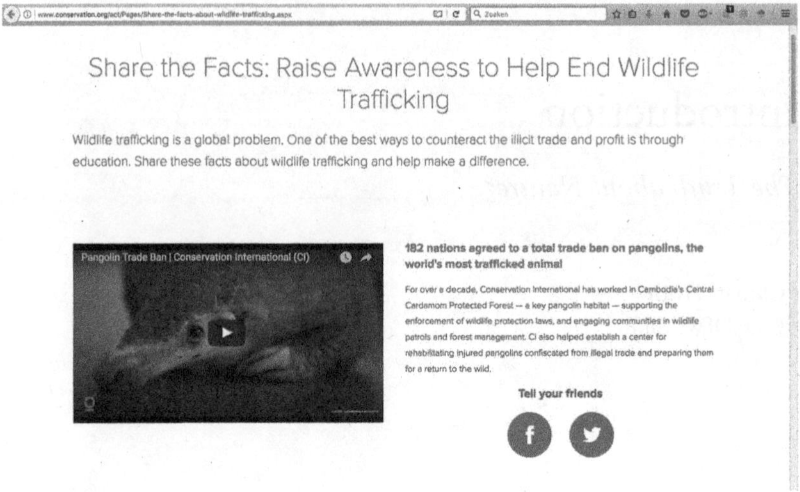

FIGURE 1. "Share the facts" about wildlife trafficking, Conservation International. Source: http://www.conservation.org/act/Pages/Share-the-facts-about-wildlife-trafficking .aspx, accessed 17 May 2017.

are generally getting worse, it makes sharing these facts and truths even more important.[2] As the quote above demonstrates, the idea is that once people understand "the facts," they are better educated and will do things that "make a difference" for the environment.

There is another reason why sharing facts and truths about nature has become more important of late. For the last several years, especially after Donald Trump's election as US president and the UK Brexit referendum in 2016, we have been living in what some have called the post-truth era.[3] Truth, it seems, has been dealt its death blow. We now live in a world where commitment to any shared understanding of "reality" or "facts" seems unrealistic. My reality *competes* with your reality, and "alternative facts" *compete* with "actual" facts. As long as one's reality or facts get traction or generate commercial success, they may seem legitimate in global information markets.

This plainly poses fundamental challenges to environmentalism in the twenty-first century. A good illustration is "an important message you can't miss" from Conservation International in early 2018. The video message summarizes the central problem for environmental action as follows: "Today's greatest threat is not climate change, not pollution, not famine, not flood or fire. It's that we've got people in charge of important sh*t who don't believe in science." The video shows what Conservation

International is doing about this and ends by stating: "If we don't stop the destruction of nature, nothing else will matter. Simple as that."[4]

Evidently, but without saying it, Conservation International here responds to the post-truth conundrum in relation to a "simple" truth about nature. This truth is revealed by science, but the problem is that there are people in charge "who don't believe in science." Hence, CI wants to "change the conversation" because, like Cynthia Barnett in the *LA Times*, they believe that "regardless of alternative facts, fake news or scientific censorship, nature tells the truth."[5] Yet the problem remains: If environmental action is supposed to be based on facts and truths about nature, how to communicate and share these in a post-truth context?[6]

This vexing problem troubles many environmental actors. Some have gone on the offensive. They argue that the dramatic consequences of the sixth mass extinction event we have recently entered into need to be communicated in a "bolder" fashion.[7] Some environmentalists indeed *demand* the truth to be heard and acted on.[8] Take, for example, the Extinction Rebellion movement. Their first of three demands is that governments "tell the truth" about our climate emergency.[9] Another illustration is the "nature needs half" community, which wants half the entire planet to become formally protected. They argue that this is the only solution commensurate with the problem of what "humanity" is doing to nature.[10] According to the Nature Needs Half website, "The magnitude of the global ecological crisis we face today—and the availability of better and more accurate ecological information—demands that conservationists provide a clear and accurate global conservation target that will realistically keep our planet viable." The conservationists behind this initiative believe they "have a duty to speak frankly about the clear implications of the science" and that this truth needs to be boldly and widely shared. "Failure to do so," according to them, "would be the ultimate disservice to people and planet alike."[11]

Other environmentalists are perhaps less bold. But they too believe that post-truth needs to be countered by truths and facts, and that these should be shared by and with as many as possible. Consider the *conservation evidence* project. It "has the wildly ambitious but conceptually blindingly obvious aim of collecting together all the evidence for how well every conservation intervention ever dreamed up actually works, for every species and habitat in the world, and making it freely available on their website." An accompanying book entitled *What Works in Conservation 2017* aims to give conservation managers access to scientific evidence in order to counter post-truth tendencies. The project encourages all of us to "stand up for science, truth and expertise" and concludes: "So if you are interested in what *really* works in conservation, and what is just hot air and wishful thinking, check out '*What Works in Conservation 2017*' or www.conservationevidence.com. Daily evidence viewing will move us cleanly and effortlessly into a post-post-truth world."[12]

Clearly, things are not this simple. And environmental actors know it.[13] This book also shows that we will not "cleanly and effortlessly" move into a post-post-truth world by digesting a daily portion of evidence (or facts, or truth). But it also demonstrates that this does not stop most environmentalists. Spurred on by new online media technologies, they doggedly and passionately continue to discover, study, and share #FactsOfWildlife, truths, and natures.

THE TRUTH ABOUT NATURE?

In its most generic sense, the truth about nature, according to many environmentalists, is straightforward: nature is not doing well but can be saved through appropriate (evidence-based) action. Looking at the scientific literature, the first part of this statement may be easily corroborated; most of today's major environmental issues are familiar and need little reiteration.[14] What does warrant emphasis is the recent tone and urgency with which they are pronounced. When conservation biologists start using terms like *biological annihilation* we may need to pay attention.[15] But whatever the precise wording, the commonly accepted and widely spread truth about nature in the twenty-first century is that we have a major problem on our hands when it comes to our contemporary environmental condition.[16] And let me make clear at the start that I, too, believe we have an environmental predicament that is intensely problematic and arguably even worse than many think. Yet this predicament does not represent "the truth about nature," let alone "the truth." While environmentalists may have ramped up their efforts to counter post-truth with truths about nature, these will always amount to generic statements that say little about the precise details of the environmental crisis in specific places, the different interpretations of this truth, how they relate to other truths, and whether they may be mediated through environmental action.

The conclusion regarding the complex question of truth and nature thus seems straightforward: there is no "*the* truth about nature" and there can never be one. This is one of the main lessons that the social sciences and environmental humanities have taught us over the last decades—if not longer.[17] Most prominently, since Bruno Latour declared that in discursive contests "the word 'truth' adds only a little supplement to a trial of strength," we have seen many scholars from poststructuralist, actor-network, critical realist, and other theoretical denominations thoroughly deconstruct ideas about truth to reveal the power relations that truth-discourses inevitably contain and often try to hide.[18] In fact, when reading contemporary environmental studies literatures in political ecology, human geography, anthropology, sociology, and the humanities, the term *truth* rarely features as a productive analytical construct. If mentioned at all, it is often in quotation marks and mostly functions as a "red cape" to prompt charges from the bulls of critique and deconstruction.[19] I myself have used it mainly in this way. And I still believe this work is critically important. We should never lose vigilance in dealing with truth claims, especially in relation to contested terms like *nature*.

At the same time, we have come to a point where this dominant type of engagement with truth—or at least its automaticity—needs rethinking. First, because all of this does not diminish the truthfulness of our global environmental predicament. And following Harry Frankfurt, we should not be indifferent to truth.[20] Indifference to truth is dangerous, especially when the environmental conditions of life on earth are concerned. Many environmental issues may be familiar, but their stakes are extremely high and we need to fully acknowledge them. Does this mean we simply accept those truths that have high stakes attached to them? In fact, the opposite: because of the stakes involved, we need to study and vigorously debate the places, interpretations of, and exceptions to consequential truth claims. Deconstructing truth claims—including claims related to "the truth about nature"—can render truth productive.[21] But this can only happen when a quest for truth is seen as legitimate; when truth is conceptualized *simultaneously as an expression of power and as more-than-power*; and when we think about truth not just in terms of power wars to be won but as tensions to be embraced, even nurtured. Part 1 of the book is dedicated to theorizing truth tensions and rendering them productive as the metatheoretical and political bearings that guide the rest of the book.

Second, the rise of post-truth politics and the specific mode of power this represents demands that we rethink the dominant engagement with truth. Post-truth, contrary to popular conceptualizations, is not some new word for age-old traditions of lying or bullshitting. It is also not, following the Oxford dictionary definition, emotions trumping facts in politics and public debate. Instead, a key intervention of this book is that post-truth is a recent phenomenon and should be understood as an *expression of contemporary forms of power.* This power, following Nick Srnicek and Shoshana Zuboff, is unprecedented and derives from a new logic of capitalist accumulation that they respectively refer to as "platform capitalism" and "surveillance capitalism."[22] Confronting this logic and the power behind it is critically important for any effective environmental politics. Not doing so will risk even the most astute environmental politics getting stuck in a debilitating vicious circle.

A VICIOUS CIRCLE (AND WHY IT MUST BE BROKEN)

The vicious circle I am referring to is a complicated and tenacious one, imbued with political economic power that works across multiple layers. Yet the basic problem, the one that prompted this book, can be summed up in one sentence: *Sharing truths about nature through online new media to counter post-truth has the unintended effect of reinforcing the structural dynamics responsible for environmental crisis.* This is a stark argument and a dire warning. Yet it might not be stark enough. Thinkers like Shoshana Zuboff and Byung-Chul Han go some steps further and warn us that while the unintended effect of industrial capitalism was the destruction of nonhuman nature, surveillance or platform capitalism could well destroy "human nature" and any idea of "free will." Zuboff refers to this, following the biological "sixth extinction," as a possible "seventh extinction," which according to her, "will not be of nature but of what has been held most precious in human nature: the will to will, the sanctity of the individual, the ties of intimacy, the sociality that binds us together in promises, and the trust they breed. The dying off of this human future will be just as unintended as any other."[23] She comes to this ominous conclusion by showing in detail how big technology corporations have reoriented their operations from *knowing and predicting* our behaviors as key products for their behavioral data markets to, increasingly, *shaping* "our behavior at scale" ultimately "to automate us."[24] Whether or how this will come to pass, I will not get into in this book. Instead, I will focus on the relations between platform/surveillance capitalism, nature, and (post-)truth, which are almost completely absent from Zuboff's otherwise stellar account. These relations are critical to understand the power of this emerging political economy and the vicious circle that it presents for environmentalists (and, indeed, all of us). A first, crude overview of the central arguments that run through the book will help to clarify the danger of this vicious circle and make the case for why it must be broken.

The argument starts again with environmentalists sharing #FactsOf-Wildlife, truths, and natures through the new possibilities provided by online media. This sharing triggers and intensifies myriad dynamics, including those related to older media, while leading environmentalists into a *political economy of platform capitalism* and its algorithmic logics. This political economy, I will show, *thrives on the sharing, cocreation, and individualization* of products and information online, including truths and natures, *while turning all these into commodifiable data.* The contradictory effect of this online sharing and cocreation is that *what is actually true no longer matters to platforms*: it is all profitable as data. To put it bluntly: *why* I would be interested to save nature becomes secondary—or totally irrelevant—to the information *that* I want to save nature, evidenced by my online clicking, browsing, and viewing choices. The truth, according to algorithms, is the latter. In this model, *any truth (or lie) could potentially be as profitable as any other truth (or lie).* Which is why I argue that platform capitalism is *responsible for the emergence of post-truth* and why I understand post-truth as an expression of power under platform capitalism. In this way, post-truth also plays into the hands of capitalist power more generally, which *intensifies rather than weakens* the overall political economy responsible for the current environmental predicament.

For environmentalists, the timing of this warning could not be worse. They already feel the environmental crisis as a colossal responsibility, and many seem to grasp at any tool that may help tackle it. Chief among these is digital technology. The largest environmental organization in the world, the Nature Conservancy, for example, appointed a chief technology officer in 2018, who writes: "We know that we can get bigger, faster and smarter with our solutions—what if action for our planet could move at the pace of Silicon Valley? Technology has extraordinary potential to play a key role in this sort of acceleration."[25] Many biological scientists, likewise, urge their colleagues to join "a new era of conservation technology," based on SMART forms of governance and data application.[26]

In other words, precisely when we should become worried about the potential effects of new platform technologies, many environmentalists feel it is time to embrace them wholeheartedly as a way of saving nature, spreading #ClimateTruth and to counter post-truth. This does not mean all environmentalists jump on board uncritically. Later chapters will show that many recognize major problems and contradictions of new media platforms. Yet the same chapters also show that they nonetheless compound it in their drive to share the truth about nature and to raise awareness about the environmental crisis. This, then, is the vicious circle we need to understand and confront. If not actively broken, this vicious circle could make matters worse for a long time to come. It is therefore vital, the book will conclude, to break the vicious circle by challenging the new forms of hegemonic power under platform capitalism by building post-capitalist platforms and by rekindling the art of speaking truth to power.

Part 2 of the book is dedicated to explaining and illustrating this vicious circle and the above arguments in detail. This is important because we can only challenge the new forms of platform power and the political economic system they emanate from if we understand them. This book does not claim to have concluded this understanding. Quite the opposite: it is offered as one step in an ongoing search that needs many more minds, especially because these new forms of platform power represent unprecedented, moving terrain that increasingly influences but does not determine environmental and conservation praxis. Conservation, after all, is not interested in saving online animals and ecosystems. Which begs the question: how do all these unprecedented platform developments influence environmental and conservation praxis, and vice versa?

PRAXIS FOR THE UNPRECEDENTED

From the frontlines of (researching) conservation praxis, whether in environmental organizations or in field situations around the globe, the above dire warning and arguments may seem rather crude and abstract. What to do with this if you are working in an environmental organization and trying to make a positive impact? How to relate to this when you are sitting behind your computer and these same organizations are urging you to click on a link to save a particular species of wildlife that you are passionate about? Or what to do if you are managing or studying a conservation area in Southern Africa, and you see that power dynamics around race, class, gender, positionality, and others seem to outweigh what is shared on online platforms regarding what transpires in actual praxis?

Questions like these are crucial. They *necessarily* complicate and complement the above political economic argumentation. We will see through diverse case studies in part 3 of the book that environmental actors are no dupes of structural forms of platform power and that they use various political strategies to try and achieve impact. It is therefore critical to investigate what transpires when environmental actors try to harness online platform forces to save nature, not just on the more abstract level of political economy but also on the level of daily praxis in different, concrete settings. For one, online action can and does lead to positive environmental impacts in some places and can inspire many people to become environmentally conscious and take action. Online truth statements about environmental crises, like those from Extinction Rebellion, the Nature Needs Half movement, or others, continue to be powerful, even when they are voiced on problematic platforms.

At the same time, part 3 of the book shows that the growing influence of new media and platforms on environmental action leads to new contradictions, including around age-old determinants of power such as class, race, and gender. Moving empirically from the daily praxis of Western environmental organizations in chapter 4 to various interventions focused on saving nature in Southern Africa in chapters 5 to 7, we will see that context becomes ever more crucial for understanding the effects and limits of more generic conduits of algorithmic platform power. In the process, any semblance of a generic "truth about nature" seems to drown in the shifting sands of the interplay between different positionalities, lived histories, and overlapping contexts. Through all this, it will become clear that the variegated political strategies that aim to mediate and employ platform power are at the same time themselves mediated and changed by this power and have little effect on its propensity to encourage post-truth. And so we are back to the vicious circle above, albeit now with a more acute appreciation for how this circle works across multiple (practical, theoretical, epistemological) layers and how all this leads us even further into unprecedented terrain.

What, then, is a "praxis for the unprecedented"? What environmental politics might lead us forward in the era of post-truth politics and platform capitalism? Wherever we search for the answer, it will require rethinking the notion of truth, to reemphasize its importance and to make it productive. After all, *it is hard to challenge power if nothing truthful can be said about this power.* All that is left is raw power itself.[27] At the same time, challenging structural formations of power is always mediated by everyday politics and praxis, where constructions of truth are anything but stable. We must therefore connect the arguments from parts 2 and 3 by conceptualizing the relations between truth, power, and nature such that they mediate between them.

This brings me, in the conclusion, back to the (meta)theoretical bearings established in part 1. Reflecting on these bearings going forward, I reemphasize the importance of basing our analysis and understanding on a metaphysics of "truth tensions." Following a close reading of Foucault's last lectures combined with tension-ridden insights from Marx, Arendt, and other thinkers, I emphasize that the importance of truth is not that it is some kind of ultimate arbiter, especially not vis-à-vis "nature." Rather and with particular reference to our problematic environmental condition, the emphasis is on making truth productive in order to confront, challenge, and speak it to power. This is a *political ecology of truth* that opens up space for structural change.

But saying this does not mean that truth must fall back into a pure construction. "Truth tensions" also indicate we must do both at once: understand the possibility of truth as something solid and as something shifting and uncertain *at the same time*. This will allow for mediation between different statuses of truth claims in parts 2 and 3 and do them justice. Based on this, I conclude that the tension-ridden space between solid ground and shifting sand, while uncomfortable, is precisely where we should locate an environmental politics moving forward, one that allows us to more effectively act on the truthfulness of our environmental predicament in an era of post-truth politics and platform capitalism. A politics based on truth tensions accepts truth as power but simultaneously rekindles the art of speaking truth to power with one ultimate aim: building post-capitalist platforms to challenge and overcome platform capitalism and so open space for a more socially and ecologically just and sustainable world.

These bearings are critical. They give direction to environmental politics and help build a narrative structure across the contingency of actual political practices and the disparate data that inform the book. This narrative structure may limit Arendtian understanding where, as I will explain, the search for meaning, history, and context is more important than the outcome. Yet this is deliberate. The call for an environmental politics that has an outcome—understanding; challenging; and, ideally, overcoming platform capitalist power—is itself part of a narrative that came out of a search for truth but simultaneously comes to direct what we see and recognize as truth. This truth tension between politics and understanding traverses the entire book; it is at the core of my metatheoretical bearings and the narrative they enable.[28] I therefore start with explaining these in more detail in chapter 1.

PART ONE

(Meta)theoretical Bearings

CHAPTER I

Truth Tensions

#PowerOfTruth
#TruthAsPower

The term *truth tensions* performs a lot of work in this book. It aims to register the deep tensions and fault lines related to the idea of truth in and behind much contemporary critical theory. It is also the umbrella that holds together the book's theoretical arguments and interventions. On a metatheoretical level, the term indicates that we need to *always* be critical of any truth claims and the powers behind them while at the same time *always* continue to search for truth. Contemporary engagements with truth focus mainly on the first part of this statement. They do so in often nuanced and sophisticated ways that I will not be able to do justice to. Yet a basic problem remains: if truth is only power, issues can only be settled through "truth wars" where organizing (counter) power ultimately trumps understanding. This is also the reason why for many others the term is so loaded that they prefer to stay away from it entirely. Both of these responses regard truth as not very productive or useful for providing meaningful theoretical bearings.

We need to rethink this stance. I argue that a metaphysics of truth tensions is crucial for any effective and meaningful environmental politics going forward. This is because, theoretically, it allows for mediating between different statuses of the term in different times and spaces and in relation to different objectives or aims, and because, politically, it provides direction in the tension-ridden space between more solid and shifting forms of knowledge. These claims may not be new, but the need to make truth productive in this way has regained urgency against the background of the emergence of post-truth. First, this emergence was deeply troubling for those who had been working hard to state that truth is nothing but power, a construction, or an (actor-)network. It has led to an emerging debate in the fields arguably most critical to this discussion, science and technology studies (STS) and the sociology of knowledge more generally. Delving into this debate in the next section will show the need for the proposed shift from truth wars to truth tensions.

This shift might seem impossible, seeing how a second major outcome of the emergence of post-truth is that political polarization has greatly intensified around the world. Yet it is necessary, nonetheless. Opposing factions seem to dig themselves ever deeper into their own, hardened truth regimes, and defend these ever more fiercely regardless of evidence or nuance. (The debates around Brexit in Britain, party politics in the United States, or climate change are just some contemporary examples that come to mind). These dynamics, combined with the urgency of the environmental crisis, render the question of how to move forward in relation to truth an equally urgent proposition, both in scientific and in public debates. The (meta)theoretical reflections in this chapter are therefore no mere abstract matter: they must be part of our collective discussions about our political bearings as we confront the necessity for urgent, structural transformation.

FROM TRUTH WARS TO TRUTH TENSIONS?

Science and technology studies and the sociology of knowledge have long reflected deeply on the relations between truth, nature, and power. In the process, and since their study objects are science, scientists, and knowledge-technology systems, they have also had a long-standing and tension-ridden relationship with other disciplines, especially the natural sciences. Steven Ward usefully chronicles some of the major developments in this relationship from the time of Emile Durkheim and argues that since early postmodernist and feminist critiques and deconstructions of science, much of this tension was situated between two basic sociologies of knowledge: a modernist one, which included more positivist social realists who believe objective truths about social reality are possible, and a postmodern approach that broadly sees truth as fully emerging from social dynamics and the textual strategies that follow from this.[1] To this, he adds a third approach based on Latour's actor-network theory, which he holds may be able to help us break through what is referred to as the "science wars" between modernists and postmodernists.

According to Ward: "One of the potential strengths of actor-network theory's approach is that it adopts a view of truth, reality, and knowledge that is allegedly void of the objectivistic expectations of traditional realist epistemology, the relativistic conclusions of postmodern theory, and the reductionistic and reflexivity-ridden accounts found in social realism."[2] I agree with Ward and Latour that actor-networks are crucial in making truths count and accepted. However, leaving behind any idea of realism outside of networks quickly brings actor-network theory into trouble. Ward states that "for Latour, if truth claims are not attacked and there is no controversy among competing truth providers, then the claims are true."[3] This is a bizarre proposition. The converse would mean that everything that is attacked is by definition untrue. In general, but particularly in a post-truth era of intensified political polarization, this is deeply problematic. It basically turns the science wars into what Peter Lee calls "truth wars" where only the power of networks determines what is true or not.

Lee views "truth as something that is produced within complex relations between the individuals who wield political power, those who manage vast economic resources, the people who control the institutions and mechanisms that validate or invalidate scientific or other knowledge claims, and those who are subject to that power."[4] For Lee, objective truth is impossible and the search for it useless. Instead, he prefers to investigate "the ways in which opposing protagonists stake their claims and make their arguments." I agree that objective truth does not exist. But the problem with Lee's argument is that it does not require the term *truth*. The concept of truth in his account has no special significance and is basically the same as "claims" or "knowledge." It does not become productive beyond it being a claim about a claim (namely, that it is important or powerful). Truth wars, from this perspective are interesting only to those who defend (a) truth and to those who attack or deconstruct it. But again, the post-truth conundrum forces us to rethink this power-only understanding of truth: it is clear that a public sphere based on ever-intensifying truth wars is highly toxic and runs a real risk of undermining what is critically important in science. A Latourian approach cannot provide the way forward here.

Fortunately, this conundrum has become subject to a growing debate within STS over the last years, with different arguments to consider.[5] Fujimura and Holmes, for one, believe that STS must "stay the course."

They argue that "STS makes scientific practices more transparent by providing knowledge that helps to locate science in its social, institutional, and material contexts."[6] Others, like Angermuller, focusing on discourses studies in STS, believe that "contemporary post-truth discourses put the constructivist foundations of discourse studies to a test." He argues for a "strong programme" "that is constructivist, without being relativist."[7] Yet others, like Palliser and Dodson, with reference to environmental conflict in New Zealand, believe that in the face of post-truth, defined as "ambiguous statements in between truth and lie," better transparency, deliberative governance and communication can lead to improved collaboration and deflect post-truth.[8] Lastly, famous sociologist of science Naomi Oreskes felt compelled to take "the other side." Her recent book, tellingly titled *Why Trust Science*, argues that the "social character of scientific knowledge is its greatest strength."[9]

Whether STS must stay the course or change is of no concern to me here. This book is not a sociology of knowledge or STS study, even though these debates have left clear traces on its content. Rather than aspire to settle the grand matter of truth, I wish to make the concept productive for understanding contemporary environmental politics within the context of post-truth politics and platform capitalism. It is, again, a *political ecology of truth* I am after. Several contributions to the debate in STS on post-truth, however, do start to point at what I am interested in. Noortje Marres, for example, argues that we "can't have our facts back" and pleads for the idea of "experimental facts" in public life: a "statement whose truth value is unstable." In doing so, she points to social media as a "truth-less public sphere by design," since its algorithms are designed to encourage the circulation of popular messages, not truth.[10] Equally important is the point by Giraud and Aghassi-Isfahana that the defense against post-truth seems to also come at the expense of "gender studies, postcolonial theory, and feminist science." This, they argue, runs the real risk of further marginalizing already marginalized knowledges and peoples or other ways of understanding the world.[11]

These two issues—the design structures behind social media and broader political economic inequalities—are key in my own reflections moving forward. A political ecology of truth, however, emphasizes nature and power in relation to truth, which adds to but also rectifies some of the major gaps in the above STS contributions.[12] For one, their engagement with political economy and power is superficial at best. Next, and remarkably, none of the studies cited here makes a clear distinction between fact, truth, and sometimes even knowledge or claims. This not only obfuscates our understanding of these terms but also makes it impossible to render them productive. Lastly, they all follow the mainstream understandings of post-truth as either the mixing of emotion and truth in public debates or as an updated variant of lying or bullshitting. A political ecology of truth theorizes post-truth very differently.

Before I get there, I must note an irony in the above critique, seeing how it may force me back to Latour. After all, this tactic resembles his when he concludes his book *Politics of Nature* with the question "What Is to Be Done" and answers it with "Political Ecology!'" Unlike Latour, however, I do not understand the world to be a flat "ensemble" of actors, networks, and their forms of experimentation with fact and fiction. For Latour, there are no "forces" that manipulate actors without their knowledge, and for him the social sciences merely serve for the collective to somehow "collect itself again."[13] Yet he hardly places any collective in context, nor does he entertain the possibility that certain forces may manipulate actors who are fully aware of this manipulation and may desire spokespersons to help them picture another world and ways to get there.[14]

Latour thus ends up with a politics where dominance, hierarchy, inequality, and power do not play a serious role and where it is unclear how these can be confronted. In short and despite the appearance of an understanding of truth as power (of networks), Latour's is an epistemology of shifting sand, with little solid rock. It is therefore not surprising that the main actor he places his faith in is the diplomat, that quintessential actor who needs to shift not just her politics but even her personality depending on circumstances. In the face of contemporary obscene inequalities and environmental crises, we must do better than that; we need to confront power directly and do so on solid grounds while also doing justice to the shifting relations between truth, nature, and power.

THE POWER OF TRUTH TENSIONS

Many scholars who emphasize the point that truth is directly connected to power often start with the work of Michel Foucault, in particular one of his most famous quotes:

> The important thing here is that truth isn't outside power, or lacking in power. . . . Truth is a thing of this world: it is produced only by virtue of multiple forms of constraint. And it induces regular effects of power. Each society has its régime of truth, its "general politics" of truth: that is, the types

of discourses which it accepts and makes function as true; the mechanisms and instances which enable one to distinguish true and false statements, the means by which each is sanctioned; the techniques and procedures accorded value in the acquisition of truth; the status of those who are charged with saying what counts as true.[15]

This quote is fascinating in many respects, especially in relation to the power of new media platforms discussed in chapters 2 and 3. But Foucault did not merely argue that truth and power are always interconnected. He also emphasized the politically liberating potential of this insight: "It's not a matter of emancipating truth from every system of power (which would be a chimera, for truth is already power) but of detaching the power of truth from the forms of hegemony, social, economic and cultural, within which it operates at the present time."[16] This phrasing is interesting. It suggests that while truth is power, it is *at the same time* more than that, which *gives* it power. Precisely what Foucault means might be gleaned from what he stated shortly before his death in 1984. In his last lecture series, *The Courage of Truth*, Foucault, according to Frédéric Gros, emphasized truth as "that which makes a difference in the world and in people's opinions, that which forces one to transform one's mode of being, that whose difference opens up the perspective of an other world to be constructed, to be imagined."[17]

I take Foucault's prompt seriously. If we wish to realistically understand and confront the environmental crisis in the era of post-truth, then the courage of truth in the sense of *speaking truth to power* is precisely what is at stake, both in theory and in practice.[18] But it is hard to promote the art of speaking truth to power if truth can only ever be uttered in brackets—as something that exists solely to be deconstructed rather than also constructed or sought after.[19] As something that only leads to wars and not (also) to understanding. And yet: much social theory, even in its most deconstructionist, anti-essentialist forms, believes that deconstructing truth-discourses brings us closer to a more truthful understanding of the world. Truth, in other words and despite its oft-proclaimed death, continues to be a normative guiding principle of theory.[20] The problem is that this acknowledgment is often left implicit, which also leaves implicit how this understanding speaks truth to power or aims to make a difference. Hence the need for an environmental politics based on truth tensions rather than truth wars: so that we may embrace the inherent and indissoluble tensions between #TruthAsPower and the #PowerOfTruth in order to rekindle and sharpen the art of speaking truth to power.

The task ahead is to theorize and empirically work through truth tensions related to currently popular forms of sharing truths and natures, especially those that allow us to get close to dominant forms of power. After all, if we need to rekindle the art of speaking truth to power in order to detach from "forms of hegemony," we need to understand, interrogate, and locate power. Building on earlier work combining (post-)Marxian and Foucauldian understandings of power and insights from literatures in political ecology and critical theory, I argue that a focus on the integrated realms of political economy and everyday praxis allows for a deeper understanding of power.[21] On both these levels, the question of post-truth in relation to sharing truths and natures leads to particular truth tensions that feed into and support the metatheoretical argument formulated above. First, however, some conceptual reflections and clarifications are necessary on the complex relations between power, nature, and truth.

POWER, NATURE, TRUTH

Power has long been central to environmental studies and political ecology. Hanne Svarstad and colleagues provide a useful overview of conceptualizations of power in political ecology and argue that three streams have been particularly important: actor-oriented perspectives focusing on the power of actors in everyday settings, (post-)Marxian approaches focusing on more structural forms of power in relation to political-economic domination and exploitation, and post-structural perspectives focusing on discursive and relational approaches to power. They argue that "the three theoretical perspectives overlap and that power is productively conceived as a combination of these perspectives," though "the weight given to each perspective may vary depending on the empirical situation."[22] I also aim to productively combine the three theoretical perspectives. The way I do so is strongly guided by two other key concepts in the book—truth and nature—which complicate and enrich our understanding of power.

Regarding nature, I adhere to a critical realist understanding that accounts for both the biophysical and social aspects of nature, and engages with them as interconnected and mutually constituting realms.[23] I follow Michael Carolan, who maintains distinctions between three categories: Nature, nature, and "nature."[24] The first is "the Nature of physicality, causality, and permanence-with-flux." The second is nature as socio-biophysical phenomenon, and the third is "nature" as discursive construction.[25] I am principally interested in the latter two, their inter-sections and mutual co-constitutions across online and offline realms (which I refer to as nature 2.0). This clearly complicates the "truth about nature" referred to in the introduction, which refers mostly to the first category of Nature. Even if knowledge of Nature may be accepted as scientifically solid, this is still mediated by and through the other two forms of nature that Carolan distinguishes, which forces us, at the very least, to accept that truth is never unidimensional.

One way to mediate these complications is by extending Carolan's categorization of nature to develop a critical realist differentiation between Truth, truth, and "truth." The first might resemble an absolute universal (always true), the second a relative universal (true depending on circumstances), and the third a discursive construction. This categorization may complement and nuance the "commonsense" understanding of the "difference between being true and being false," that Harry Frankfurt proposes in his defense of truth.[26] There are important benefits to such a commonsense understanding: it saves one the impossible task of coming to a remotely satisfactory definition of the term and, as I will argue below, there are certain elements to truth that can only ever be "commonsensical." At the same time, there are serious downsides to these conceptualizations of truth. Commonsense may be an excuse to not interrogate truth claims, while the proposed categorization might allow environmentalists (or others) to say that the higher Nature equals the higher Truth and that these should override all other understandings of those terms (as, indeed, often happens). Both do not take seriously that truth and nature cannot be seen outside of power. If taken too seriously, they would lead to even fiercer wars over who gets to speak for and about Nature and Truth in the context of environmental crisis and current debates about the Anthropocene.[27]

Another way to illustrate the downsides of a more commonsense understanding of truth in relation to nature is to compare truth to "facts" (which is how many environmentalists often frame truths about nature: #FactsOfWildlife). Following Mary Poovey's brilliant *History of the Modern Fact*, we can understand facts as references to "actually existing realities" that are "recorded in a language that seems transparent"— especially numbers—and without context or history. Poovey shows how the modern fact came into existence historically, and how it became "modernity's most favored unit of knowledge."[28] Following Foucault, Poovey, and work in science and technology studies, this decontextualized, ahistorical, and apolitical understanding of knowledge has been critical in the development of contemporary forms of (capitalist) social order and political power.[29] And while facts do not equal (and can be used to challenge) capitalist power, there is a reason why it makes no sense to "speak fact to power." The relations between truth, nature, and power, as shown by Steven Shapin, are simply too dependent on history, context, positionality, and other sociopolitical and -economic dynamics.[30]

More than that: I argue that a major difference between fact and truth is precisely this dependency. In my conceptualization, truth distinguishes itself from fact by incorporating history, context, positionality, and other sociopolitical and -economic dynamics to the extent required to gain a full, meaningful *understanding*. Here, then, is where I part with Harry Frankfurt. His discussion is "concerned exclusively with the value and the importance of *truth*, and not at all with the value or the importance of our *efforts to find* truth or of our *experience in finding* it."[31] In contrast, I argue that it is precisely the effort to find truth that gives it value and importance, as it is this effort that forces one to acknowledge context, history and other sociopolitical and -economic dynamics left out by mere facts.

This does not mean that every effort in finding truth is the same: some efforts may seem more easily accepted than others. It also does not mean that everything that is accepted as truth actually equals truth. Truth is not *dependent* on acceptance, because some truths are more universal and objective than others, even if these are always mediated by and reached through distinctly less-than-universal and less-than-objective forms of knowledge and understanding. This is an insight transposed from what is arguably the environmental studies predecessor of the current post-truth discussion: the "social construction of nature" debate in the 1990s and 2000s that also led to environmentalists feeling compelled to defend a semblance of an autonomous and objective "truth about nature."[32] From this basis and in relation to nature, Proctor argued that we should "accept the paradoxical truths that nature is, so to speak, *both* autonomous and socially constructed, that our knowledge of nature speaks to *both* secure objectivity and slippery subjectivity, that our caring for nature is based on values fully arising from our particular and hence limited perspectives yet also fully aspiring to some claim of universality—that, in short, we must all found our environmental ethics in a dual spirit of confidence and humility, with one leg standing surely on solid rock and the other perched tentatively on shifting sands."[33]

I extend Proctor's metaphor about solid rock and shifting sands from being paradoxical truths about nature to paradoxical truths about truth itself. The uncomfortable space between solid rock and shifting sands is precisely what I refer to with the term *truth tensions*. Placing ourselves within this space means that any effort to find truth can only be done by acknowledging, building on, and working through these tensions. This effort, by definition, can never be complete and at no point will I therefore proclaim any kind of *the* truth. The point of still trying to *search for* truth is to look for solid rock amid shifting sands in order to elevate a *scientific* effort to gain knowledge into a *meaningful* effort toward understanding. To explain this, I build on Hannah Arendt's distinction between knowledge and understanding.

THE MEANING OF UNDERSTANDING

According to many environmentalists, it is up to science to produce the knowledge, evidence, and facts that will allow all of us to see and share the truth about nature. In turn, this will allow us to counter post-truth and, according to Conservation International, challenge "people in charge of important sh*t who don't believe in science." They themselves know it is not this simple but do not communicate why. Hannah Arendt's distinction between knowledge and understanding can help clarify. She argues that "understanding, as distinguished from having correct information and scientific knowledge, is a complicated process which never produces unequivocal results." It is "unending and therefore cannot produce final results"; "it begins with birth and ends with death."[34] This is the opposite of how environmentalists habitually talk about science and how the latter unearths Truths about Nature as absolutes. It is, in my opinion, also at odds with several (nonhuman, new materialist, ontological, and other) turns in contemporary theory that seem to sacrifice a holistic, dialectical understanding for monist commitments to particular parts, actors, or epistemological preferences.[35] Arendt explains:

> True understanding always returns to the judgments and prejudices which preceded and guided the strictly scientific inquiry. The sciences can only illuminate, but neither prove nor disprove, the uncritical preliminary understanding from which they start. If the scientist, misguided by the very labor of his inquiry, begins to pose as an expert in politics and to despise the popular understanding from which he started, he loses immediately the Ariadne thread of common sense which alone will guide him securely through the

labyrinth of his own results. If, on the other hand, the scholar wants to transcend his own knowledge—and there is no other way to make knowledge meaningful except by transcending it—he must become humble again and listen closely to popular language . . . in order to re-establish contact between knowledge and understanding.[36]

Two insights from this quote are important going forward. The first is Arendt's point that understanding makes knowledge meaningful. In my words: understanding puts knowledge in context, renders it historical, and relates it to positionality. Similarly, I argue that the difference between facts (or evidence) and truth is that the latter contains meaning by being situated in context, history, and relation to positionality. The second insight is Arendt's emphasis on the "popular" or what I refer to as everyday praxis. Truth and understanding acquire meaning if they make sense in broader contexts, as part of a bigger story and longer history, and if they relate to popular praxis or everyday life.[37] It is this conceptualization of truth related to Arendtian understanding that allows us to hold on to an idea that truth is simultaneously power and more than power.[38] This is because, according to Arendt, truth depends on an idea of shared reality. In her words: "Without reality shared with other human beings, truth loses all meaning."[39] This does not mean that truth *is* shared reality, just that without it, truth cannot attain commonsense meaning beyond power.

This powerful yet tension-ridden insight will play a critical role in the analysis. After all, new media platforms thrive on the idea that we can share our realities with others; that, indeed, these media are social *because* they allow our "friends" to partake in our reality on a near-constant and immediate basis. Sharing is the sine qua non of new media platforms and what allows them to extract data from its users. And yet, most of us now know that these platforms have not actually facilitated a more shared world or shared reality; quite the opposite. They have shown that this sharing is deeply mediated by power, which in turn also deeply implicates and complicates one of the most dominant environmental strategies to counter post-truth: sharing truths and natures through new social media platforms. By delving into several tensions and contradictions related to sharing truths and natures, I can explain more precisely why I locate power on the levels of political economy and daily praxis. In the process this will lead to a set of arguments that do not constitute truth but are the outcome of an effort to find it, which aim to foster understanding in Arendtian terms.

SHARING TRUTHS AND NATURES

"Sharing truths and natures" has more connotations than at first meets the eye. These connotations contain many interesting, perhaps even surprising contradictions. I start with the sharing of nature itself, which at first glance appears as a straightforward proposition. It seems an intuitive truth that we (humans) all share nature, especially since humans *are* (also) nature. But on inspection, it is not at all clear what this means. For one, the long historical development of the global ecological crisis seems to have rendered the sharing of nature progressively more difficult.[40] Extraction, wildlife crime, land-use change, forest conversion, and climate change are intensifying in most parts of the world, thereby heavily impacting on the natural word, including the last wild, remote places.[41] In this context, the idea of sharing nature pales compared to the many and often intensifying conflicts over increasingly smaller, isolated or threatened pockets of nature. The field of political ecology from which this book draws inspiration has long been centrally concerned with these issues and their effects on the distribution of access to, control over and benefits from (nonhuman) nature.

At the same time, sharing nature has never seemed easier. Due to the rise of the internet and online new media platforms, we share nature images, ideas, and experiences as never before. Pristine, wild, and well-conserved nature may seem increasingly scarce in our Anthropocene world, but it is remarkably abundant online. Moreover, these natures are fully embedded in and contribute to digital network technologies that allow for so-called cocreation of images and information. Stimulated by the recent development of the interactive web 2.0 and beyond, much information on the internet is no longer passively consumed, but actively cocreated or coproduced through online possibilities of sharing, liking, modification, and so forth.[42] At the same time, more and more natures are fitted with "smart" sensing technologies, monitored and tracked so that they can "share" data that is used for the "optimization" of environmental governance.[43] All this allows for the production of even more natures, to the extent that we are witnessing what I call a "digital nature-glut": an excess of online natures increasingly amenable and accessible to online netizens. I refer to these cocreated natures as "nature 2.0."

These examples were chosen to make two points. First, the precise meanings of nature in them are multiple and include human nature, nature as nonhuman ecology, socio-ecological nature, discursive "nature," animals, and more. All these have different connotations in different contexts and different consequences for how they might be shared.[44] Sharing any truths about them could rightly be regarded as pointless, especially since these different connotations are mediated by power in complex and multifold ways. Second and seemingly contradictory, there is still truth in these diverging forms of (non-)sharing nature, one that drives much of the empirical investigation in the book. This truth derives from the observation that environmental actors have rapidly embraced the possibilities of social media and platform technologies to pursue their goals; that they increasingly rely on nature 2.0 to conserve, share, or tell the truth about nature offline.[45] Many conservationists even hail the web 2.0 as a game changer in global environmental politics, one that may lead to a "digital conservation movement." All of this is premised on sharing truths and natures, about which I have just concluded that their diverse connotations make it pointless to try to search for any shared reality among them. Why then pursue this search anyway?

Because this contradiction is actually understandable—and could become a shared reality—if we understand it as being fundamentally embedded in, and the outcome of, historical developments in the capitalist political economy. Both the increasing difficulty of sharing nature offline and over-shared "digital natureglut" are deeply tied to changing contemporary dynamics of capital and power. The first part of the paradox relates principally to capitalism's history of uneven geographical development and how, according to David Harvey and Jason Moore, this is unevenly embedded in the web of life.[46] The second part relates to capitalism's more recent restructuring to increasingly derive value from forms of platform organization. Google, Amazon, Facebook, Twitter, and other online platforms have not just changed the internet. They have also transformed global capitalism to the extent that scholars are starting to refer to "platform capitalism." In part 2 of the book, I will show that the tension-ridden connotations of these forms of sharing truths and natures become comprehensible through these political economic changes. Moreover, these changes have brought us into the post-truth era and hence lead to some of the key arguments I will develop along the way.

THE SOLIDITY OF POLITICAL ECONOMIC POWER

Following Nick Srnicek, I use the term *platform capitalism* to signal one of the defining characteristics of contemporary capitalism and the concomitant workings of political economic power.[47] The platform—in its most generic form—is an organizational structure that depends on the internet, especially so-called 2.0 possibilities of two-way communication and cocreation. Social or new media organizations, like Facebook and Twitter, but also Amazon and Google, are the quintessential capitalist organizations of our time and all depend on a platform model. They have drastically reorganized global capitalism over the last decade.[48] They will therefore form the basic context for my explorations into the relations between nature, (post-)truth, and power in the next two chapters.

Platform capitalism, I argue, is also the context in which we can start making sense of the emergence of post-truth. Of course, questions of truth and power are of all ages and all societies. From this perspective, I agree with Jasanoff and Simmet that it is wrong to see post-truth as an alarm signal that we are losing an age where truth once preceded construction and power. This age has never existed; truth tensions have always characterized environmental politics and will continue to do so. Yet, unlike Jasanoff and Simmet and many other STS scholars, I distinguish post-truth from age-old traditions of lying, deceit, and bullshit.[49] Post-truth, as I conceptualize it, is a *particular expression of power under platform capitalism*. This has significant implications. For one, as argued in the introduction, it makes one of the main environmental strategies to deal with post-truth ineffective at best and can lead to a debilitating vicious circle at worst. This strategy is to spread facts more widely, more vehemently, and more forcefully as to their truthfulness (#ClimateTruth!). Post-truth, as mentioned, is commonly countered by spreading ever-larger quantities of truth and #FactsOfWildlife. Yet this strategy is premised on the idea that post-truth is something done by people who have a blatant disrespect for truth: people like Donald Trump. Post-truth in this rendition is an individual character trait. It is something that people in power *do* rather than an *expression of structural power*.

I argue the opposite. Post-truth as an expression of power reflects how contemporary capitalism has been changing over the last decades and, following Karl Marx, how it leads individuals to take on specific roles.[50] In other words, Trump—or rather: the Trump phenomenon—is an expression, not the source, of our contemporary political economy of platform capitalism. Speaking truth to power, therefore, crucially depends on how we understand not just those in power—though that obviously matters too—but how political economic power has developed to its present state and continues to change. I will work this out in the following two chapters. It will lead to a key argument of the book: *that some of the most dominant ways in which environmental actors currently share truths and natures derive from the very forces that undermine truths and natures in the first place.* They are part of why we presently live in a post-truth era marked by integrated environmental and social crises. Our ability to act effectively on our socio-environmental predicament depends on whether and how we are willing to confront this fundamental contradiction.

Does this mean that (understanding) political economy equals truth? No. Instead of seeing it as truth, I regard political economy as a particular form of *solid rock*, namely as accumulated, institutionalized power over time. It is about *structural* power, which in the rich tradition of historical materialist analysis can provide deep insight into our contemporary condition. Yet this insight still only partially allows for understanding. Platform capitalism is not just a mode of power taking place within an abstract political economic context. Platform capitalist logics intersect with yet others and become part of everyday dynamics that are highly influenced but never determined by this context. Identity, class, race, age, gender, and more infuse, steer, and color environmental politics in empirical praxis. We therefore need to pay specific attention to them. Understanding conservation in the post-truth era thus requires connecting more solid, structural political economy to shifting, day-to-day politics by actors in specific settings. This also means that power is not just structural. It also emanates from, disperses into, and is mediated by everyday forms of praxis. And these lived realities, as ethnographic traditions in anthropology, geography, and political ecology emphasize, are messy, contingent, and contentious, and can only be studied as such.

THE SHIFTING POLITICS OF EVERYDAY PRAXIS

A common critique of more structural understandings of power is that they do a bad job of reflecting everyday praxis and the manifold dynamics that influence people's daily lives.[51] How, for example, do the structural imperatives of platform capitalism matter to professionals working for environmental organizations and their worry to reach young people on social media who increasingly understand the world through online platforms? How do online efforts by European environmentalists to try and save elephants in Southern Africa affect and reflect daily conservation realities locally? How does the everyday sharing of nature in the Kruger National Park in South Africa through social media affect power relations around the park? And how do racial and class dynamics intersect with online efforts to save the rhino from poaching pressures? These are the questions that guide the empirical cases I will work through in part 3 of the book (chapters 4 to 7) in order to gain grounded knowledge of some of the contexts, histories, and positionalities that constitute and influence everyday attempts to share truths and natures using online new media platforms.

What matters here, however, is that these questions highlight very specific places, actors, and issues and that, since most of them relate to Southern Africa, this may smack of randomness. Media platforms, after all, are distinctly global, and so I could have picked myriad other places or issues to illustrate the everyday dimensions of using nature 2.0 to save offline natures. The reason I picked Southern Africa is straightforward and relates to my own history and positionality as a scholar: I have done research in this region for a long time and hence built up a deeper understanding of conservation in this specific context. This allows me to give meaning, color, and depth to the political economic arguments in part 2 in a way I could not with other regions. But while this may be a valid reason, my point about randomness goes further than personal history and bias, namely that *any* randomly chosen region could reflect and give meaning to global, structural, political, and economic forms of (capitalist platform) power. The search for truth works *dialectically*: it should lead one deep into the "shifting" contexts, histories, and positionalities that give meaning to more structural forms of power. But out of these complexities, we should at the same time strive to extract elements that allow us to cut to the core of issues and hence *create* more solid "shared realities" that give meaning to everyday praxis.

This provides yet another connotation to the term *truth tensions*. Besides an umbrella for my arguments and the basis for a politics going forward, the term also captures my methodological and epistemological outlook. This outlook builds on Marx's and Harvey's dialectical method, combined with insights and methods from Foucault, Arendt, and others as well as a multilevel ethnographic sensitivity to everyday praxis. In short, the tensions between the more abstract, solid structures of political economy and the concrete, shifting forms of everyday praxis are what allow me to locate (structural, relational, and actor-oriented) power *and* search for truth. What this outlook does not do is provide a specific direction one might take this search into. How to direct one's search in order to create shared realities out of the seeming randomness of shifting empirical complexities? My strategy in this book, inspired by Chantal Mouffe and Erik Swyngedouw, is to centralize politics. Two key elements in Mouffe's project are also central to my own idea of politics, namely that it is about (dealing with) conflict, power, and antagonism and that it takes place within the framework of (challenging) hegemony. I apply this both on the level of the cases and in terms of the overall objective of the book itself.[52]

On the level of the cases in part 3, I follow environmental actors in their everyday struggles to employ, direct, and use online platform tools. These actors passionately strive to convince people to join them to save elephants and rhinos; share discursive constructions of these and other natures online; and aim to do so based on their specific ideas of what constitutes evidence, facts, and truths about nature. Every chapter in this part conceptualizes a dominant form of politics that I argue captures the essence of the particular struggles over sharing truths and natures that these actors are engaged in. The four forms of politics I thus unearth from the cases are, I believe, illustrative of the types of environmental politics that characterize our platform capitalist world. They are not meant to be exhaustive but rather to give direction to how I give meaning, color, and depth to the more structural platform capitalist dynamics highlighted in part 2. Moving through these chapters, the reader will notice that the notion of truth seems to lose weight compared to the histories, contexts, and positionalities that are supposed to give it meaning. How, then, to relate this back to the book's objective to rekindle the art of speaking truth to power?

HEGEMONIC DATA

Speaking truth to power is about challenging hegemony. But if truth, as I have argued, is caught between solid rock and shifting sand and if it can merely be approached by going on a journey to find it, how can we ever hope to speak it? Let alone to power? The full answer to this question will have to wait until the book's conclusion; until after we have actually covered the entire journey. The short answer is that speaking truth to power, in essence, is about the art of compressing the understanding that is the basis of truth into commonsense kernels that challenge hegemony. These kernels reflect the building blocks of any journey toward understanding: the facts, evidence, and data that allow for the construction of knowledge related to histories, contexts, positionalities, and more. Speaking truth to power, therefore, relies on and can be expressed through these kernels of data and knowledge, though at the same time also always needs to transcend them. An appropriate way to explain this process is by comparing it with how platforms deal with the data they gather by providing online services.

As different environmental actors share natures and truths via new media platforms in order to save nature offline, they help turn complex realities into *data*: isolated and individuated pieces of "information *that* something has happened."[53] Data, in Marxian terms, translate use value into pure exchange value so that it becomes capital for platform corporations.[54] But because people always live in worlds with history, context, and positionality, platforms must translate data back into daily praxis to provide meaning for them. Again, Marx noted this long ago: exchange value never works without use value; the drive toward successful exchange value based on isolated, individuated commodities must be infused with use value. For platforms, this means that endless amounts of data need to be collected in order to build *knowledge* (information *why* certain things happen), which is done through electronic algorithms. It is the reason platforms continuously encourage all of us to share all of our activities, thoughts, whereabouts, truths, and natures.[55]

Platforms and algorithms are good at turning data into knowledge, and rapidly becoming better at it over time. In this process, however, they create a specific form of *algorithmic* knowledge that Antoinette Rouvroy refers to as "knowledge without truth."[56] Drawing on Foucault, she argues that this is so because it is knowledge that does not challenge content or people; that does not challenge hegemony and hence cannot speak truth to power.[57] It is literally *post*-truth knowledge, at least for the platform. And this, in turn, is convenient for those in power and one reason why post-truth should be conceptualized as an expression of power under platform capitalism. Consequently, data and knowledge in algorithmic form can never lead to Arendtian understanding. Understanding happens when the search for meaning, history, and context is more important than the outcome; when embedded use values are more important than disembedded exchange values.[58]

Obviously, under capitalist conditions, the latter is paramount, which platform capitalism takes to new levels by turning social realities into commodities, precisely by hollowing out the things that give people's lives meaning, context, and history. This also means truth is hollowed out by breaking up the possibilities for shared realities into what Pettman refers to as "countless dispersed micro-experiences" through online media platforms. He argues this is a deliberate strategy of "hypermodulation," which itself is an intensification of older forms of Debordian spectacle that enable "common grounds of separation."[59] It ensures that "the nebulous indignation that constitutes the very fuel of true social change can be redirected safely around the network, avoiding any dangerous surges of radical activity."[60] Hence another reason for post-truth as an expression of power under platform capitalism: this power not only enables the hypermodulation of truth into countless, dispersed micro-realities but by doing so it also diminishes our ability to speak truth to power.[61]

Algorithmic platforms can never transcend the knowledge they create based on the data they incessantly collect. They may pretend to do so or become part of more-than-platform attempts to do so, with substantial and important effects. But platforms cannot challenge contemporary hegemony and the power of capital that animates it—they *are* it. Indeed, platform capitalism thrives on the fact that it hollows out truth; it thrives on degrading truth to the incessant flow, capture, and commodification of data. Platform capitalism is the embodiment of post-truth, which expresses its power. This, I suspect, is why social media, especially Twitter, are so often characterized by destructive truth wars.[62] It is also the reason why overcoming post-truth means that we need to build our politics on truth tensions: on the need to *always* be critical of any truth claim and the powers behind them while at the same time *always* continue to search for truth in order to speak truth to power. Doing so relies on data to construct knowledge in order to narratively transcend it, and so enable the journey toward understanding. And this journey, Arendt warns us, never ends. But it can always begin.

PART TWO

The Political Economy of Platforms, Post-truth, and Power

CHAPTER 2

Sharing Truths and Natures

#ConservationMatters
#NatureRocks

INTRODUCTION

New social media have rapidly become the prime instruments for spreading truths, natures, and the importance of conservation.[1] Facebook and Twitter are the most dominant platforms. But others, such as Pinterest, Snapchat, Instagram, and YouTube, are equally important for reaching people, for getting—in new-media lingo—clicks, likes, and eyeballs on nature. All major environmental organizations nowadays have digital media specialists, even departments, as part of their overall communication strategies.[2] They see this as vital to getting the message across to the public, to making it clear that #ConservationMatters and #NatureRocks. Indeed, many are convinced that the new media technologies constitute a breakthrough in global efforts to save threatened natures. Take Dex Kotze, influential South African environmentalist and chair of Youth 4 African Wildlife. Under the title "A Digital Conservation Movement: The Holy Grail for Wildlife?," he argues:

> Modern discoveries of the Internet, smart phones, digital cameras and the ease with which anyone can broadcast image messages to the world on social media platforms such as YouTube, Facebook, Vimeo and Google Plus, may just be the platform to educate the inhabitants of Earth to preserve wildlife for future generations. Never before did the tools exist to so effortlessly convey messages to different parts of the world at the click of a button. Facebook has over a billion users, a community larger than most countries.

Twitter, Google Plus, Instagram and YouTube communicate billions of messages and images per day. A conscientious "Digital Conservation Movement" is required amongst all different cultures across all social media platforms to initiate a paradigm shift in human behaviour to save wildlife species from extinction.[3]

Kotze has hailed digital media as a game changer, as have many others: Caroline Fraser, writing in Yale's *Environment360* magazine, argues that we should tap "social media's potential to muster a vast green army"; well-known environmentalist Paul Hawken in his book *Blessed Unrest* writes, "The Internet and other communication technologies have revolutionized what is possible for small groups to accomplish and are accordingly changing the loci of power. There have always been networks of powerful people, but until recently it has never been possible for the entire world to be connected."[4] At the 2014 World Parks Congress, a once-in-a-decade major conservation event, there were many sessions built around the idea of new media as environmental game changer.[5] One session, titled "Networking for Nature: The Future Is Cool," aimed to "showcase game-changing ocean initiatives to support the discovery of and connection to nature through new technologies." Another session, "Technology without Walls: Drawcards to Nature," sought to "highlight key lessons and insights from professionals developing the latest digital tools to generate passion and engagement with nature." Many more sessions and workshops did the same, often sharing "successes," "tips," and "experiences" about specific projects, initiatives, websites, or apps.[6]

Further examples of "environmentalism 2.0" will be explored in chapters to come, from interactive web tools to nature apps and the gamification of conservation.[7] The starting point for the analysis in this chapter is the one I emphasized in the introduction, namely that many environmentally conscious citizens, organizations, governments, and companies are enthusiastically embracing new media in their fight to save the natural world. Even Naomi Klein, generally not one to uncritically take up any new trend, argues at the end of her book *This Changes Everything* that "thanks in particular to social media, a great many of us are continually engaged in a cacophonous global conversation that, however maddening it is at times, is unprecedented in its reach and power."[8] But what exactly is unprecedented in new media? And what, precisely, is its reach and power, especially when it comes to sharing truths and natures? New technologies have every so often been seen as game changers—for good or bad—only to be reinterpreted later in light of more careful reflections and considerations. In order, then, to gauge more accurately what is unprecedented or powerful about how new media technologies share nature and how this makes a difference, we need to better understand what new media do, how they work, how they differ from other (older) media forms, and what impacts these factors have on sharing truths and natures.

Throughout the chapter, I argue that the sharing of nature through any media form also influences the relations between truth and nature. A related argument of the chapter is that both the sharing of nature through different media and its implications for truth will change alongside developments in the global political economy. I start, however, by going back to the main environmentalist response to the post-truth conundrum, namely that post-truth needs to be countered by sharing truths and facts about nature and that these are based on the idea that we all share nature. This idea is powerful because it is seen as a basic truth not just of environmentalists but more generally. By first exploring the manifold connotations of the idea of "sharing nature" and next how new social media and internet platforms have influenced these, we will start to see several key tensions emerge in attempts to save nature in the era of post-truth politics and platform capitalism.

SHARING NATURE

"Nature belongs to us all." This rather antiquated phrase—or variations on it—is still uttered frequently by many.[9] It supposedly indicates something foundational about nature: that it inherently transcends individual human beings, that it is something we all share, something we all *need* to share. But what does this mean, above and beyond the fact that it moves beyond sharing *online*? What does it mean in the early twenty-first century when most of the world is demarcated in material, discursive, legal, sovereign, and other ways as never before? Legally, for example, it is not true that we all share nature. Most consequentially, after several famous and far-reaching court cases in the United States in 1980, it became legally possible to privately own the genetic building blocks of nature.[10] Since then, we have seen a massive growth in private ownership through patenting of (genetic and other aspects of) nature that can be used productively and profitably in cosmetics, biotechnology, and broader bio-economies.

More generally, questions around access, ownership, control, entitlement, and use have long overshadowed, even sidelined discussions over *sharing* nature.[11] In actual capitalist practice, moreover, we have histor-ically seen more competition, privatizing, and enclosing than sharing.[12] Capitalist uneven geographical development fundamentally depends on putting boundaries in, on, and around nature and land.[13] Concomitant dynamics of land, forest, ecosystem, and biodiversity conversion, frag-mentation, enclosure, and degradation are intensifying in most parts of the world, thereby heavily impacting on the natural word, including the last wild, remote places.[14] In such a global context of ecological crisis, examples of sharing nature seem to give way to intensifying conflicts over increasingly smaller and isolated pockets of nature.[15]

Calls to address the crisis and to conserve and connect what remains of important biodiversity and ecosystems are ubiquitous. Importantly, this includes calls from those in positions of (political economic) power. An increasing number of them, too, underwrite the generally accepted truth about nature in the twenty-first century that I posited in the intro-duction, and call for measures to halt the crisis. Currently the most dominant of these are based on the neoliberal premise that saving shared global nature is best done by allowing market actors to account for and trade abstracted pieces of it as "natural capital." In much of my earlier work, I have tried to show how and why this move amounts to a fundamental contradiction that will do little to rein in the structural causes of the ecological crisis.[16] To truly appreciate the depth of this contradiction it is important to dwell a bit more on how "the truth about nature" is shared with and rendered visible to power.

SPEAKING NATURE TO POWER

Sharing the truth about nature with those in power makes sense to many environmentalists, since their actions have (potentially) the largest effects on how we cope with environmental crises. Yet this is not easy. Despite an increasing number of exceptions, most of those in positions of power are generally considered to see nature or conservation as externalities to more important (and more *profitable*) preoccupations around economic growth, capital accumulation, finance, security, and so on.[17] In the words of former EU environment commissioner Stavros Dimas: "Too often, nature is considered as having little if any economic relevance, but the truth is it sustains and underpins our economies and societies, and can offer effective protection against climate change."[18] He spoke these words after launching the findings of the influential study "The Eco-nomics of Ecosystems and Biodiversity," or TEEB for short.[19] TEEB's principal aim has been to render "nature's values visible." As remarked by TEEB study leader and former Deutsche Bank senior executive Pavan Sukhdev: "The economic invisibility of ecosystems and biodiversity is a major reason for their alarming loss, despite their tremendous economic value to society. Our stock of natural assets, or natural capital, is as important as man-made assets or physical capital. Recognizing and rewarding the value of benefits flowing to society from natural capital must become a policy priority."[20]

And a policy priority it has become. The language of "natural capital" has now become the dominant discourse for sharing the truth about nature with and between those in power. A resolution adopted at the 2016 World Conservation Congress in Hawaii, for example, notes that "concepts and language of natural capital are becoming widespread within conservation circles and IUCN [International Union for Conservation of Nature]."[21] At the Congress, a global "natural capital coalition" was launched to further establish the idea of natural capital as a policy priority. Now encompassing over two hundred different organizations, this coalition started from a "TEEB for business" network, but "evolved to become the Natural Capital Coalition in 2014, as it had become clear that it was not just business, but the entire system that needs to come together, in order to tackle these issues and mainstream natural capital thinking."[22]

This nature shared with (and by) power, is a "nature that capital can see"; an economized natural capital that provides environmental services.[23] Power here is *capitalist* power, across "the entire system." And the natural capital coalition aims to push this system to become more conservation oriented. Many critics, myself included, have argued that this effort is flawed because it helps to commodify nature and subject it to capitalist market dynamics.[24] But proponents have retorted that they do not necessarily intend to commodify or put a price tag on nature. Indeed, Pavan Sukhdev believes "this is a fundamental misreading of the concept which conflates placing a value on something with putting a price tag on it."[25]

According to Sukhdev and many others, the fundamental point about using natural capital language, is that the *value* of nature can be communicated more effectively with the business world.[26] As explained by Gerard Bos, director of the Global Business and Biodiversity Program at IUCN: "It's going to be a language that every company in the world can use to see 'How does my business influence, impact nature?' What damages do we do? What benefits do we create? How do we measure these things? And once you can measure them, how can we manage them? That needs to come out in the reports of companies. How well do you do this? So a consumer can compare one company to another because we all use the same language."[27]

Using economic language as a sharing mechanism has been highly effective. The language of natural capital helps to "speak nature to power," and therefore, at the same time, aims to speak the truth about our environmental predicament. Or in the language of natural capital: "If we keep drawing down stocks of Natural Capital without allowing or encouraging nature to recover, we run the risk of local, regional or even global ecosystem collapse."[28] The ultimate assumption is that sharing and collaborating around natural capital will render nature visible and capitalist practices sustainable; it will enable all of us to share nature sustainably and at the same time profit from it. This, as I will explain in more detail in the next chapter, is an important Foucauldian "truth regime" in many (especially, but not exclusively) Western societies, one where truth and power are clearly seen as mutually reinforcing.

THE POWER OF CONTRADICTIONS

One might be inclined to readily dismiss this type of discourse as wishful thinking or, worse, simple hegemonic propaganda. And given the fact that capitalist systems of power have a long-standing, fraught relationship with the idea of sharing, including sharing nature, this might be correct. Yet fundamental contradictions related to sharing nature remain. In commonsense and public discourse, there is still the idea that nature belongs to us all, that we all share nature in a foundational way—no matter how strictly some natures are protected from others by their legal owners; no matter how hard many actors fight over the use of, access to, or control over pieces of nature; and no matter the irony in "natural capital" trying to avoid environmental destruction by legally and symbolically enclosing nature to render it fit for accounting sheets.[29] So even as we—rightly—criticize the contradictions in natural capital thinking, we can and should be open to the idea that the actors behind these discourses can have a deeper idea of *sharing nature* in mind.

What is more: privatizing nature can work for conservation. Take the rhinoceros as an example. As I will discuss in chapter 7, rhinos in South Africa have for a long time been bought, sold, and owned. They are, quite literally, forms of natural capital to their owners, who use them to make money through tourism, hunting, or breeding.[30] In fact, their private ownership and income-earning potential is regarded as having been crucial in saving the species from extinction.[31] Yet the rhino as a species and an element of nature seems more fundamental than the ownership of individual rhinos. Yes, individual rhinos can be possessed privately. But the species, as one part in the intricate web of life, is something that cannot be owned. It can only be shared by all of us, including future generations. Elite capitalist actors keep on repeating this, and arguably might honestly believe it, even as their utterances sound contradictory or elitist. Prince William of Great Britain, for example, believes it is unfathomable that *his* children might someday live in a world that does not contain rhinos and elephants.[32]

The idea of sharing nature thus comes quite "naturally" to most people, including capitalists. This should not come as a surprise. After all, humans *are* (also) nature. Perhaps many of us "get back to the wrong nature," as William Cronon so famously put it.[33] But getting back to nature, in one way or another, most of us do (and, in the end, all of us must). It is therefore perhaps no major surprise that we so widely and passionately share nature through new media. But before we start analyzing this online sharing, it is important to take a step back and more clearly define the key concept of "media." So far, I have been using the term rather generically. But in order to gauge the difference *new* media makes within the context of platform capitalism, we need to understand two things: how the mediation of nature has worked historically, and how this developed into specific natures that were gradually adjusted to different forms of media, with due consequences for the relations between truth, nature, and power.

MEDIATING NATURE

The term *media* literally means "in between," its etymology being *medius*, or "middle." In this generic sense, media could practically be anything. From consciousness and ideologies to political or institutional structures: if one digs, one can always find something "in the middle" between that which is mediated and what this mediation is aimed at. Yet conceptualizing "mediating nature" in this way would be problematic, as it dichotomizes nature and humans into stark opposites.[34] A more robust conceptualization comes from Lisa Gitelman, who defines media as "socially realized structures of communication, where structures include both technological forms and their associated protocols, and where communication is a cultural practice, a ritualized collocation of different people on the same mental map, sharing or engaged with popular ontologies of representation." This definition, as Gitelman points out, emphasizes media as social and political.[35] *Mediation*, therefore, is equally social and political but not to be confused with *representation*. In its most basic sense, Noel Castree notes, the representation of nature "entails a simultaneous 'speaking for' and 'speaking of' what we call nature." This means "that what apparently different forms of representation (e.g. scientific or artistic) have in common is that they're both constructed and political. They are 'constructed' in the sense of being purposefully fashioned by epistemic workers of various kinds, and they are 'political' in the general sense of secreting—or, in some cases, reflexively questioning—the representers' particular goals, values and preferences."[36]

Representation in this sense is a key element of the mediation of nature, with the main difference that with "representation" there is usually a clearer idea of agency. It takes certain actors to represent nature (in both meanings of the word).[37] Mediation, conversely, is done both by actors and by "technological forms and their associated protocols."[38] It is the combination of (human and nonhuman) actors with technologies and protocols that is key in understanding the mediation of nature.[39]

The principal ways in which these come together in the book is through the lens of environmentalism and, especially, conservation. Conservation, in essence, is about how to (not) use (nonhuman) nature in such a way that aesthetic or ecosystemic properties and species populations are maintained. This means that (mediating) conservation is always a struggle between and in relation to different "natures" as defined by Carolan.[40] At the same time, environmental conservation is also an industry or "sector" with dominant actors, particular cultures, narratives, networks, meeting spaces, politics, and so forth. I am interested in both meanings of conservation (as a way of using nature and as a broader, environmental sector), since both are relevant in understanding the mediation of nature.[41] After all, in mediating nature, conservation actors simultaneously mediate ways of using nature and the sector itself. How, then, have different media done this over time, and how is this changing with new media?[42]

Before answering this question, we need to be clear about the parameters of what will follow. Again, I take my lead from Lisa Gitelman, who resists "thinking of media themselves as social and economic forces" or "the idea of an intrinsic technological logic." Media, she argues, "are more properly the results of social and economic forces, so that any technological logic they possess is only apparently intrinsic." Having said this, Gitelman at the same time stresses the "materiality" of media and resists "taking a reductively antideterministic position." This means that "at certain levels, media are very influential, and their material properties do (literally and figuratively) *matter*, determining some of the local conditions of communication amid the broader circulations that at once express and constitute social relations."[43] In other words, the material technologies and associated protocols that constitute media together with the way in which these are the results of broader social, historical, and political-economic forces is what will guide the discussion.

TENSIONS IN NATURE MEDIATION

The argument by Gitelman that media—and how they frame nature— are "the results of social and economic forces" could be traced back historically, all the way to the role of media in the origins of environmentalism, under the political economy of colonialism.[44] It could also be exemplified by investigating how subsequent political-economic formations influenced a wide range of nature representations around emerging forms of conservation and the complex politics involved in this.[45] More important here, as it became clear during the late nineteenth and early twentieth centuries that natures and environments were coming under increasing pressure, is that "the possibilities for mass communication were quickly picked up by conservationists."[46] This was done in many ways, across a wide variety of media, including the printing press, the phonogram, radio, and television, all of which sent shockwaves through social and political systems upon their invention and introduction.[47]

One tension has become especially apparent in the historical development of mediating nature. This tension, according to Gregg Mitman and Cynthia Chris, typifies much nature mediation but especially the genre of the wildlife documentary; that between *mediation as a truthful reflection of nature* and *mediation as entertainment or spectacle* aimed at making a connection with audiences, often to solicit support for conservation or care for nature.[48] A key moment in the history of this tension is the founding of the BBC Natural History Unit in 1957. According to Beinart and McKeown, over time, "the unit increasingly distanced itself from earlier wildlife filmmaking strategies in its pursuit of representations that were 'true to nature.'[49] Film was directly used to present, and educate the public about, scientific findings." This type of education, focused on communicating the truth about nature, rapidly morphed into more entertaining and, later, increasingly spectacular productions.[50] Summarizing and simplifying at least four decades of development of nature documentaries, Bagust argues, "We can contrast old didactic, science-led, 'unmediated spectacle' nature documentary conventions which played on a fictive, but still powerful deceit that what was being captured was entirely 'natural' with newer 'converged' forms emphasizing instrumental technologies, (often self-referential) pure spectacle, the construction of emotional attachment, celebrity-driven narration, website-driven interactivity and community building."[51]

This argument about the development of the nature documentary form from more "realistic" to more spectacular and entertaining is widely accepted in the critical literature on the mediation of nature.[52] Yet this generalization says little about the elements and changes that have led to or accompanied this transformation. Moreover, it also says little about how the relation between the mediation of nature and claims to speak the truth about nature has changed concomitantly. One of the most foundational of these changes is the rapid proliferation of the amount and types of media available. Even before the arrival of the internet, we have seen a rapid increase in, for example, newspapers, magazines, and television and radio channels, all clamoring for the attention of potential viewers, readers, and listeners. This competition impacted greatly on the mediation of nature, particularly through the focus on narrative.

NATURE'S NARRATIVES

According to scholars of wildlife films and other wildlife media, narrative is key: "In wildlife films it is nearly always story that matters most."[53] This focus on narrative makes sense in the context of competitive media industries and how wildlife media needed to start competing with increasingly spectacular, drama-filled, and recognizable stories in films, documentaries, soaps, and much more. Spectacle became as important as giving an accurate reflection of "nature." In Bagust's interpretation of Bousé's work, this "moved the form well away from documentary convention, and 'tended to place more emphasis on dramatic action, on storytelling, and in later decades on the creation of animal characters,' steering the nature film towards the conventional structures of 'regular' genres like comedy, drama, melodrama and tragedy, but with animal, not human, protagonists."[54]

One implication of this change is that story and narrative started determining what truth about nature is shown or represented. In Bousé's words: "Story is king, and science its servant."[55] This same conclusion is drawn by Jeffries, who argues that the BBC holds "contrasting paradigms" of science between its natural history work and other scientific programs. According to him, science-informing natural history documentaries promise "a window onto an awesome and beautiful natural world" and build on the "Romantic movement's attitudes towards nature such as aesthetic enjoyment combined with ideals of order, associated with an escapist tradition viewing nature as a source of renewal." Building on Coates, Jeffries argues that these representations are "old ecology," "based around the ecosystem science of the mid-twentieth century, which was dominated by notions of balance and equilibrium." By contrast, other science programs are based in "new ecology," rooted in ideas of "disorder and turmoil, derived primarily from chaos theory in the 1980s." The subsequent gap in scientific credibility, Jeffries suggests, was effectively closed by having many of the main BBC natural history blockbusters narrated by Sir David Attenborough, "the voice of scientific authority."[56]

There are two further important reasons why science in nature mediation serves attractive narratives and not the other way around. The first is that much nature mediation, particularly that focused on wildlife and biodiversity, serves to elicit care for nature and support for conservation. This is what Weeks refers to as "Jeremiad discourses," focused on the evocative and implementational, geared toward emotions and toward action.[57] The second is that much nature mediation is caught up in capitalist logics that respond to what makes commercial sense. This is what Bousé points at when he argues that "media scholars have long expressed concern that as television has become our primary storyteller the stories we are now told no longer reflect the values of communities, or even have their origins in communities, but are instead the products of a complex process of industrial manufacturing and marketing."[58] The programs that result are ones like *Mad Mike and Mark* where "The programme seems to be about nature, but the commercial imperative drives the programme's focus on the limited aspect of Dangerous Animals. Nature is sacrificed to 'eyeballs.' The mass TV audience needs to be titillated by danger and excitement in order to keep watching and thus to maintain viewer ratings. In order to do this, the programme borrows elements from a range of different sources such as extreme adventure, reality shows and MTV that appeal to contemporary TV audiences."[59] The mediation of nature, in sum, is highly influenced by the same political economy that leads to the need for much wildlife mediation in the first place.[60]

SPECTACULAR MEDIATIONS

We have hit a strong contradiction: to convince people to care about conservation focused on the truth about nature, mediation has increasingly had to construct alienated, adulterated spectacles of the same. This is one way in which conservation and capitalism have jointly reshaped the mediation of nature over the past decades. Goodman and colleagues use the term *spectacular environmentalisms* to characterize the outcome of this mediation. Spectacular environmentalisms, for Goodman et al., are on the one hand, "forms of mediated, visual media that work across affective registers to frame not just environmental issues but offer up pedagogical narratives about how we should go about caring for more-than-human nature." On the other hand, spectacular environmentalisms give emphasis to "the effects of capitalism on media production and ideology and to the possibilities for its disruption."[61]

An added reason for employing "spectacular environmentalisms" as a signifier of the contemporary mediation of nature is that it historicizes new media and shows what is unprecedented about them. Following Papacharissi, we should be wary of the "mythology of the new." She argues that "evoking the metaphor of a *new world* or *new frontier* suggests both an exercise in abandon and an exercise in power, as past inhabitants of new worlds traveled there to forget, start anew, and inevitably reshaped and were reshaped by new worlds in doing so."[62] At the same time, newness in general, and especially in relation to online, cocreative 2.0 media and technology, is often heralded as innately positive.[63] As described at the start of the chapter, this can lead to excitement, anticipation, and grand statements about game changers, paradigm shifts, and revolution. In reality, "the opposition between old and new obscures the practices and settings of technologies, the ways technologies are used (ways that are often diverse, conflicting, and unexpected), and the ways these uses produce different sorts of subjects."[64] Building on the idea of "spectacular environmentalism" helps us to overcome this opposition and to more carefully analyze where nature 2.0 differs from "pre-2.0" mediation of nature and to place these differences in a larger political economic context that helps explain why they occurred.

All this means that the co-creative 2.0 element *intensifies* rather than fundamentally changes spectacular environmentalisms. And intensify it has. As shown through the examples at the beginning of this chapter, the internet allows us all to share sights, sounds, and experiences of nature—and to share truths and facts about nature. If something negative happens to some important nature in any part of the world, this is often shared almost instantaneously. Nature is continuously part of the overall maddening cacophony of online new media, leading to a venerable "digital natureglut."

DIGITAL NATUREGLUT

The term digital *natureglut* refers to the abundance, even excess, of nature online. This primarily relates to the sheer *volume* of nature that is produced, consumed, and shared online. Equally importantly, it has to do with *how* nature is produced, consumed, and shared online. Let me use an illustration to explain what I mean. While writing an early draft of this chapter around Christmas 2014, I received an email from the Nature Conservancy, stating: "This Cyber Monday, with just a click of your mouse, you can also save nature and support The Nature Conservancy while doing your online holiday shopping."[65] At first blush, this simply amounted to customer-friendly online conservation: saving nature while shopping and clicking. But its significance for the analysis in this book goes further, a point that becomes clearer when describing what happened as I clicked on the provided link. I first got directed to a URL that registered my click, after which the actual website it wanted me to see appeared.[66] The "Ghostery" add-on in my Firefox browser told me that, as soon as I landed on this webpage, seven "trackers" had been notified of my visit, including Facebook Connect, Google Analytics, Google Tag Manager, and advertising companies such as Google subsidiary DoubleClick. This data is fed into the algorithms employed by Facebook, Google, and other platforms that use this to construct knowledge of who I am and what I am interested in, which in turn is used to direct me to particular conservation-related sites or commercial products.

All of this is also sharing nature: without my knowing I helped cocreate online content that may in future searches direct me (and my "friends") to certain aspects of nature and not others. I did so without giving it a second thought: I simply clicked on a link to understand how Christmas shopping and saving nature come together and what kinds of nature I would then help to save. In that split second, I became one of thousands of similar actions feeding the algorithm that influences how nature is shared online. Yet that split second is important: "Every action performed by a user, no matter how minute, is useful for reconfiguring algorithms and optimizing processes."[67] The next chapter delves deeper into algorithms and how the platform capitalist dynamics they enable influence sharing nature. Important here is to recall the contradictory truth I introduced in the previous chapter: as biodiversity, landscapes, and ecosystems are disappearing or degrading and many environmentalists accept Anthropocene "post-wilderness" as a given, we are confronting a true digital natureglut.[68] To put it bluntly: as nature is degrading and disappearing around us, it brightly and diversely proliferates on our screens. All these online natures may serve myriad purposes, such as informing conservation campaigns and strategies, fundraising, tourist advertisements, and much more. Yet, as they do so—often successfully—they also become pawns in a bigger game.

As mentioned, *natureglut* refers to the overabundant natures on the internet *and* to the endless possibilities for cocreating further natures. Both these elements have consequences for sharing nature that need to be explored. Starting with the former, the term *natureglut* is my variation on Mark Andrejevic's concept of "infoglut," through which he aims to understand "sense-making strategies for an era of information overload" and "the new forms of control they enable."[69] This excess of possible information has led, according to Andrejevic, to an increasing "fragmentation and "nichification" of audiences in the contemporary media landscape." He adds that this shift was not simply an outcome of the proliferation of (new) media outlets but a (neoliberal) "reconceptualization of news as a customizable commodity subject to the vagaries of taste that govern other forms of consumption."[70] Put simply, infoglut forces actors to be selective. The process of selection, however, is a complicated game between users and providers of information and the online platforms where they meet. The specifics of this game are important but will occupy me in the next chapter.

Here I highlight a significant result of this game, namely that many actors increasingly buy into those news and information channels that already correlate with their worldview (and ideas about the truth) and exclude those outside of it.[71] This evidently influences the online sharing of truths and natures. It forces (potential) conservation supporters to choose from an excessive variety of natures that they may like, share, or want to support. Hence, in times of digital natureglut we can increasingly expose ourselves to or get involved with those natures we believe matter to us. Whether or how this links meaningfully to offline natures is an important question that part 3 of this book investigates in detail. At the same time, it forces environmental actors to frame their messages such that they become visible to potential users, for example by relating it to other things we like (such as Christmas shopping). When we respond to potential hints (such as the email from the Nature Conservancy above) it tells conservation organizations something about how to customize the presentation of nature so that we feel compelled to support them and not their competitors.[72] In the process, many conservation organizations are happy to contribute to the digital natureglut, especially out of a drive to embed their objectives deeper into (potential) supporters' lifeworlds.[73]

In sum: conservation organizations and the online platforms they employ greatly influence what natures we get exposed to and how. But they do not fully determine this, which brings me to the other element of digital natureglut, the endless possibilities for cocreating further natures.

NATURE 2.0

With the rise of web 2.0 and social media technologies that allow for two-way communication facilitated by the internet, information online is increasingly cocreated. This element of cocreation is also referred to as *prosumption*—simultaneous production and consumption—and is a crucial element in the analysis: it is the ability for online netizens to partially coproduce or influence, through modifying, sharing, liking, commenting, and so forth, the information, images, or products they consume.[74] And even though it is important to emphasize that these features are not historically unique to the internet, nor clear-cut in practice, this 2.0 element profoundly influences contemporary environmental politics and practices.[75]

For one, it means that the sharing of nature online now more accurately becomes the cocreation or prosumption of nature. The resultant natures become "customized commodity subjects," wedged in between conservation actors that wish to share truths and natures with (potential) supporters, and the behaviors, likes, customs, preferences, and individual or collective experiences of these supporters. This further complicates the sharing of truths and natures online, since these become part of and *mediated* by the technological, political, and economic dynamics and interests of new media platforms. Indeed, it could be argued that these dynamics and interests lead to a new form of nature altogether, what I refer to as *nature 2.0*. Nature 2.0 comprises new online forms and manifestations of what political ecologists refer to as "second nature": "a nature that is *humanly* produced (through conceptualization as well as activity) and that therefore partakes, but without being entirely, of the human."[76]

Several elements in this definition are worth unpacking. "New online forms and manifestations" of second nature refers to the online cocreative element of new media. As noted, with web 2.0, internet citizens or "netizens" do not just "consume" content produced by others; they actively modify, share, link, like, or otherwise influence this content. Online cocreated "second natures" therefore are (supposed to be) reimagined natures, tailored to suit the individual "prosumer." A good illustration is the Nature Conservancy's My Nature pages, which described itself as "the intersection between you & nature." By building your own personal web page, the site declares that you can get "green living tips, nature images, invitations and conservation news tailored to your interests!"[77] This has implications for these same organizations' drive to share the truth about nature: What if prosumers are not interested in the truth about nature? Or what if the truth about nature is not tailored to their individual interests? More generally: is there not a stark tension between the idea of the "truth about nature," the #FactorsOf-Wildlife that are revealed by science, and cocreated nature 2.0?

Conservation organizations could respond that the point about tailoring nature to individual interests is to get them interested in nature and conservation. Once interested, they will educate themselves, or be educated, about "the" facts based on scientific evidence. Leaving aside for the moment how these facts are constructed in the first place—an important issue that I will come back to—this might of course be the case. Yet this response does not diminish the contradiction between the imagined, engaged netizen who helps environmental organizations reach her by coproducing *individualized, abstract, and idealized nature-signs* and the corresponding *generic, particular, truthful natures* that these organizations say they help to conserve. It merely indicates that this contradiction can be overcome. Whether this actually happens depends on many different contextual and other factors.

One important factor that limits the freedom to cocreate is digital natureglut itself: the sheer amount of potential natures and conservation initiatives to engage with. Conservation organizations compete over the limited attention span of (potential) online supporters by continuously providing new and attractive content, which gets ever harder with ever more content out there. At the same time, Andrejevic argues that "as users shifted from consuming mediated images to creating them, they gained a self-conscious, practice-based awareness about their constructed character." They become "post-deferential" about "dominant media representations."[78] Content providers respond to this by allowing yet further possibilities for cocreation. This leads to another important limitation, namely that cocreation is directed and facilitated by technological possibilities and broader structures of political economy that employ these technologies in particular ways and for particular ends. Not only is there politics at play between facilitators of cocreative nature 2.0 spaces and online prosumers about how nature gets to be shared and reimagined, to what ends, and to whose benefit, but all this happens within a larger political economic context. The "politics of platforms" that could result will be empirically illustrated in chapter 5.

What about the second part of the above definition, the nature in nature 2.0? How does this influence the truth about nature that many conservation actors talk about? For one, as Jim Igoe emphasizes, nature 2.0 is always both symbolic/virtual and material *at the same time*.[79] It includes the material flows that comprise the internet/computer economy, the inner workings of the technology undergirding web 2.0, and the ways in which material offline natures influence virtual/imaginary online natures and vice versa.[80] The "without being entirely of the human" thus emphasizes that online discourses, images, and conservation products almost always derive from particular material natures, which themselves have been produced, changed, mediated, conserved, or destroyed in multiple and complex ways.[81]

But not only are we talking about material or virtual/imaginary natures in nature 2.0. The speed, reach, and technological possibilities of new media enable all forms of hybrid "technonatures," a concept that according to its originators points to the idea that "we are inhabiting diverse social natures but also that knowledges of our worlds are, within such social natures, ever more technologically mediated, produced, enacted, and contested, and, furthermore, that diverse peoples find themselves, or perceive themselves, as ever more *entangled* with things—that is, with technological, . . . urban, and ecological networks and diverse hybrid materialities and non-human agencies."[82] Nature 2.0 is such a technonature and leads to myriad "technonatural" forms of environmentalism. I am, however, not interested in developing a detailed conceptualization of the type of "hybrid nature" that constitutes nature 2.0. Rather, I am interested in using nature 2.0 and the various techno-natures to which it leads to understand the changing politics of saving nature in the era of post-truth and platform capitalism. In other words, my search is to understand how within structural power constellations *and* different contexts and histories environmental actors define, employ, manipulate, or endorse nature 2.0 to share truths and natures, and with what consequences and possibilities. The following chapter continues this search. The next section rounds off the current chapter by emphasizing one of the main differences brought by new media.

NEW MEDIA AND THE COMPLICATION OF NARRATIVE

One of the most consequential changes brought by new media—at least for environmental organizations—is the complication of narrative and an associated loss of emotional, rational, or other appeals to care about or conserve nature. As mentioned, Bousé talks about "nature as narrative"—how wildlife films depend on narrative, either through storytelling, or through particular types of production, editing, or camera angles to deliver a nature that is suitable for and can compete with mainstream films and TV.[83] With other media also, be they print or audio, conservation organizations often try to frame nature according to particular narratives aimed to elicit response or action. Yet narrative is complicated on the internet. Even when not taking new media into account, it is clear that "infinite distraction," as Pettman refers to the "hypermodulation" of the internet, does not favor straightforward narrative structure.[84]

People often only see parts, even fragments of narratives, for example through watching YouTube videos. Many people no longer sit and watch films or clips in full. When at the computer, most people nowadays get interrupted by emails, Facebook messages, and tweets, or they are simply busy doing several things at once (writing an email, checking the news, reading Facebook updates, downloading data, and so forth). All this distorts the idea of concentrated attention to, or focus on, narrative. Moreover, because many narratives are familiar, especially in wildlife cinematography, people often feel they need not watch a whole clip to know where it goes.[85] They know more or less what they can expect and might skip ahead to the kind of shots they are interested in (especially the so-called money-shot[86]), which are often the most spectacular ones to which they know the narrative is leading.

But many YouTube wildlife films these days are not narrated at all. They are amateur films, where all sorts of sequences—spectacular, mundane, well shot, shaky—are posted online. These films often receive dramatic or spectacular titles such as "Lions Attack & Bring Down Buffalo: Absolutely Crazy Ending!," but there are also completely mundane or straightforward ones. YouTube, in turn, strings these videos together, so the next video will start playing automatically when you have finished the one you clicked on initially. Hence, you can, for instance, watch a series of videos on how anacondas eat humans or on shark attacks. Some videos are not even about these actual things but simply use the titles to draw your attention. While watching YouTube clips, viewers' attention is further distracted by hints and messages in the clips, often referrals to other clips. Moreover, people often move on when the highlight of the clip they were watching has passed. In this way, viewers might build their own narrative in relation to nature and wildlife, it seems, but it is a narrative of a string of not necessarily connected clips and online activities.

To be sure, the arrival of the internet is not the only complication of narrative; (prior) print and broadcast media themselves also changed (the consumption of) narratives, especially through increased competition and choice, and the subsequent rise of spectacular environmentalisms. Yet the arrival of the internet has specific complications that accompany its ability to transgress "the limits of the print and broadcast models by (1) enabling many-to-many communications; (2) enabling the simultaneous reception, alteration, and redistribution of cultural objects; (3) dislocating communicative action from the posts of the nation, from the territorialized spatial relations of modernity; (4) providing instantaneous global contact; and (5) inserting the modern/late modern subject into an information machine apparatus that is networked."[87] Clearly, these elements are at the basis of the complications and tensions I started outlining in this chapter. But actors have also responded to these challenges by trying to develop narrative forms fit for the internet age. These include the simplification of narrative so that it becomes clear(er) in a short video, a 140-character tweet, a cartoon, or an image that can easily be shared and consumed online. Also, many actors bring out a flurry of messages across various media and platforms to enable repeated exposure to elements of a broader narrative or story.[88] This means that the effectiveness of individual media campaigns cannot be assumed beforehand. Yet the total picture of the (new, internet-based) media landscape is one of excessive choice and dramatic representational velocity that does impact on the production and consumption of narratives. These impacts change even more when we speak of prosumption and cocreation, where individual viewers customize—to different degrees—the images and signs they encounter on the internet.

The complication of narrative is not just about fragmentation and simplification. It also relates to what Kang argues is "the distinctive feature implicit in storytelling," namely "its capacity to facilitate companionship between audiences, which is attained through corporeal actions like listening and speaking."[89] It is, in short, about creating *shared realities* and thus the conditions for truth. These are often lost in new media: the corporeality is taken out and it is not clear who is listening (even if some communicators think carefully about their audience) or speaking. The possibilities for infinite distraction online render narratives fragile and problematic and can defuse radical political action.[90]

There is another, related change brought by new media, namely how the intended effects of narrative—care, political action, civic behavior— also change in the internet age. As Papacharissi argues:

> The emerging model of the digitally enabled citizen is liquid and reflexive to contemporary civic realities, but also removed from civic habits of the past. Most civic behaviors originate in private environments, and may be broadcast publicly to multiple and select audiences of the citizen's choosing and at the citizen's whim. The emerging political conscience is not collective, but privatized—both by virtue of its connection to consumer culture and in terms of the private spaces it occupies. The contemporary citizen adopts a personally devised definition of the political, and becomes politically emancipated in private, rather than public, spaces, thus developing a new civic vernacular."[91]

Web 2.0, therefore, has not just implications for narratives, but also what (some of) these narratives are supposed to inspire, namely joint or common *political* action. And these complications multiply with more complex forms of nature 2.0. So even as it is true, as Kotze, Klein, and many others argue, that new media can potentially reach billions of people, how and to what *political* effect is unclear. Connectivity, as Van Dijck shows, is hardly the same as community, and can enable both engagement and numbing vis-à-vis all the signs and messages that people encounter on a daily basis.[92] Thus the question of political action is raised anew under web 2.0 conditions: How can conservation organizations, in a context of digital natureglut, ensure that narratives are not only seen and understood, but also followed up on to enable conservation buy-in? Or in the language of political economy: how do conservation organizations enable the *realization* of the signs that they put before potential conservation supporters?

Before delving into these questions, it is important to explicate what they signpost, namely, what could be referred to as a "double alien-ation" from the truth about nature. As I established earlier, develop-ments in the political economy of media have led to an increasing gap between the truth about nature and spectacular mediations of nature to compete with other media offerings and remain attractive to viewers (and potential conservation supporters). Yet, for even these spectacular mediations to reach their audiences, conservation organizations must overcome or deal with the digital natureglut that, in effect, doubles down on the alienation from the truth about nature.[93] How this works is the focus of the following chapter.

CONCLUSION

In this chapter, I have shown that sharing nature is fraught with con-tradictions and tensions. Sharing nature in general has been highly constrained by historical and contemporary enclosing, privatization, and marketization of natures and lands, while online there is so much nature to choose from—a venerable natureglut—that both producers and consumers of online natures must go through complex processes of selection to meet each other and engage in actual sharing. More-over and ironically, the nature 2.0 that results is not necessarily shared; it is customized to individual preferences, subject to broader political, economic, and technological possibilities and interests. Still the idea of sharing nature remains powerful. It animates many attempts to con-vince people to support conservation efforts, while it remains centrally important in the mediation of nature over time. In a sense, we could say that there is a certain basic truth in the idea that we all share nature. Yet this does not make the relation between sharing truths and natures any more straightforward.

The chapter emphasized the long and complex history in the media-tion of nature, where one central tension stands out: to balance doing justice to the "truth about nature" with other imperatives and pressures that accompany media more generally. A conclusion based on this chap-ter is that we have moved a long way from the juxtaposition of science and truth and commercial pursuits to precisely the opposite. As Gregg Mitman argues in relation to early twentieth-century cinematography and natural history, "as a science, natural history offered a path of adventure and a secular, yet ascetic pursuit of truth, far removed from the commercial excesses of modern society."[94] Now truth is what makes commercial sense: nature has become natural capital; natural capital has become the new truth regime in mainstream conservation; and commodified natures as *spectacular environmentalisms* are (seen as) *realistic* attempts to employ media technologies for conservation purposes.

Explicating this tension allowed me to juxtapose new media to older media in their mediating of nature in order to understand more precisely what is new about the former. One of the most consequential changes is the loss of narrative, or at least the fact that narratives are more scattered. At the same time, the chapter argued that new media are not actually new in the sense of being different from what was before but rather a specific *intensification* of older dynamics, particularly that of spectacular environmentalisms. These are perhaps narrated in less organized ways. But they are spectacular, nonetheless. Much of this is the result of a broader intensification of the capitalist political economy more generally.[95] Yet, in order to communicate the truth about nature more widely, this does not stop environmentalists from rapidly embedding the sharing of nature into platform capitalism, with due consequences for the relations between truth, nature, and power. One central contradiction here is that the main online social media platforms for sharing the idea that we all share nature seem to work against the possibility of coming to any shared understanding of any truth about our environmental situation. In fact, they may help to undermine it. To help us comprehend this, the next chapter will explore and theorize the above in relation to platforms, post-truth, and power.

CHAPTER 3

Between Platforms, Post-truth, and Power

#EndangeredEmoji
#LastSelfie

INTRODUCTION

These two hashtags represent some of the more successful recent World Wide Fund for Nature (WWF) social media campaigns. #Endangered-Emoji was about retweeting seventeen different animal emojis that represent endangered animals, as depicted in figure 2. Social media users are encouraged to donate ten cents for every one emoji they tweet and so "help WWF protect the seventeen Endangered Emoji and many other species from extinction."[1] According to Hootsuite, "During the #EndangeredEmoji campaign, WWF received 59,618 signups within the first two months of the campaign; garnered global press coverage and influencer attention"; and "inspired similar campaigns from other nonprofit organizations."[2]

Clearly, getting into social media worlds and how they are used and experienced is important for conservation organizations. Adrian Cockle, digital innovation manager at WWF International, explains this in a powerful way. At the 2015 Social Media Week London, he made the following remarks, worth quoting in full:

> If organizations were looking to attract younger audiences, I think one of the key things that we've learned through the research that went into #EndangeredEmoji and also since then is looking for behaviours that exist already and looking at ways of taking your core message to them in a way that resonates with how they are using the platforms, the values that they hold, and in a way that comes across as authentic, or is authentic, I should

Western gray whale   Blue whale   Bluefin tuna   Galapagos penguin   Maui's dolphin   Spider monkey

Green turtle   Siamese crocodile   Antiguan racer snake   Sumatran tiger   Amur leopard   Tiger

Asian elephant   Bactrian camel   Giant panda   African wild dog   Lemur frog

FIGURE 2. WWF #EndangeredEmoji animals. Source: http://endangeredemoji.com/, accessed 31 December 2017.

say. So, as well as #EndangeredEmoji, which is very much using people's use of emoji to connect with our work, another one of our offices, around about the same time, actually, launched a campaign called The Last Selfie [see figures 3 and 4]. So, using snapchat, and the concept of how snapchats are ephemeral and the messages delete themselves, they had pictures of very iconic species with the countdown timer and a message, connecting that to the fact that the time is running out for these species. And without some action on our part to conserve them we will lose these species in our life- times. And that is quite a scary thought, especially so for the younger audi- ences who, obviously, their lifespans going out slightly further than mine. So we don't want to be the last generation that knows rhinos. And that is quite a stark point. And if you can make that in a way that is engaging and gets them in the heart and the head I think that is one of the key things."[3]

Cockle explains that both campaigns are about employing platforms in a way that makes sense to the platforms and hence resonates with how users employ these platforms. #LastSelfie is powerful in this respect. It uses Snapchat's unique feature of messages that self-delete after ten seconds to make the point that time for endangered species is also run- ning out (figures 3 and 4). In this way, WWF argues, "snapchat is a mir- ror of real life." Just like the images we share on Snapchat, the selfies of endangered species are ephemeral, "their plight heightened by the fact that before your eyes they simply disappear . . . as they will do in real life if we don't take action."[4] Taking action then entails, among other things, sharing this truth about nature further on the user's other social media networks.

According to Cockle, this type of social media use makes the mes- sage "authentic," a point that is reinforced by others who praised the

FIGURE 3. #LastSelfie campaign by WWF. Credit: Grey Denmark.

FIGURE 4. #LastSelfie campaign by WWF, explained. Credit: Grey Denmark.

campaign. Praise cited on the website includes: "selfies just got real"; "The most contextually relevant branded use of @Snapchat I've seen"; and "Love when medium = message."[5] According to WWF, the campaign was a major success: "WWF Snapchat accounts became an active awareness & donation channel. After one week, 40,000 tweets hit 120 million twitter timelines meaning 50% of all active twitter users were exposed to it. With headlines in more than 6 languages #LastSelfie raised global awareness and in just three days WWF reached their donation target for the entire month."[6]

SIGNPOSTING POLITICAL ECONOMY

Based on these two innovative social media campaigns, we could revisit the central point made toward the end of the last chapter and ask: What does it matter if social media and the digital natureglut they enable break down narratives in environmental communication? Were these not fake in any event—anthropocentric fantasies by humans depicted onto animal lives? Is it better to embrace social media and make "medium the message," as these WWF campaigns do? Certainly, through these types of campaigns, conservation organizations like WWF show that they are very creative in dealing with digital natureglut. But is it also proficient to share truths and natures? Perhaps it is possible that 50 percent of active twitter users learned about certain animals being endangered. But what does this exposure signify? What types of action, other than further sharing, does it encourage? And how does it make a difference in actual conservation situations *in their multiple, overlapping contexts*?

The last question will form the starting point for the third part of the book. But to begin these empirical explorations, we need to gauge more accurately what is unprecedented and powerful about new media technologies and the platforms that host them. Based on discussions in the previous chapter, we are now in a better position to understand what social media do, how they work, and what impacts they have on sharing nature generally and sharing the truth about nature specifically. I now need to substantiate how the specific mode of sharing nature online, which has led to digital natureglut and nature 2.0, undermines the idea of any truth about nature by promoting post-truth. As I elaborate toward the end of the chapter, post-truth should be understood as a *particular expression of power under platform capitalism*. Sharing the truth about nature through online 2.0 platforms, therefore, harbors a stark contradiction, even if—or especially when—they are as creative as the WWF campaigns.

Thus, a large part of this chapter focuses on platforms and their mediating role. If indeed social media are not just used to *share* (the truth about) nature but we have come to the stage where medium = message, we need to make sure we understand the medium.[7] In a sense, then, the medium becomes the truth, a "mirror of real life." But it is a specific truth and real life, namely, the truth and reality of political economy. More to the point: it is the truth and reality of *platform capitalism* that conservation organizations are employing to share the truth about nature. And it is platform capitalism, building on the long historical run-up to this form of capitalist political economy, that undermines the idea of any "truth about nature" by promoting post-truth, with far-reaching consequences for understanding and acting on our current environmental predicament. This is the central argument of the current chapter, which complements the previous chapter. We start the discussion by revisiting the argument that the cocreative "2.0" element *intensifies* rather than fundamentally changes the spectacular environmentalisms produced by new media platforms.

SPECTACULAR INTENSIFICATIONS

As we have seen, new media platforms have dramatically enhanced the ability to produce spectacular environmentalisms whereby connections are made and multiplied between myriad natures, conservation interventions, actors, temporalities, and spaces. Jim Igoe has theorized and investigated this most perceptively. He argues that "conservation NGOs engage in spectacular accumulation, through which images of spectacular landscapes and exotic people and animals are used to communicate urgent problems in desperate need of the timely solutions that these organizations claim to be uniquely qualified to offer. They present an audience of potential supporters with compelling virtual opportunities (problems that need to be solved) and the resources necessary to realize these opportunities, provided they make the necessary investment (a generous gift)."[8] The basis for these linkages—and hence for spectacular environmentalisms—is Debord's conceptualization of the spectacle as not merely "a collection of images," but "a social relation between people that is mediated by images" (1967: 7, thesis 4).[9] Igoe expands this definition to include the mediation of relationships between people and the environment by images or signs.[10] Through new platform possibilities, conservation prosumers cocreate this mediation. They codevelop the imagery that expresses their relationship to (imagined) natural environments, thus adding value to the work of conservation organizations in "aleatory and subtle" ways.[11] However, Debord also argued that the mediation of relationships by images depends upon significant concealment of connections and contexts that define those relationships.[12] "This creates unique possibilities for elaborate and pervasive presentations of connection and context, which are visually compelling to the point of being mistaken for the connections and contexts that they simultaneously draw upon and conceal."[13]

Conservation actors are now experimenting with and exploiting these unique possibilities in manifold ways. A true "virtual smorgasbord of media productions" has developed, accompanied by a rapidly increasing production and circulation of sign values—like the #EndangeredEmojis above—meant to inspire people to become better caretakers of nature.[14] This further stimulates digital natureglut. And due to digital natureglut, potential conservation supporters often no longer see the forest for the trees, which makes it harder for conservation organizations to reach people and ensure their buy-in. Perhaps WWF "exposed" 50 percent of twitter users to #LastSelfie, but precisely what this message was competing with, we do not know. It might, for all we know, be various popular twitter hashtags promoting international air travel, car sales, or other things not so good for the environment. The point is that the mediation of relations between people and nature through images via platforms may conceal more than they reveal, even as they expose people to the truth about nature. I became acutely aware of this during my research on the social media side of the rhino-poaching crisis (the focus of chapter 7).

In my interview in January 2014 with Dr. Ian Player, the godfather of rhino conservation in South Africa, he stated that social media "have shown to the world that this is going on—nobody can say they don't know about the rhino killing[s]."[15] At first reflection, this seemed perfectly true to me. Social media clearly expose many people to the plight of endangered species like the rhino. In fact, many times during my research, when people asked me why I studied the rhino-poaching crisis, I mentioned that it was hard for me to go online and *not* be exposed to the topic. It simply seemed everywhere, all the time. And to a good degree it was: all the conservation organizations I studied, all the conservation news I followed, and all the online conservation groups I was part of regularly, if not continuously, covered the rhino crisis.

But this immediately exposed my own bias, namely that most of my social media use was already focused on the topics that rhino poaching is categorized under. Those who are not interested in conservation, or for whom conservation is but one of their pursuits, might not feel it is so ubiquitous. Many might not even have heard of the problem at all. I became aware of this on a research trip to Kruger National Park in February 2014. To understand how tourists experience social media in the park, I joined a tourist safari where, to my surprise, many of my fellow travelers had no idea that there was a problem with rhino poaching. Several of them had in some way used social media to prepare for the trip but had not encountered the poaching crisis. This, to me, was very interesting, especially in the light of the above statement by Dr. Player—a statement repeated by several other informants when asked about the importance of social media in relation to the rhino-poaching crisis. It indicates, quite fundamentally, that social media are *cocreated* by and for individuals; that sharing with "the world" may be much more limited than is often realized.[16] The other tourists and I shared the same space but not the same reality.

In other words, conservation messages do not automatically reach those potentially interested in conservation, apparently not even some tourists traveling in the Kruger National Park, who arguably would be interested. This also shows that all those exposed to certain messages are not necessarily aware of the (import of the) message or realize that the problem is most acute in the very park they have booked a safari to. This is what spectacular environmentalisms do: they may make some connections ("the rhino is endangered due to poaching") but conceal others ("most of the poaching happens in the park I am booked to visit"). To comprehend this, as well as its fundamental impact on the idea of truth, we must study the fundamental technological device that organizes social media platforms, the algorithm, and the basic unit that populates it, "data."

DATATRUTHING NATURE

New media platforms allow for the sharing of signs or images, which in turn—as spectacle—allow for new relations between people and between people and nature. Yet for the platforms themselves, the meanings of these signs and images, or what they are supposed to lead to, is not important. Even if they will say they care about you and what you do—and all the signs and images you attach to your activities and identity online—the way new media platforms work renders this care empty and superficial. This has to do with algorithms and the basic unit that populates them: data, the raw material for platform capitalism. We therefore must be clear about what data are. Srnicek distinguishes "*data* (information that something happened) from *knowledge* (information about why something happened). Data may involve knowledge, but this is not a necessary condition."[17] The more data platforms can access and record, the more they can link patterns and (try to) predict our behaviors, preferences, and "likes." This is why it is crucial for Facebook, LinkedIn, and other platforms to push you to "complete your profile." This allows them to become more useful to you, and hence entice you to spend more time on or through them, which renders you more useful—and more *profitable*—to them.[18]

This definition of data has an important connection to the idea of "the truth about nature" as I have been using it in the book so far. On social media, we now constantly hear *that* certain environmental facts have happened and that this—often but not always—portends bad consequences. Precisely *why* certain facts have happened we do not know, as the connections that are made and unmade between different pieces of information are hardly traceable and never straightforward. This is not just because we do not know local or contextual details, but because of how these facts come to us through algorithms. As Judy Wajcman emphasizes, "Software algorithms are not impartial."[19] How they work, however, is not clear, partly because their precise functioning is the most guarded secret platform corporations keep. Yet the basic logics that inform algorithms are known.

Put simply, algorithms are procedural and calculative decision mechanisms or sets of rules that sort data and process these according to particular modes of reasoning. These modes of reasoning, in turn, are based on sorting data according to (perceived) relevance. This allows algorithms to not only approximate what we want, but indeed predict what we want before we may even realize it ourselves. Algorithms thus "enact political choices about appropriate and legitimate knowledge."[20] And yet, because this "knowledge" is ultimately based on data combined with (for us unknown) algorithmic rationalities for reasoning and selection, it becomes a knowledge focused on correlation between keywords, hyperlinks, and other recognizable pieces of data (place, likes, browsing history, etc.). What emerges, claims Andrejevic, "is a model in which correlation takes the place of correspondence (between symbolic representation and that which is represented) and effective intensity comes to stand in for and displace referential "truth," authenticity, and factual evidence."[21] What comes out as relevant or "trending" in social media is not related to any idea of truth but to logics of algorithmic relationships and calculations.

Algorithmic knowledge, in Antoinette Rouvroy's words, is "knowledge without truth" because it does not challenge content or people.[22] It is, in a sense, antipolitical, which corresponds with the self-proclaimed positionality of platform corporations of being "objective," since algorithms—unlike people—make decisions based on facts.[23] This, evidently, is consequential for the argument developed in this book. Sharing truths and natures through online social media becomes data for platforms in precisely the same way that sharing videos of large plumes of black smoke by so-called "coal-roller" communities who modify car engines does.[24] For platforms, love for nature and love for coal are equivalent as data. As such, the importance of algorithms goes much further than sorting data. They fuel a paradigm change that Rouvroy refers to as "algorithmic governmentality" that affects knowledge production, the exercise of power, and "the way we become subjects."[25]

While it is not necessary here to explain this mode of governmentality in detail, what links these three elements for Rouvroy is that they promote an ontology of the world that is without meaning, intentionality, or understanding, and even history and causality. She argues: "we don't want to understand phenomena anymore, we just try to predict their appearance" based on a computerized, algorithmic "transcription of the social world."[26] Why I would be interested to save nature becomes secondary—or totally irrelevant—to the information *that* I want to save nature by virtue of my online clicking, browsing, and viewing choices. The truth, according to algorithms, is the latter; this is the objective fact. The question of why (and hence, of meaning, intentionality, etc.) is sidelined or at best estimated through forms of "profiling" based on categories of personalities and generically associated wants, needs, preferences, and so on. As a result, "the concept of truth is increasingly wrapped up at the expense of pure reality or pure actuality, to the extent that eventually things seem to be speaking by themselves."[27] The platform world that is being built, to borrow from Thomas Friedman, seems to be a "flat world." Yet, contra Friedman, this is no reason to rejoice. Instead, I argue that it is the perfection of the death of nature, ironically by making it livelier than ever.

SPECTACLES OF DEAD NATURES

Sharing the truth about nature through social media encourages and strengthens new media platforms, whose mode of operation is based on creating algorithmic relations as "knowledge without truth." The truth (about nature or whatever else) becomes a piece of data on platform servers that has to compete with any other piece of data (whether truthful or not). This, as we will establish below, is the basis for post-truth as an expression of power with effects on our ability to distinguish between truth and lie. Since for algorithms there is no difference between truths and lies about nature, they make it harder for all of us to understand any truth about nature and how it may inform conservation interventions. Both truths and lies—and anything in the middle—might become popular or trending on social media because people or commercial interests buy into it. They amount to equivalences without meaning or intentionality (and obscene profits for platforms in the process).

This contradiction, however, needs to be developed further still. As the enthusiastic and passionate sharing of the truth about nature continues online, it (calculatedly or inadvertently) strengthens not just new media platforms, but *the power of platform capitalism, which in turn strengthens the power of the capitalist political economy more generally*. Capitalism, after all, has a long history of rendering qualitatively different things equivalent. Back in the 1940s, Horkheimer and Adorno wrote that "bourgeois society is ruled by equivalence. It makes dissimilar things comparable by reducing them to abstract quantities." And as we saw in the previous chapter, the capitalist way of saving nature is by turning qualitatively different natures into universally exchangeable forms of natural capital to enable the value of nature to become visible (represented in practice—and despite proponents' insistence to the contrary—in money).[28] This core capitalist contradiction lies at the basis of the algorithmization of nature and conservation through platforms and is, I argue, further intensified by the latter.

To explain this, I go back to Horkheimer and Adorno. They quote Francis Bacon, who asks: "Is not the rule, 'Si inaequalibus aequalia addas, Omnia erunt inaequalia,' [If you add like to unlike you will always end up with unlike] an axiom of justice as well as of mathematics?"[29] Horkheimer and Adorno argue that it is not. But what is interesting here is that "like" as used on Facebook (an expression of affection or support) is not the same as "like" in this quote (an expression of equivalence). Yet, for an algorithm, both are true at the same time, though it understands only the latter (equivalence). Hence, for the Facebook algorithm, when you like something it is not an expression of affection but an expression of relational equivalence between you and something or someone, which is *interpreted* as affection. This is a crucial difference. It led Facebook, for example, to introduce a "dislike" and various other buttons, since it became painful for many people, when they shared bad news on Facebook, that others "liked" this (whereas now, they can be "sad" as well).

If we transpose this logic to the sharing of nature online, we will see how nature is mediated and commodified on a deeper level through an intense dialectic of equivalence and difference. As mentioned, for algorithms it does not matter whether truths or lies about nature are shared: both are profitable for platforms as both are pieces of data. Both also indicate, following Carolyn Merchant's classic formulation, a deepening of the "death" of nature, which I earlier—with Murat Arsel—defined as "the reduction of nature to an inanimate, technocratically manipulable object."[30] In Merchant's own words: "The removal of animistic, organic assumptions about the cosmos constituted the death of nature—the most far-reaching effect of the scientific revolution. Because nature was now viewed as a system of dead, inert particles moved by external, rather than inherent forces, the mechanical framework itself could legitimate the manipulation of nature. Moreover, as a conceptual framework, the mechanical order had associated with it a framework of values based on power, fully compatible with the directions taken by commercial capitalism."[31]

Murat Arsel and I argued that the death of nature is a precondition for the production of commodified natures we referred to as "Nature™ Inc." Here I take that further by venturing that the death of nature is a precondition for sharing nature online. For platforms, all natures that are shared are dead natures without truth: inanimate pieces of mechanical data that provide clues upon which users may be understood and advertisers may be directed. At the same time, for most users, the natures they share are very much alive. As I will show in detail, they passionately follow, like, share, and defend them even if the online natures they defend have little to do with the offline natures they are supposed to represent. What is more, as the examples in the beginning of the chapter show, mediated natures have become increasingly spectacular in order to keep people interested and attracted. It is this disturbing contradiction, *the intense, lively spectacle of dead natures without truth*, that conservation through new media platforms represents and stimulates.

Yet even this contradiction is only a stepping-stone to help explain the greater contradiction that sharing the truth about nature stimulates the very forces that undermine the truth about nature by promoting post-truth. These forces, as mentioned, are *the power of platform capitalism and the power of the capitalist political economy more generally.*

THE RISE OF PLATFORM CAPITALISM

How can we explain the rise of the digital intermediaries through which nature 2.0 sign values travel, the platforms that have become integral to our lives (Google, Facebook, Uber, Amazon, Airbnb, and so forth)? Platforms, as mentioned in the last chapter, are "digital infrastructures that enable two or more groups to communicate" and are hence positioned as "intermediaries that bring together different users: customers, advertisers, service providers, producers, suppliers, and even physical objects."[32] As such, they are also the infrastructures through which sign values increasingly get produced, consumed and, indeed, prosumed or cocreated. To explain the rise of platform capitalism I follow Nick Srnicek's argument that "twenty-first century advanced capitalism came to be centred upon extracting and using a particular kind of raw material: data." He explains the background to this necessity for data as follows:

> Data were a resource that had been available for some time and used to lesser degrees in previous business models (particularly in coordinating the global logistics of lean production). In the twenty-first century, however, the technology needed for turning simple activities into recorded data became increasingly cheap; and the move to digital-based communications made recording exceedingly simple. Massive new expanses of potential data were opened up, and new industries arose to extract these data and to use them so as to optimize production processes, give insight into consumer preferences, control workers, provide the foundation for new products and services (e.g. Google Maps, self-driving cars, Siri), and sell to advertisers. All of this had historical precedents in earlier periods of capitalism, but what was novel with the shift in technology was the sheer amount of data that could now be used. From representing a peripheral aspect of businesses, data increasingly became a central resource.[33]

To make use of this vastly expanded potential for capturing, recording, and using data, new forms of (digital) organization were needed, and this became the platform model. Why? Because they were best suited to do the job: "rather than having to build a marketplace from the ground up, a platform provides the basic infrastructure to mediate between different groups. This is the key to its advantage over traditional business models when it comes to data, since a platform positions itself (1) between users, and (2) as the ground upon which their activities occur, which thus gives it priviliged access to record them."[34]

As the world's most powerful search engine, for example, Google has long moved on from allowing one to find things on the internet. It has become a powerful, tentacular platform that aims to—literally—become the background to all our activities. If we want to know something, we search Google. If we want to go anywhere, we use Google Maps. If we want to browse for academic articles or check citations, we go to Google Scholar. If we want to translate anything, we go to Google Translate. And so forth. And everything we do through Google gets recorded, organized, and fed into Google's algorithms, which, in turn, try to predict what we want to know, where we want to go and what we would like to buy. Google, in short, wants to be in between all of us (literally!) and everything we would like to do (literally!). In that way, Google allows us to cocreate and customize more of our activities but can also direct them through sponsored links, ads, places on maps, and so forth.[35]

This, then, points to another essential characteristic of platforms, namely that they "produce and are reliant on 'network effects': the more numerous the users who use a platform, the more valuable that platform becomes for everyone else." Srnicek points here to the example of Facebook. This platform aims to become the background to our social lives, which it can do because so many of our friends and family are (also) on Facebook. And again, everything we do on Facebook is recorded and feeds into Facebook's algorithms, which in turn determine what our Facebook walls look like. This makes these and other platforms powerful, since they have a tendency to expand into divergent areas (to access more data) and hence the potential to grow very quickly. "And as more and more industries move their interactions online . . ., more and more businesses will be subject to platform development."[36]

It is in this specific political economic context of platform capitalism that conservation now has to share and convince people of "the truth about nature." This has deeply affected the conservation sector and "industry," as well as the sharing of nature more broadly. It would, in fact, not be too much of an exaggeration to say that contemporary conservation is increasingly becoming "platform conservation" or what in the next chapter I will refer to as "conservation 2.0." This broad term signifies the rapid integration of conservation action, fundraising, awareness, education, and implementation with new media platforms. The dominant platforms, such as Facebook, Twitter, and Google, are included here, but also dedicated do-good platforms oriented toward charitable causes, such as causes.com, pifworld.org, givengain.com, and others, featured in chapter 4. In this way, conservation's sharing of signs that lead us to understand the truth about nature and act on it has become increasingly intertwined with these platforms. But, as I will explain in the next two chapters, this does not mean conservation is only determined by platforms; the term *conservation 2.0* equally relates to the negotiation of the distinction between online and offline.

Before we get there, however, the rest of this chapter explores the more structural elements that the power of platform capitalism is bringing to the conservation world and how this relates to notions of truth and post-truth.

(POST-)TRUTH AND POWER

Even though it seems to have lost much ground, the concept of truth is still one of the most debated concepts in the long histories of science and philosophy. I am, however, not interested in recounting these histories. Rather, following the metatheorertical bearings in chapter 1, I will place the above discussions in the context of the relations between (post-)truth and (capitalist) power. A good starting point to examine what is changing in these relations is the quote by Foucault already cited earlier:

> The important thing here is that truth isn't outside power, or lacking in power. . . . Truth is a thing of this world: it is produced only by virtue of multiple forms of constraint. And it induces regular effects of power. Each society has its régime of truth, its "general politics" of truth: that is, the types of discourses which it accepts and makes function as true; the mechanisms and instances which enable one to distinguish true and false statements, the means by which each is sanctioned; the techniques and procedures accorded value in the acquisition of truth; the status of those who are charged with saying what counts as true.[37]

To a good degree, this is still "true," as we saw, for instance, with the truth regime on natural capital. At the same time, there is an increasing disconnect in many societies between "the discourses which it accepts and makes function as true" and "the techniques and procedures accorded value in the acquisition of truth." Moreover, in a world with a nichification of audiences and an increasing amount of "fake news," "the mechanisms and instances which enable one to distinguish true and false statements" also seem to be breaking down.[38] US president Trump is the obvious example. His statements are generally seen as containing many falsehoods, yet this did not hamper him getting elected. Of course, the fact that we have serial liars as political leaders is historically nothing new. As Steven Shapin notes, "In France, Montaigne brilliantly analyzed untruthfulness and the breakdown of trust this caused and expressed as the most serious subversions of social order."[39] He next quotes Montaigne as follows: "Lying is an accursed vice. We are men, and hold together, only by our word. . . . Since mutual understanding is brought about solely by way of words, he who breaks his word betrays human society. It is the only instrument by means of which our wills and thoughts communicate, it is the interpreter of our soul. If it fails us, we have no more hold on each other, no more knowledge of each other. If it deceives us, it breaks up all our relations and dissolves all the bonds of our society."[40] This is a quote from the sixteenth century. Yet it rings eerily familiar. We can today also see serial lying breaking down the "hold on each other" in many societies. But lying is not the same as post-truth. Lying, as Montaigne argues, is a vice with powerful effects. Post-truth is an expression of power with effects on our ability to distinguish between truth and lie. It derives, inter alia, from the point by Andrejevic that "as users shifted from consuming mediated images to creating them, they gained a self-conscious, practice-based awareness about their constructed character."[41] In other words, since we are all today able to generate or at least cocreate news, facts, and truths, we understand better that all other actors producing news, facts, and truths also go through processes of construction. This leads to a generalized "postmodern" acceptance that all truths are constructed and, importantly, are *nothing more* than constructions."[42] If this is the case, "market-legitimacy" creeps in, meaning that if people buy into certain ideas, whether truthful or not, it can make them *seem* legitimate or truthful, even if they are not.

Andrejevic shows that this affects power and specifically the critique of power in peculiar ways. For those in power, "the goal is not so much to propose an authoritative counter-narrative as to use the expanded media space to engulf any dominant narrative in possible alternatives . . . not to 'cut through the clutter,' but, on the contrary, to suck critique into the clutter blender; not to 'speak truth to power' but to highlight the contingency, indeterminateness, and, ultimately, the helplessness of so-called truth in the face of power." He concludes: "Post-truthism is fundamentally a 'small-c' conservative strategy in the sense that it tends to work in the interest of existing power relations: there's not much point in neutralizing the power of critique if you want to challenge or transform existing power relations. But if you happen to be in power already, the thorough debunking of deliberation and the dismantling of truth claims is more threatening for one's enemies than one's allies.

When the truth crumbles around you, the assumption is that you'll still be holding the reins."[43]

How, then—to reiterate but also expand my earlier question—is the environmental movement supposed to deal with this "post-truth politics," especially now that much of its truth-telling is shifting to the online realm, the clutter blender par excellence? In the conclusion of the book, I will come back to this in detail, particularly around the notion of speaking truth to power. For now, it is important to emphasize that post-truth politics has already had major implications for global environmental politics.[44] One potential implication is outlined by Jodi Dean, who writes, "Today, the circulation of content in the dense, intensive networks of global communications relieves top-level actors (corporate, institutional and governmental) from the obligation to respond. Rather than responding to messages sent by activists and critics, they counter with their own contributions to the circulating flow of communications, hoping that sufficient volume (whether in terms of number of contributions or the spectacular nature of a contribution) will give their contributions dominance or stickiness."[45] She argues that politics is foreclosed because of new media. Or, more precisely, that "the intense circulation of content in communicative capitalism forecloses the antagonism necessary for politics."[46] To some extent this is true, and certainly always a danger. Yet later empirical chapters will show that despite a lot of circulation leading to sometimes-impermeable natureglut, the argument that politics is foreclosed is too drastic. By presenting case studies of how truths about nature get circulated in order to support conservation, I will show that antagonistic politics abound within and through new media. Yet, like Dean, I too doubt their efficacy within the context of what she refers to as "communicative capitalism." Any specific political agenda, for example the pressing for a particular truth about nature, could be seen as just another niche that one could occupy and that might, from this perspective, be equal to any other niche (whether or not positive for the environment).

THE NATURES OF PLATFORM CAPITALISM

We have come to another major tension in the dominant ways of sharing truths and natures: not only does power have a fraught relation with sharing, it also has a fraught relation with truth. Online cocreation through the web 2.0 is central to both these sets of contradictions, and this will further intensify as it increasingly permeates the functioning of the capitalist political economy as a whole. The next step is to render more explicit the power that animates this political economy. This is needed to more fully appreciate why some of the most dominant ways in which we currently share truths and natures derive from the very forces that undermine them in the first place. Dean refers to this political economy as "communicative capitalism." I prefer "platform capitalism." The reason is that platform capitalist power is not built on the fact *that* we communicate but rather on extracting rent from *how* we communicate. How, then, can we understand not just the rise of platform capitalism, but also the power it wields?

Again, I go back to Nick Srnicek. He has convincingly argued why digital platforms are far more than just one (technology) sector in the broader economy but have swiftly become fundamental to capitalism more generally: first, "the digital economy appears to be a leading light in an otherwise rather stagnant economic context"; second, "digital technology is becoming systematically important, much in the same way as finance"; third, "the digital economy is presented as an ideal that can legitimate contemporary capitalism more broadly."[47] The popular way of expressing this is that all things must become "smart" by allowing platforms to optimize their functions and interactions. Environmentalism is not exempt from this trend, especially since nature as "natural capital" increasingly ought to be positioned in "smart" ways vis-à-vis other forms of capital to render capitalism sustainable.[48]

It is important to work out in more detail how platform capitalism and sharing nature come together. Interestingly, this is not (just) through the concept of natural capital. While increasingly the lingua franca to "speak nature to power," the concept of natural capital seems mainly important for environmental organizations as a *legitimate and truthful form of representing nature* in relation to power. Natural capital, in order words, signifies a "truth regime" and is actually seen by proponents as such. Therefore, the critique that natural capital might have to do with capital-*ism* or commodification is deemed erroneous by its advocates. It is really just a language to bring nature and power together, as Mark Gough, the executive director of the Natural Capital Coalition, argues:

> The suggestion that we "put a price on nature," is one I am often confronted with. While these concerns are well-intentioned, I believe the charge is a category error. We don't price nature, we illuminate the value that we already receive from it. This is a vital distinction. Price and value are not one and the same. You don't pay a price for the air that you breathe, but does that mean that it holds no value? In this way, we *can also communicate* the value

of clean air, without assigning it a price. This is the aim of natural capital in a nutshell.[49]

The problem for many critics, however, is not (just) with price. It is, precisely, with value. After all, the hallmark definition of capital is "value in motion," which is central in understanding capitalist power.[50] What is therefore missing in these defenses that focus on communication and language, is a *critical* understanding of how political economic power actually works and changes. Most fundamentally, the way political economic power works and has been changing undermines efforts to conserve nature by sharing its importance via new media and the language of natural capital. This undermining is due to three intermediate reasons and one overarching one. First, as I showed above, both new media and natural capital have fraught relations with the sharing of nature. This makes it difficult not only to come to a common understanding of the state of our environment but, even more, to do something about it in (offline) practice. Second, new media platforms and natural capital both work with, rather than against, contemporary capitalist power. This means that if there is truth in the argument that capitalism is inherently environmentally unsustainable, this is not even considered. Third, capitalist power has a fraught relation with truth, which further reinforces and complicates the previous two points.

The overarching reason is that platform capitalism brings these three elements together and intensifies them. In fact, it can even profit from them, with fights over the truth about nature increasingly played out on online platforms. Platforms grow and become more valuable as more circulation of communication and data occurs through them. So even if new media are also used for anti-capitalist organizing and activism, this could, ironically, bring just as much value to platforms like Facebook and Google as the online circulation of ideas about natural capital. Platforms are therefore not just intermediaries. They are expressions of the power of being "in between." Which gets us to the crux of the post-truth conundrum.

POST-TRUTH AND THE IN-BETWEEN

For platforms and their algorithms, truth is of little concern. They produce "knowledge without truth." But this is far from how platform corporations see themselves, which brings me to the political basis of their economic platform model. To continue to grow *economically* as capitalist communication infrastructures, platforms like Facebook and Google need to and indeed do present themselves *politically* as twenty-first-century bastions and defenders of free speech. In their view, whether something is true or not is up to platform users.[51] Yet the cocreative, 2.0 features of these platforms technologically mediate what types of information people get to see; hence, it is evident that the pairing of data involved in the outcomes of searches, Twitter feeds, Facebook walls, and so forth, are not based on their truth quotient. Instead, they derive from complex interactions between individual user preferences, commercial (advertising or other) interests and yet further value judgments we simply do not know.[52] And because we do not know, platforms can and do claim a neutral, in-between position. Yes, they may admit they have interests. But they will simultaneously insist that they do not want to decide for users what they should regard as important, interesting, or truthful. The technologies, they say, are meant to help *us* decide what *we* believe is important.[53]

This is fallacious. But the precise reasons why are important. First, the platform, as an "in-between," is also a massive *infrastructure*, one that can be owned and shielded from others. This is crucial, as Srnicek explains: "Today every area of the economy is increasingly integrated with a digital layer; therefore owning the infrastructure that is necessary for every other industry is an immensely powerful and profitable position to be in." And it is not just the economy: it is nearly every aspect of society that is "increasingly integrated with a digital layer."[54] Second, 2.0 customization, even though it helps to "organize the world for us, and we have been quick to welcome this data-driven convenience," has significant social consequences. As mentioned, it has led to a nichification of audiences, where our online realities—and how these depict the world around us—are increasingly customized as well, leading to increased insularity, reinforced prejudice, and enhanced potential for social polarization.[55]

These two points clarify why post-truth is an expression of power under platform capitalism, and hence why it is qualitatively different from lies and bullshit. As Harry Frankfurt explained, bullshit is no longer about true or false. The liar cares about and knows the truth but lies because he does not want others to know the truth. The Bullshitter "is neither on the side of the true nor on the side of the false. His eye is not on the facts at all, as the eyes of the honest man and of the liar are, except insofar as they may be pertinent to his interest in getting away with what he says. He does not care whether the things he says describe reality correctly. He just picks them out, or makes them up, to suit his purpose."[56] Post-truth differs from both because it is connected to the functionality of the platform. Online platforms, ultimately, do not care whether those active and leaving data online are honest, lying, or bullshitting. As long as they traverse the platform and leave behind data that can be sold.[57]

In a sense, then, post-truth derives directly from the importance of *data*. To repeat Srnicek's definition, data "(information that something happened)" must be distinguished from knowledge "(why something happened)," and hence also from truth (which is linked to Arendtian understanding). It means that platforms as "extractive apparatuses for data" are, quite literally, *post* truth (and beyond lying and bullshit).[58] Moreover, the nichification consequences of platform cocreation imply that each individual user can customize their own online reality. But as Hannah Arendt warned, "Without reality shared with other human beings, truth loses all meaning."[59] Hence, on platforms, truth, reality, or facts lose much of their power: we (can) each build our own.

Post-truth, as a function of the relation between platforms and truth, becomes powerful in the context of contemporary capitalism. It is now, after all, widely accepted that "twenty-first century advanced capitalism came to be centred upon extracting and using a particular kind of raw material: data."[60] Or as *Wired* magazine put it, "Data is the new oil of the digital economy."[61] To capture this "new oil," enormous (technological, physical, software, and other) infrastructures are needed, and these are precisely what the major platform corporations have been building. In a short span of not even a decade, this led them to become some of the most profitable and powerful companies on the planet. It is clear, therefore, that their basic mode of operating, and how this affects the relation between truth and nature, is tremendously powerful as well.

CONCLUSION

This chapter sought to gauge more precisely what is unprecedented and powerful about new media technologies in relation to sharing truths and natures. Through detailed discussions of algorithms, data, and platforms, I have tried to open up the social media black box to show how it has led to an intensification of spectacular environmentalisms as well as the acute contradiction of *intense, lively spectacles of dead natures without truth* that environmentalism through new media platforms represents and stimulates. The even bigger contradiction we end up with should be a sobering one for environmental actors—namely, that the zeal and passion with which they share truths and natures online supports the very platform capitalist model that not only promotes post-truth but also does little to challenge capitalist development more generally. Worse: it runs the risk of reinforcing the very foundations of our ecological crisis. This is a debilitating vicious circle if ever there was one.

As I will show in the next chapter, these contradictions are not easy for environmental actors to share or act on. First, the sharing of this knowledge often moves through the very same platforms—whether in book form through Amazon or key messages on social media—that further aid "algorithmic governmentality" and platform power. Second, most conservation actors have little time for these complications. After all, a core element characterizing conservation is its zeal and urgency. Nancy Peluso argued over two decades ago that "the urgency called for to defend endangered species, endangered habitats, or whole ecosystems, is a common component of the discourse of conservation."[62] Robert Nelson, a decade later, talked about the "crusading energy of current environmentalism."[63] Fast-forward another ten years, and we have the start of the half-earth movement and its desperate call to "save the planet."[64] If one is so busy rooting for conservation, and if this is supposed to be based on *the* truth about nature, it may be difficult to see or acknowledge the many complicating dimensions conservation is part of.[65]

The analysis in this chapter, however, shows that this zeal and urgency may further undermine the conservation enterprise, due to its being embedded in platform capitalism, and that this can lead to a debilitating vicious circle. It does so by hollowing out any sharing of the idea of "the truth about nature" that conservation action is based on and by stimulating capitalist uneven development more generally, which degrades many of the natures that conservation aims to save. But while this threat is very real, it is not one-dimensional or all-determining. Both conservation 2.0 and natural capital are taken up in myriad ways by different conservation actors, often half-heartedly, sometimes hardly at all; sometimes they are actively resisted.[66] As Nancy Peluso reminds us, even once commodified, the "forms and extents of what will change in entangled webs of social and socio-natural relations are not predetermined."[67] This is important to emphasize: as new media are enlisted in the larger project of saving nature under (platform) capitalism, the resulting neoliberal technonatures and social and socio-natural relations are not set in stone. Indeed, nature 2.0 not only stimulates the commodification of biodiversity and ecosystems, it also complicates it. Hence, while the internet "is still a medium constructed in a capitalist era," its media change the forms and extents of possible socionatures and technonatures that together lead to different conservation actions, possibilities, politics, and outcomes.[68]

The analysis of the political economy of platform capitalism in this part of the book is therefore meant not to conclude but to open up further empirical scrutiny.[69] This is especially important for conservation, which is not interested in saving online animals and ecosystems. Platform capitalism may highly *influence* nature and conservation, it does not *determine* them. It takes shape differently in and through different contexts, histories, and positionalities and intersects with many other conditionalities of power, including those of race, class, gender, and many others, in important and sometimes surprising ways. To gauge this influence more accurately, we must study the politics and everyday praxis of saving nature in the era of post-truth and platform capitalism in a variety of empirical settings.

PART THREE

Environmentalism 2.0

CHAPTER 4

Conservation 2.0

The Politics of Cocreation

#ConservationAction
#MakeEarthGreatAgain

INTRODUCTION

> I recently had a conversation with a friend . . . who talked about a virtual
> litter game where you had to pick up litter. But the litter is still virtual! So,
> for some, it helps to share messages about conservation, spread the word,
> but in other ways, people think they are helping by liking . . . something like
> the litter game, but that is not the same as picking up litter outside! So the
> question is: how can you be compelling enough to get the person playing the
> litter game in order to get their heart and mind and to get out from behind
> the computer and experience real nature.[1]

This is a quote from an interview with a senior social media officer
at one of the worlds' largest conservation NGOs. It corroborates an
important argument in this book: that the distinction between online
and offline matters and that the negotiation of this distinction is a major
challenge for environmentalists.[2] Most conservation work, after all, does
not take place online. It is, by necessity, focused on offline environments
and how human and nonhuman natures impact each other's lifeworlds.[3]
Until now this book has been rather abstracted from these lifeworlds
and the daily praxis of actual conservation organizations, interventions,
and causes as well as the people that act in them. This was necessary
to understand the more structural pressures and dynamics brought by
platform capitalism, and the consequent contradictions. To develop a

holistic inquiry, it is equally necessary to bring people's experiences and real-life situations into the analysis.

There is another important reason to do so. As platform capitalism is changing the way the global political economy works, environmental actors have not been sitting back and letting platform dynamics wash over them. As I show in this chapter, they are active players in all of this. Environmental actors not only employ, direct, or manipulate the technological, political, and economic developments in their favor but also continue to "#ShareTheFacts" about wildlife and nature and put pressure on other actors to join or respect #ConservationAction. In doing so, they navigate many different dynamics and issues; those around platform capitalism are increasingly important, but they are not the only ones. Hence, we need to broaden the context within which real-life conservation unfolds vis-à-vis other political-economic, social, and ecological dynamics that come into play when trying to conserve nature in actual places and contexts. How do those interested in doing justice to what they believe is the truth about nature mediate conservation politics in an era of platform capitalism? This chapter provides a first attempt at answering this question. Subsequent chapters delve into details around specific conservation initiatives, areas, and issues in (relation to) Southern Africa.

Specifically, in this chapter I want to highlight important conceptual and empirical aspects of the politics of conservation in the era of platform capitalism—conservation 2.0 in short. How do conservation organizations relate to this?[4] How do they manage the relations between online and offline? How do they do justice to science and truths about nature in this process? Importantly, I will show that questions of history, context, and positionality come back with a vengeance. They might not be visible for algorithms. But they are very visible and real to the people who employ nature 2.0 to save offline natures. These histories, contexts, and positionalities are, in turn, imbued with manifold interests, ambitions, and sensitivities that need to be recognized. By focusing on these elements, the chapter shows that conservation organizations often do recognize the contradictions of conservation 2.0, yet nonetheless compound them in their drive to share the truth about nature. Thus, environmental actors might subversively try to turn #MAGA into #MEGA—#MakeEarthGreatAgain—this subversion still stimulates platform development of the kind that might undermine conservation goals. This last point becomes even clearer toward the end of the chapter when we take a look at the total sum of online conservation actions—the world wide web of nature 2.0.

This chapter is informed by data derived from over a dozen interviews with conservation actors at influential conservation organizations in the Netherlands, the United States, and South Africa between 2012 and 2015.[5] The rest of the data come from online sources collected since 2012. It is important to emphasize that the data that inform this chapter are partial and biased. While I did manage to interview new media staff at many major conservation NGOs, this was not initially part of my research plan, so I may have missed crucial voices. Moreover, the data are influenced by my own online behavior—which informs the algorithms that subsequently (co-)direct my search results, Facebook wall, Twitter feed, and so forth—and thus not truly representative of the digital natureglut out there.[6] This makes the data even more biased and partial.

I devised two strategies to deal with this problem: one analytical and one methodological. The analytical strategy was to let the tentativeness and the rapid rate of change that characterizes the digital natureglut influence my analysis and argument. In other words: the fact that my data are biased, partial, and selective in ways that are hard to comprehend, even for myself, is part of the argument I make in this chapter. As I will illustrate, *the choices that conservation organizations make in sharing truths and natures online renders both nature and truth biased, partial, and selective.* These choices become part of a politics of cocreation that is at the center of conservation 2.0. In the next chapters, however, I aim to move beyond this tentativeness and present more grounded arguments in their multiple online and offline contexts. The methodological strategy to do so entailed "ground-truthing" online data with offline data. Focusing these offline ventures on a region I know well helped me to understand the broader contexts within which actors pursue conservation initiatives and share truths and natures.

THE RISE AND PROFESSIONALIZATION OF SOCIAL MEDIA IN CONSERVATION ORGANIZATIONS

A simple observation: environmentalism is much older than social media. Trite though this observation may be, it is crucial in understanding how the latter came to influence the conservation world. Thus, while many see social media as a game changer, even the holy grail for conservation, many others are skeptical. This was clear during several of my interviews. Most conservation organizations, and especially the more senior people who had been working there for long(er) did not (immediately) see the potential of social media, or even the necessity to take it seriously. As one community manager responded after I asked him how he got into managing social media:

'Well, you are young—do social media. . . .' I came to [conservation organization] to do a project with a social media component, and before I was a web-writer, and social media at the time was an afterthought. So I was tweeting and finding my voice and [conservation organization's] voice. Many older people in the organization didn't grow up using it, but I did. People on lower levels do the programmatic stuff; they are closer to the ground— the CEO has other responsibilities, traveling the world, meeting important people, etcetera.[7]

The idea was that since my respondent was young, he knew and could therefore manage social media. A similar experience comes from an online marketing and social media advisor at a Dutch environmental organization, who stated in 2012, "I started about two years ago, sort of secretly behind my job. At first, nobody knew about it, but it grew and started becoming a success, and then people started noticing. When that happened, we needed to make a plan about why we used the page, and how many people we reach."[8]

Other interviewees, recounted similar experiences, showing that social media needed to be integrated into and learned by conservation organizations. This happened differently in different organizations, though a common thread seems to be that social media engagement evolved from younger whiz kids in the organization who took it up and then convinced senior management that this was important. In a rapid timespan, from about 2006–2008 to about 2012–2014, the turn to social media has notably changed most environmental organizations. As one respondent recalls the changes (who refers to his organization as "the brand"): "I just used it personally and started thinking we can use it for the brand as well. That was three years ago, when you could still mess around and try out things; now you have to have a strategy and think about what you are doing. And now I give courses to the rest of the employees on Facebook, Twitter, etcetera, for example about what is smart to post."[9] And another one: "People used to write and phone to ask questions, but that has shifted to Facebook. . . . We try to do more crossmedia communication here, bringing the right message to the specific audience of each medium. But although we are trying to bring more structure in our media strategy, for the last years we learned in social media by stumbling forward in it."[10]

Yet, after some stumbling, pioneering, and trying out, many organizations rapidly professionalized their social media engagement. This entails, for example, a greater coherence in how people within the organization communicate via social media, as an interview with two respondents from the same organization illustrates:

Respondent one: The question is, what do you communicate? You have to be critical about that, not everything is suitable for twittering.

Respondent two: We have now developed a protocol: when do you tweet, when do you answer on Twitter? The latter is something you have to do, so it is also quite demanding on employees. To some of them it comes naturally, but for others not, and that is sometimes forgotten. A lot of people start off enthusiastically but then gradually lose interest. But when you start, you have to make sure the whole organization is with it as it is a "diffuse" mechanism.[11]

The professionalization of social media engagement is not just about coherence across the organization. It is—importantly for the argument in this chapter—about understanding and mediating platforms such that they support the strategy of the organization. In other words, conservation actors are no dupes of platform developments outside of their control; they actively try to mediate, manage, and change the possibilities that platforms provide, especially the possibilities for cocreation. To illustrate these possibilities, we can refer to Google. Google helps us receive search results that fit with our preferences (tracked through cookies and other trackers) and that reflect the interests of businesses and organizations that either pay Google directly or know how to influence its algorithm. Indeed, a whole cottage industry has developed around managing the cocreation of online profiles and, for that matter, online "truth." Take the UK company Reputation Defender. They introduce their services as follows: "Search engines decide which version of the truth people see. How do we find out about someone these days? We Google them. What appears may not always be to our liking. Most people don't look beyond page 1 of search results, so whatever appears will influence their opinion of you. We help you control your online reputation by creating a more balanced and true reflection of who you are."[12] Reputation Defender focuses on individuals and their reputation. But many conservation organizations now employ these types of services. According to a social media staff officer, "Tracebuzz helps you trace how it buzzes around on websites, tweets, etcetera. This weekend I was on the monitor—thousands of websites and messages that need your attention—by tracing it, we can respond to the buzz. It is something else, quite incredible. It is pretty expensive still to use—we have a good deal with the organization that sells the license—about €5,000 per month, which is a lot for us, but will become cheaper (see https://www.tracebuzz.com/)."[13] This program alerts the organization to specific dynamics in online discussions so that these can be managed and intervened in, if deemed necessary. This same strategy was also mentioned by others, and hence a great deal of attention goes into social media monitoring to ensure that online discussions stay on course— meaning: in tune with the goals (and associated truths about nature) of conservation organizations.

Another social media expert at a large Dutch environmental NGO also explained how they analyze social media data and how this is a "prestige thing" because they compete with other social media users, including political parties: "We use the IPM (interaction per mile—per 1.000 fans) so that we can compare Facebook pages with each other. It is a complex formula that helps to calculate the interaction rate on your page, so you can compare the quality of the fans on Facebook pages. Right now, we are the second-best page in the Netherlands. The VVD [a Dutch political party] is first, but that is because of the election, with many people congratulating them. But next week we will hope- fully be first again."[14] Interestingly, WWF keeps track of the number of supporters on their key social media channels (Facebook, Twitter, and YouTube). On the website http://wwfsocialstats.appspot.com/ you can see that, according to WWF, "it's busy at the watering hole"—boasting figures in the millions in terms of Facebook likes, Twitter followers, and YouTube views. But in interviews it was not just about the figures and the number of fans or likes. The question is how these translate into meaningful engagement:

> One can look at the number of likes for a page as a whole; the total number of followers is important, but the engagement percentage is for me much more important—the people liking, sharing, commenting, etcetera. There was a study ["Study: Only 1% of Facebook 'Fans' Engage with Brands," http://adage.com/article/digital/study-1-facebook-fans-engage-brands /232351/], that looked at the largest commercial entities with significant name recognition and said that from all people that like them, only 1 percent are really engaged. Our goal is 3–5 percent—to do a little bit better, so that is the benchmark. We can spike anywhere to 10–14 percent. So I am also very focused on the engagement numbers.[15]

A staff officer at a Dutch environmental organization corroborated this point: "Liking an organization on Facebook is not a very big step for people; you can't really give very much meaning to it, it's just one click. The next much more interesting step is getting people involved and leading them to your own website eventually. There you have more opportunities for fundraising and other forms of involvement."[16]

What this signifies is that online behavior—down to every individual click—is monitored, and that it is not just the exposure that matters. It is also, and arguably more importantly, engagement and action that conservation organizations are after. Hence, the rapid rise of social media at conservation organizations—at least from my interviews—shows precisely this: that its use has risen swiftly and gone through rapid processes of professionalization. How this happened in organizations differs tremendously. It stands to reason that certain organizations do this better than others and that the bigger organizations have more resources to manipulate and influence new media.

CHANGING CONSERVATION WORK

The rise and professionalization of social media in conservation organizations has changed environmental organizations and the way they work in many ways. One noticeable change is that social media continues 24/7. Many of my interviewees mentioned this, including the benefits and challenges this brings:

> I try to find the appropriate balance—not always to work in the weekend, but it doesn't stop after 5 p.m., so I try to get balance, so if I don't respond to someone immediately, then I cut myself some slack. Sometimes I take some time and get discrete chunks of social media time.[17]

> The weekends we also work if needed—we worked yesterday [Sunday]. So yesterday we had a press release and then we communicated with each other, in order to get it on the website and then on Facebook.[18]

> Three people work on the web team, but also on social media. So we have shifts of three weeks—you are responsible to reply and post stuff on all accounts, so this is also in the weekends. Social life is possible in those weekends but it can be busy sometimes. That is why you do three weeks and then you have six weeks off. But we do that with company phones.[19]

These three different quotes indicate that staff had to get used to working more outside of office hours, and that organizations plan social media engagement to keep on top of things, including over the weekends. Most respondents did not really mind, though one remarked that "the boundary between work and private life is fading."[20]

Another way in which social media have changed conservation organizations is that there is now more pressure on them to be accountable, transparent, and on top of things. For example, in response to my question whether social media put pressure on the organization, three social media experts with a South African environmental organization stated:

Respondent one: Yes, especially because people want answers yesterday—it is the whole impatience thing [respondent three] referred to. So, for example, you might be working on getting information together in order to get people the full story, but they want it now.

Respondent two: And it even happened that if you stay quiet for half an hour, they think you are hiding the facts!

Respondent three: It is about things going viral, so if you don't respond, then it has happened that somebody spread rumors, which then go viral and then people get mad with [environmental organization] without actually knowing what is going on.

Respondent one: The point is just that people want it, and want it now, and that they are really impatient.

Respondent two: What we have noticed is that the inputs you give are critical—if you reason with them, and if you give them the right information, and give it to them soon, then you can turn a critic into a supporter. It is human nature; people want to be heard and acknowledged. And then you can turn them around (only for reasonable, constructive opinions) and then you build ambassadors for the organization (especially in relation to how quickly you respond).[21]

Similarly, my respondent from a large American conservation NGO also mentioned that social media pressurizes the organization to be(come) more accountable and open:

[The CEO] said, for example, that not everybody has to agree, but at least people should believe what we say is truthful. If you don't, people can now use social media to amplify issues and responses. So, if you have something to hide, you should reevaluate—you should be transparent and truthful. Like with corporate actors, [conservation organization] doesn't believe it can change actors, but we are willing to listen how it can change better, but this is still this approach, which we should be open about. The option on social media is there—many don't use it, but they can.[22]

Interesting about this quote is that "being open" is equated with being "truthful." This seems to imply that being open about *what* organizations do also provides legitimacy for truth claims in relation to their conservation solutions and *how* these (re)present nature. I will come back to this point below. For now, it is important to emphasize that new media have significantly changed conservation organizations and how they interact with supporters and the broader public. Another outcome from the discussion so far is that social media have brought new pressures on conservation organizations and that they are not passive in all of this. They employ the same new media platforms that have changed them to affect the types of change they are after.

PLATFORM POSSIBILITIES FOR EFFECTING CHANGE

The above interview quotes show that environmental organizations have had to learn quickly and that they are active players in the brave new world of social media platforms. Many conservation organizations have specialized staff who understand how they work and how to use them. These professionals are often very creative and use their knowledge to mediate and influence new media platforms to affect environmental change in the offline world. A senior communications manager aptly illustrates this point: "With other NGOs we worked on prohibiting the Brazilian forest code, we wanted the Brazilian president to veto the forest code, so together with other NGOs and all our constituencies we could put more pressure. Also, through AVAAZ, we created a petition to put pressure. We call our online followers our friends, so we asked our friends to sign that petition on AVAAZ. And Greenpeace were doing the same, also driving traffic to that site, and so combined voices become stronger"[23] This interview was in June 2012, and the action the interviewee was referring to sounded familiar to me. Back home, after the interview, I checked my emails (I had, in the year prior, subscribed to many organizations' listservs to keep up-to-date on their social media activities) and found an email I had received from Greenpeace on 19 April 2012. It stated that the Amazon needed 1.4 million friends and urged me to take action. The problem was that Brazilian landowners were "doing everything in their power to amend the current law that protects the rainforest. These changes would give them carte blanche to chop down an additional area of forest the size of Great Britain."[24] The goal was to collect 1.4 million Brazilian signatures in favor of a Zero Deforestation Law, which would force the Brazilian parliament to discuss the law and put pressure on them to reject the alternative, destructive option. Online petitions have, of course, become ubiquitous, so, at first, I thought this was just another attempt to get me to sign something online. But Greenpeace was not interested in my signature. They wanted *Brazilian* signatures. The reason the email was sent to me was to make use of my social media networks and urge me to urge my Brazilian friends to sign the petition. "Do you not know any Brazilians?" the email asked. "We will help you. Through our website, the *Brazilian Friend Finder*, you will easily find Brazilians on your social networks."

I never did use the Brazilian Friend Finder. Yet it stuck with me as an intriguing example of how new online media have changed the politics of conservation. Greenpeace used specially designed Facebook and Twitter apps to locate online and "unique individual" Brazilians to expand their reach and put pressure on the Brazilian president and legislature.[25] Several weeks later, the news broke that "Brazilian president Dilma Rousseff had partially vetoed a bill that would have weakened her country's efforts to protect the Amazon and other forests."[26] Whether this was due to the Brazilian Friend Finder is speculation. But certain is that online new media were crucial in orchestrating, amplifying, and communicating the pressure on Rousseff, while allowing those concerned with the fate of the Amazon rainforest to take action and be involved in efforts for its conservation.

A similar example comes from Indonesia, where conservationists have also been putting pressure on the government to protect rainforests and the species they contain. One of their strategies has been to take companies destroying rainforests—in most cases for palm oil—to court and then applying media pressure to ensure that corrupt judges will not be bought off by those same companies. After explaining how several documentaries were produced about the deforestation and shared on their social media channels, one senior conservationist told me: "The judges were monitoring our Facebook; things would get quiet, and then BANG, we blow them up again; keeping pressure on the court cases going." In this way, he explained, "social media was instrumental in getting the government to take action because it was becoming embarrassed," simply because of the "armada of media pressure."[27]

Clearly, conservation 2.0 means that new media can inspire offline action. And this is not just action from professional conservationists, as other interviews also indicate. For example, after I asked the question whether more people have a relation with nature areas through social media, a staff officer at a conservation organization in the Netherlands answered: "Yes, indeed. There is an example of people buying square meters of nature in Bilthoven [A Dutch town], triggered by Twitter and especially Facebook, which have had an effect on these people even if perhaps they haven't been to those areas—they still feel they have some attachment to those areas."[28] An online marketing and social media advisor at another Dutch conservation organization is even more outspoken about this issue:

> The corporate Twitter is mostly corporate news, for people interested in the corporation, while Facebook is more for fans of nature in the Netherlands; that is the main difference. Twitter is also used by rangers. Forty-two rangers have iPhones and are twittering, they share stories about what they experience and see, and they post pictures. They also answer a lot of questions, for example in relation to pictures that people have taken. So they are kind of a webcare team, but independent of the organization. Most of their followers are people from the forest or reserve in their neighborhood, so it is hyper-local. We also have Facebook pages for many individual reserves and forests. Corporately, we brand nature in Holland in total but if you live next to nature, then you go to nature over there, for example in the Veluwe, and then you are not as interested in nature in Groningen (for example). We see that people are mostly interesting in the areas where they live. You don't reach as many people, but the quality of the fan is higher.[29]

This shows that social media can make local connections between people and nature, something that is different for more internationally focused NGOs, like WWF, who must resort to new media to bring "far away natures" closer: "In the case of WWF, a lot of our work is done abroad, where the biodiversity value is highest—Amazon is more valuable than the Veluwe [a Dutch nature reserve]—but for many supporters it is very far away, so it is also a means to bring that closer to them"[30]

More examples could be given, but the point remains the same: environmental organizations actively employ new media to effect (offline) change.[31] At the same time, online conservation activism and activities are also challenged. As environmental organizations become smarter in using cocreation possibilities to pursue their goals, so those same possibilities are used to complicate if not counter and actively challenge conservation messages. Thus, while the above example of the Brazilian Friend Finder may seem like a smoothly organized campaign, actual social media practice is never very smooth. Social media campaigns are, by definition, part of the broader maelstrom of online digital natureglut—and the online infoglut more generally—and hence always partial for those supporting the campaign online (save, perhaps, for true diehards that focus on a specific campaign for a period of time only). This is because the supporters and receivers of well-orchestrated online conservation campaigns can also use the cocreation spaces to complicate or challenge the campaign, with consequences for the truths and natures those campaigns (aim to) embody.

COCREATING TRUTHS AND NATURES

Environmental actors are savvy. They study and learn about the contexts they are in, and work with and try to influence those in different ways.[32] This obviously includes new media, as books like James N. Levitt's edited volume *Conservation in the Internet Age: Threats and Opportunities* points out. It is within these contexts that conservationists, as stated in the introduction, doggedly and passionately continue to study and discover truths and facts about nature. But this is only part of the picture. In these same contexts, it is clear that many actors do not share and even actively challenge (aspects of) "the truth about nature" as depicted by (mainstream) conservation. And these actors have also become savvy online. Put the two together and what we get is a more concrete understanding of the politics of cocreation unleashed by conservation 2.0. This is a politics based on the *creativity* and *originality* (as well as the volume) of online sharing. What this means is not only that online sharing is (often) coordinated and monitored, but also that the success of defending or challenging certain interests—and their corresponding truth-discourses—greatly depends on the creativity and originality of online social media practices. Evidently, the practices included in this politics are extremely wide ranging.

An appropriate illustration is the #Selfie campaign, discussed by Roberta Hawkins and Jennifer Silver. They argue that indigenous peoples and others, by changing the conservation frame attached to a famous "selfie" to the Twitter Hashtag #Selfie, opened space to challenge a strong, and engrained conservation narrative against sealing in Canada. They explain: "The emergence of #Selfie is characterized by a cultural politics wherein posters seemed motivated to speak back against engrained narratives about baby seals and barbaric sealers, and in some cases, to explicitly call into question the authority of individuals and organizations that advocate an end to commercial sealing in Canada. Because the #Selfie phenomenon was picked up and reported in journalistic media, broader national and international attention was drawn to their concerns and challenges."[33] In this way, indigenous Canadian seal hunters used new media to challenge anti-sealing celebrities such as talk show host Ellen Degeneres directly. Creative use of hashtags, Hawkins and Silver show, can and does change conservation politics in favor of those normally marginalized in global debates.

Another way in which the truth about nature is challenged is through new online forms of culture-jamming. One example is through games on http://www.molleindustria.org/. The website describes itself as "a project about games and ideology, it's a bit of art, media activism, research, and agitp[r]op. The idea is to apply the culture jamming/tactical media (remember tactical media?) treatment to videogames: spreading radical memes and, in the process, challenging the language of power, the infrastructures, the modes, genres and tropes of the dominant discourse which was omnipresent in videogame culture." Importantly, not only does this website challenge truths about nature generated by conservation videogames, it also challenges the neoliberal ideology often espoused by conservation organizations. Other interesting examples in this regard are Tinnell's initiative to use "eco-blogging" as part of an "ecopedagogy" to "critique established, consumeristic online communication" and the attempts by activists to hijack the Twitter hashtag of the World Forum on Natural Capital, held in Edinburgh in the November 2013, to force them to address environmental justice issues.[34] A final example in this category is an anonymous twitter account that calls itself The Panda Bare, who started following me sometime in 2017 and clearly shows itself critical of mainstream conservation and its general mode of communication online. Its profile text reads "Not impressed by corporate green PR, vacuous 'motivational quotes' or wildlife pics for self-interested fundraising."[35]

These counterexamples, however important and powerful, are few and far between. They are rarely if ever found on the social media spaces of the large environmental organizations that attract the majority of global conservation funding. Most conservation actors employing new media tools openly espouse their neoliberal vision for conservation (like Conservation International and The Nature Conservancy), while others do not explicate their stance for fear of sounding political (and consequently often do not resist the dominant political economy). This does not mean that those working for conservation organizations do not recognize that moving along with—rather than challenging—the dominant political economy, including how it translates into the platform model, is problematic. Take the following interview excerpt: "There is a principal contradiction in the personal profile and the commercial nature of

Facebook. Their business model has a tendency to destroy the feeling of intimacy people are looking for. So we will see how long people are comfortable in that environment and keep trusting Facebook."[36] Yet despite this more critical comment, the same staff officer also noted that online supporters do try to create intimacy:

> A side effect is we discovered bird watching on the internet attracted people that are less nature oriented and more animal oriented—it is not birds, but *that* bird, more like a pet—it is a way to make birds personal. Sometimes people even like to give a name to a wild bird, and people talk about the bird getting a baby—the original birders would never call a young bird a baby. . . . But our mission is not to protect individuals, but *nature* so that we can conserve species. But people relate to *one* bird through social media—feeling compassion for animals in that sense is double. We are a *nature* conservation organization, we want to conserve nature, but pressure from the outside is strong. We try to stay science based in our decisions and policy, and not sentimentally or emotion driven.[37]

This is a very interesting quote. It shows the types of intimacy people foster online—focusing on individual birds, giving them names—and that this does not quite fit with "the truth about nature" espoused by the organization. The truth here is that nature is not about individuals but about (the survival of) species. The latter is "science based" while the former is "sentimentally or emotion driven."[38]

Overall, critical remarks in my interviews were rare, and they seem even rarer online. Most conservation actors still appear quite content to move with the neoliberal "spirit of the time."[39] As one interviewee from a South African platform development organization with clients in the conservation sector argues, "Times have changed, and we need to now focus on the greatest impact. And the greatest impact can be done by being more business-like."[40] But going with the spirit of the time, also means going along with its (algo)rhythms. And one of the key elements that many interviewees kept emphasizing—and that I encountered in my own research as well—is the pace of change of new media. How do environmentalists deal with this? And how does this affect the relation between truth and nature?

THE CHANGE NEW MEDIA MAKE

Things change very quickly online, and it is hard for organizations to keep up. This relates not just to content, but also to platform features or trends in the social media landscape. Environmental organizations employ programs to help them make sense of social media or learn from those actors who see themselves as visionaries, who walk ahead of the crowd by staying up to date on new features and trends and relay these to others. One of my interviewees mentioned that she learns a lot from such gurus and specifically recommended me to take note of Daniella Brigida, who calls herself a "net naturalist." Brigida self-describes as "an early adopter of social media with creative, engaging campaigns that are grounded in meaning." Her website states that she is "recognized as one of the 10 Most Generous Social Media Mavens by Fast Company; one of the 75 Environmentalists to follow by Mashable" and "one of 10 People to Follow Who are Saving the World by Mother Nature Network."[41] On her site, Brigida collects tips for engaging with social media and posts on things like how to "create Facebook interest lists," "common mistakes to avoid while tweeting," or "5 Tools for Tracking Hashtags Like #WildlifeWeek."

One of the consistent elements in Brigida's posts is how to stay up to date on social media features and how to use these for effective, organized, and structured social media communication. A typical post in this respect is one that I received over email on 7 May 2015, titled "Trail Guide for Facebook."[42] Brigida writes that, as "Facebook is constantly changing . . . it's apparent that some things are working better than others." She next encourages us to "be social" (by tagging pages, nurturing comments, etc.), "post more videos" (as these "are doing well on Facebook's algorithm right now") and to "post often," among other recommendations. These, many other posts, and similar blogs by other social media gurus aim to keep conservation professionals and interested amateurs up-to-date on changing platform features and how to effectively instigate environmental change through new media. In doing so, they help us to "explore the social media ecosystem," as Brigida refers to it.[43] To a good degree, they also naturalize the pace of change of social media and the ways in which this ecosystem allows for sharing (the truth about) nature. The ultimate expression of this is when medium = message, as the #LastSelfie example showed.

While these tips and lessons may allow for more control over and reflection on social media by conservation actors, this does not mean that supporters also experience social media communication in the same way. For them, any one message or tweet still becomes part of the "overload of parallel information sources."[44] Moreover, building on Judy Wajcman's remark that "the speed of Google's search engine so enthralls us that we seldom reflect on the fact that it favors some content over others," the pace of change in this overload may lead many to simply believe certain #FactorsOfWildlife, even though the context that renders these facts meaningful is absent.[45] This is where carefully and creatively crafted social media campaigns may still falter under the weight of algorithmic relations as "knowledge without truth."

This brings us back to the idea of spectacular environmentalisms: as conservation actors, prodded and aided by social media gurus, become more astute in understanding *and* (co)creating spectacular environmentalisms, and hence the mediation of relationships by images, they also further encourage the concealment of connections and contexts that define those same relationships. Or rather, to quote Jim Igoe, they create "unique possibilities for elaborate and pervasive presentations of connection and context, which are visually compelling to the point of being mistaken for the connections and contexts that they simultaneously draw upon and conceal."[46] While they may not say it in this way, conservation professionals show that they are aware of this reality, as the following quote illustrates: "Twitter has been great because it has been more immediate. With Facebook I try very hard to not overwhelm people with information—I post twice a day, spread it out every day. With Twitter it is more a scrolling news feed, and people have been used to it, so it is great, because it allows us to talk about events in real time. We can communicate when things are happening."[47] This informant tries "hard not to overwhelm people with information" on Facebook, while Danielle Brigida, in her above blog post, advises her followers to "play with the platform and strive to be different." This, together with the data presented in prior sections, suggests two things. First, conservation actors, even if they are aware of the pitfalls of platform capitalism, continue to share "the truth about nature" online. Second, in doing so, creativity, originality, and volume are crucial in the politics of cocreation; of promoting particular conservation interests within and through the fast-changing constraints and possibilities of social media platforms and the digital natureglut they have facilitated. Some campaigns, like #LastSelfie, fit these criteria and become a success. Other campaigns may also fit the criteria but, as I will show below, fail miserably.

All this, however, does not (necessarily) lead to more control over the sharing of truths and natures or generate more desired effects. Quite the opposite: no matter how creative, active, and astute conservationists' tactics in sharing truths and natures are, this sharing—together with attempts at resistance—still thickens the digital natureglut. The reason for this is not necessarily clear from the analysis so far, because many of the above quotes relate to the dominant types of social media, especially Facebook and Twitter, and how they are used by established conservation NGOs.[48] If we restrict our analysis to these, however, we get only a limited sense of the variety of possibilities in the worldwide web of nature 2.0 that is currently being built online. It is therefore important to provide a brief glimpse of this variety.

THE WORLDWIDE WEB OF NATURE 2.0

In earlier work, I have argued that next to the major platforms there are four main categories of nature 2.0 online: search engines, online games, online communities, and apps.[49] Integrated into these categories are technologies such as webcams, real-time live streams, augmented or virtual reality, and more that offer further possibilities to render nature 2.0 (even more) spectacular. Next to the many longer-standing conservation NGOs, countless other organizations, including new (online) start-ups, are experimenting with these possibilities. What follows are some examples across these categories that stood out in my research. The point will not be to present a representative sample of (further) nature 2.0 possibilities (if this were at all possible), but to present a sample of the types of initiatives out there, and the conservation discourses they espouse.

Ecological search engines such as www.ecosearch.org and www.ecosia.org promise that every search done through their engines leads to advertising income that is subsequently used for environmental projects. This is nature 2.0 lite: some input is needed—a query—but that is as far as interactivity goes. Online communities dedicated toward environmental ends are more interactive but follow the same basic principle as Facebook. The longstanding platform www.care2.com has over 44.7 million community members, while www.nudge.nl and www.ampyourimpact.com are more focused communities that try to help share sustainability resources. A similar category relates to dedicated web 2.0 platforms aiming to give (potential) supporters new cocreative possibilities to engage in conservation action. These have certain peculiarities that are interesting to discuss, but this will come in the following chapter. The focus here will be on the most interactive categories: games and apps.

The gaming industry is massive, and games are increasingly used for conservation. Early on in my research, I came across a Facebook game called My Conservation Park. The aim was to run an online park that, supposedly, had a direct link to offline conservation. As the narration went: "Today, you are part of our virtual conservation team. Living right here, in My Conservation Park, working hand in hand to protect and defend the same species offline." What this means was also explained: "Together, we must counteract the destructive impacts of encroaching human population." The accompanying video was unambiguous about what this looks like: as the player, you are a little green man protecting nature. In one scene, the little man successfully stops desperate hordes of people trying to get into nature. While doing so, it is smiling, having fun.[50] The game is no longer active, possibly because this representation of what saving nature looks like in practice was problematic. My Conservation Park was one of the examples I had hoped to investigate over a longer period but the game's disappearance from the web prevented this.

A game I was able to follow for longer was Rhino Raid (figures 5 and 6). This game for mobile phones was designed by Flint Sky for WWF South Africa. You, the player, are the rhino, who tries to "thump" poachers. Google Play describes the game as follows:

> It's about the most Rad-ical rhino to run across your screen—ever! And he's on a mission for good—to save the rhinos of Southern Africa. Brought to you by the World Wide Fund for Nature (WWF) South Africa. Play now and save the rhinos. Rad keeps up a running charge against poachers and their arsenal of weapons. With the help of his trusted ally, Horn Bill, Rad has to dodge the flying hand grenades and automatic rifle fire; jump over exploding barrels . . . then thump the poachers as you chase after their getaway trucks and get one charge closer to Mr Big, kingpin behind the international rhino poaching syndicates. Rad's adventure across the African savannah is punctuated by WWF's key insights into facts about rhinos and the truth behind the rhino poaching scourge. Rhino Raid aims to create awareness of WWF"s rhino conservation projects in South Africa. It's fun, it's for good . . . and it's RAD![51]

The game, according to WWF South Africa, was meant to target new audiences that spend a lot of time behind computer screens in order to do "transnational, cross-cultural messaging that would subliminally or not so subliminally provide messages that would lead to change."[52] The (not so) subliminal messages all have to do with the rhino-poaching crisis, though the promotors of the game admitted that they did not know whether it had any impact on behavior change.[53] One could argue that another subliminal message of an action game like this is that problems can be solved—besides through gaming—through heroes who "thump"

FIGURE 5. Rhino Raid still. Credit: ©Flint Sky Interactive; http://www.flintsky.com
/projects/rhino-raid/

FIGURE 6. Rhino Raid still. Credit: ©Flint Sky Interactive; http://www.flintsky.com
/projects/rhino-raid/

poachers in the poaching war. This messaging, whatever else it may achieve, runs the risk of adding to the racialized hysteria that I will argue in chapter 6 characterizes the online dimension of the rhino poaching crisis.

There are, obviously, many other conservation games around, some of which can be found on sites like http://ecogamer.org/ and http://www.gamesfornature.org/. One further intriguing example combines an app and a game. My Green World is about allowing "users to participate in real-world wildlife conservation and habitat restoration scenarios, and each action that a user takes in the game will assist affiliate charities to emulate those actions in real life." It explicitly says it "gamifies the concept of saving animals, and will allow users to rescue, rehabilitate and care for animals and habitats within their own carefully crafted world." The makers of the game are anything but modest: "This game will revolutionise the way that the public connects with wildlife, environmental and animal welfare issues, and will make it possible for anybody to make real, positive changes in the natural world. This game will empower the global community and transform game culture while restoring the natural world. This app truly is a change to the status quo; utilising online activism to achieve tangible results in conservation."[54]

Next to games—or apps-as-games—there are many (mobile or web-based) environmental apps with varying degrees of cocreative possibilities. Important is that these are available on mobile phones, and thus (even) more omnipresent than laptops. Within these apps, but also on platforms and general websites, many other possibilities are tested, including webcams, livestreams and augmented reality. An interesting example bringing several of these elements together is Safari Central by Internet of Elephants. Acknowledging digital infoglut, they relay the "challenge for conservation" as follows: "With intense competition for the attention of today's consumers, getting people to pay attention to wildlife and its conservation is not easy. It can be a constant struggle for wildlife conservation organizations to keep their existing donors truly engaged, develop future donor pipelines, bring attention to their work and educate local and global audiences."[55] The answer, according to Internet of Elephants, is "technology and games." The reason: "Tomorrow's conservationist needs to be attracted on their terms. Online games are played by over 2 Billion people worldwide and have a proven capacity to captivate an audience. Games are social, emotional, participative, fun, accessible and lasting."

The game app developed by Internet of Elephants transports "real wild animals" into your mobile camera frame through augmented reality technologies. Through your mobile camera, you can "follow" the routes of actual wild animals through the city you live in and see augmented versions of these species moving through your screen. You can also make selfies and pictures of yourself and friends with the augmented animals and share these on your other social media. In the words of Internet of Elephants, "We partner with leading conservation organizations to create awe-inspiring digital versions and stories of the animals they study and protect to make them famous; and put the work of our partners in the limelight of global audiences."[56] Unlike the people behind My Green World, who seem to believe they can singlehandedly "empower the global community," Internet of Elephants focuses more on supporting existing conservation NGOs. They state that they have a "number of products that can be customized to fit your campaigns and digital engagement strategy."[57]

A final illustration is an app called Tails Up! The app was developed by the international Association of Zoos and Aquariums (AZA) and self-describes as a "fun way for kids of all ages to learn about all kinds of animals."[58] In an interview, Gregg Oosterbaan, a member of the AZA TailsUp! Creative Task Force, introduces the app: "We were challenged by the perception that an online and mobile app component to a wildlife conservation grant could be considered an oxymoron, but we were also realistic about the prevalent use of 'screens' by today's young people."[59] Hence, again, while being aware of the possible contradictions, conservation actors still feel they have to be "realistic" and compound the digital natureglut. Not only that, they also encourage users to share their cocreated natures. Oosterbaan again: "Video is recorded of the players acting out the animals they see on the screen, which is resulting in some pretty hilarious content people can share." Also: "You can review the animals you just acted out and share interesting animal facts on social media with your friends and family."[60]

These are just some samples from my research. Multiply this by hundreds, if not thousands, and we start to get a sense of the thickness of the digital natureglut out there. Many initiatives, clearly, are ambitious, like My Conservation Park was before it vanished, and My Green World, at the time of writing. Moreover, many of these initiatives are not meant to encourage people to think critically about conservation, but to engage users in "the truth about nature." Many games or apps often do not provide space for responses and comments, although Facebook,

Twitter and Instagram are almost always attached to or integrated in these possibilities. But what types of change do these initiatives—and yet others—instill in the offline world? Some are extremely confident that they will change the world. Is this justified?

If we look at the early literature on conservation games and apps, we should be doubtful. Sandbrook and colleagues argue that "conservation games may mislead if their modeled or synthesized environments oversimplify or misrepresent real-world problems." In this way, "conservation games might succeed in raising awareness, but at the same time reduce understanding of an issue."[61] According to Fletcher, "digital games may at times actually inspire more affective commitment to environmental causes than the direct experiences most conservationists advocate." Yet, at the same time, "engagement with digital games can create a false sense of agency in that belief in the efficacy of one's virtual engagement may discourage more direct entanglement in the complicated and contentious politics of 'real' natural resource management."[62] Finally, Stinson, who studied augmented 2.0 wilderness experiences, argues that "this new ontology of wilderness does not just allow for nature to be represented and experienced in novel ways, but has opened up wilderness and wilderness-based recreation to new forms of governmental rationality and economic exploitation." In particular, "the increasing visibility of wilderness-based recreation afforded by social media and apps (and the data created by their use), has allowed it to be exploited as a form of virtual labour."[63]

These are important arguments, and much in this book undergirds them. Yet they do not have a basis in extensive empirical research, nor do they capture the online elements in a broader context that includes offline dynamics. These factors, I argue, are critical to put arguments with respect to the digital natureglut in perspective and create a more holistic picture of conservation 2.0. The following chapters take up this aim.

CONCLUSION

This chapter sought to understand how those interested in doing justice to what they believe is the truth about nature mediate conservation politics in an era of platform capitalism. Importantly, the chapter showed that conservation actors are no dupes, but actively mediate the possibilities they have. They are creative, smart, and often critical about their engagements with social media. And they get social media to work for them and achieve actual conservation aims in the offline world. They are also often aware of challenges. Environmental actors know they cannot fully control the cocreative possibilities of social media, which can and do put pressure on organizations, and they admit that staying abreast of discussions or new features is not easy (not even with supporting programs). More generally, many conservation organizations lament the reality that most young people look at their screens more than at nature. But since it is the "reality," they continue to share nature and to use the tools provided by new media to get others to share, like, and cocreate nature.

In the process, conservation 2.0, or the integration of conservation with platform development, continues apace, and with it digital nature-glut thickens. Most directly, this is through conservation organizations' pages or accounts on Facebook, Twitter, Instagram, and so forth. But it has gone much further. The integration of the Facebook "like" button or other social media plug-ins on their websites is one example.[64] Adjusting messages to fit the medium, as in the #LastSelfie campaign is another. Next to these, many new entrepreneurial start-ups have come up with creative and innovative ideas to promote conservation online. Some of these work by themselves, others with major conservation organizations. Nearly all of them see new social media as a game changer for nature, with some—like My Green World—even believing they will change the "global community." What all of them have in common is that they play with the cocreative possibilities of new media and try to mediate these to promote their interests. This is the politics of cocreation.

The next question is how this affects truths and natures. First, we have seen glimpses of how meanings, intentionalities, and histories, themselves imbued with race, class, gender, age, and other differentials, infuse behind-the-scenes decisions and the types of discourses and images developed online (My Conservation Park, Rhino Raid). Second, we have seen how the creativity allowed by social media is used to turn "the truth about nature" into forms that target audiences can understand and relate to. Through their new media offerings, conservation organizations often help facilitate the alignment of nature with other familiar narratives or emotions, including violence, action, competition, playfulness, and more, leading in turn to violent, competitive, playful, and other natures.[65]

The point here relates to Foucault's and Shapin's argument that truth is situated in social contexts of power and that these contexts overlap and intertwine without people necessarily being aware of them. At the very least, it corroborates the argument that the choices that environmental organizations make in sharing truths and natures online render both nature and truth biased, partial, and selective. From this conclusion it may be hard to see how and why we should still search for something so elusive as truth. Yet we have only scratched the surface. We need to delve far deeper into the messiness and lived realities of daily praxis. The next chapters continue this journey, taking us deep into specific conservation histories, contexts, and positionalities in Southern Africa.

CHAPTER 5

Elephant 2.0

The Politics of Platforms

#DoGoodFeelGood
#Twelephants

INTRODUCTION

"Elephants go!" Cheers for elephants were plenty on the elephant corridor project on www.pifworld.com around May 2010. Pifworld.com is an online crowdsourcing platform that enables its members (called "players") to support and raise funds for conservation and development projects around the world. The elephant corridor is one of these and aims to crowdsource €430,000 for the establishment of an elephant conservation and migration corridor from Chobe National Park in Botswana via the Caprivi Strip in Namibia to the Kafue flats in Zambia. While giving support to the project, players can leave comments behind, chat with and support other players, and share and like comments or other things happening on the site. One player congratulates her friend for becoming a player as well and writes: "Those elephants are very happy with your donation, thanks!!" Another player uses the "support" function to show his appreciation for someone who just donated €10 to the corridor. He comments: "This update on Pifworld rocks! Thumbs up for making it happen! Now let's make that corridor happen too!"

At the top of the page, right below a picture of the globe with the (then) Pifworld slogan "Do Good Feel Good," we see a status bar indicating that, so far, €9,190 have been donated, 3 percent of the overall target of €430,000.[1] It seems that "making the corridor happen" might take some time still. Yet, like several of the initiatives referred to in the last chapter, the ambition for the project was sky high in the early days of Pifworld. Along with the website, a Twitter campaign was launched: "Twelephants." Said one of Pifworld's program officers: "Twelephants is one of the most ambitious projects on the Pifworld platform . . . established to raise awareness for the Elephant Corridor, enabling elephants in Botswana to roam freely across the border to Zambia."[2] A supportive blog post stated: "With an aggressive goal of attracting 100,000 followers on the microblogging platform and securing 430,000 Euros (approx. $645K US) in donations by summer 2010, this campaign needs the support of as many members of the Twitterati as possible. Presently with only 311 followers (as of this posting), Twelephants needs to scale at almost 15,000 followers per month to reach its target"[3] With only 3 percent of the funding and 0.3 percent of the desired Twitter followers secured, confidence that the project would be "the first major step in the realization of the world's largest wildlife park" was nonetheless tremendous around 2010.[4]

Fast forward to 20 December 2013. The elephant corridor is finally funded, with €422,730 raised. After almost four years, this is considered sufficient. Since July 2012, the target counter for the project hovered around 92 percent thanks to a €370,000 donation from the MAVA Foundation. One player—a director of the organization that will receive the funds—responded to this donation by encouraging others to "go the last mile": "We are almost there. Pifworld players lets go for the last mile. 100% after summer? lets go for it!" Other players, too, were excited and exclaimed: "Let's get to the 100%!" "Almost there, let's make the Elephant Corridor a reality!" But "after the summer" was again too ambitious. It would take yet another one and a half years before the counter would rise from €399,100 to €422,730 and the project was considered funded.

DIVERGENT TRUTHS?

This chapter tells the story of the elephant corridor project on Pifworld and how it unfolded from its beginnings in 2010 until and after it was considered funded in December 2013.[5] The elephant corridor project was a typical nature 2.0 initiative. On the Pifworld website, online players co-constructed ideas and imaginations of elephants and landscapes in Southern Africa and so constructed natures that were partly but not entirely of their own making. In the first part of this chapter, I analyze the online and offline dimensions of the elephant corridor over time and show that there was a large disconnect between the natures shared online and the offline natures they were meant to conserve. The elephant corridor was a spectacular environmentalism *in extremis*: the truth presented on the platform had very little to do with the truth offline.

At first glance, the elephant corridor seems a relatively straight-forward case and in line with lessons from political ecology and development studies.[6] It is one where online rhetoric and on-the-ground realities are starkly different and often incongruent—two different worlds that sit at odds with each other, contrary to what online players like to believe. But this is only half the story. Behind the elephant corridor and many similar online projects and crowdsourcing initiatives is a politics of platforms and a battle over the control of doing good online. This politics of platforms is about the ability to be(come) central in the online conservation and development capital and data flows that influence how and where nature lovers spend their time, money, and energy. In the case of the elephant corridor, the penultimate section of the chapter shows that (material) elephants in Southern Africa recede into the background; they become underlying assets for the objective of the Pifworld platform to acquire a central position within the world-wide web of nature 2.0.

In the conclusion, this leads to the argument that what is most inter-esting about the elephant corridor case is not that there are divergent truths, that online philanthropic gestures are far removed from offline realities, though this in itself is important. What the case reveals is how the organization of conservation funding flows have been changing due to the rise of new media platforms. This resembles a broader process where elephants and their plight merge with numerous other conserva-tion and development projects to become the background against which platforms compete over the capital flows that determine the possibilities for "doing good" online. This process, I argue, is post-truth in action, or an expression of power under platform capitalism. This power resem-bles an intensification of older dynamics around development and con-servation aid but also goes beyond it in several ways. In the conclusion, I spell out the implications of this new beast—the elephant 2.0—and the way it affects the politics of platforms focused on online "doing good."

ONLINE PLATFORMS FOR GOOD

The first time I stumbled on Pifworld must have been late 2009 or early 2010. Around that time, many online platforms and initiatives oriented toward developmental or environmental causes emerged or consolidated and started competing with established nongovernmental organizations.[7] While diverse, what united these platforms was their innovative use of new interactive web 2.0 tools to pursue development cooperation, environmental conservation, or general social giving objectives. The 1% Club, for example, referred to this trend as "international cooperation 2.0." Organized around the idea that if we all spend 1 percent of our money, time, and energy on doing good things, the world would be a better place, one of its directors argued: "Through the website you can choose yourself which projects you want to support, so you know exactly where your 1% is going. The website combines Web 2.0 elements with the rise of people and organisations who want to contribute to development cooperation, and is therefore really in itself a form of International Cooperation 2.0."[8] Other examples include Givengain—with the slogan "raise funds, do good"—and Greater Good South Africa, which aimed to achieve what its name suggests.[9] Like these organizations, pifworld .com is an online platform that enables netizens to do good in the world through interactive online media tools. The idea behind Pifworld revolves around what the website called "playing it forward" (PIF, now changed to "paying it forward"), which, in 2010, they explained as an intuitive and seemingly self-reinforcing sharing mechanism: "Playing it forward is doing good in a simple way. Join Pifworld and invite three friends to do the same. It's power in numbers. If your friends also invite three friends and these friends invite three others we will reach the number of ten million people in no time. Together we could do almost everything, imagine the power of that!"[10]

"Doing good" involved many different things and never seemed easier: "Pifworld offers all kinds of projects: enable kids to go to school, free child slaves, protect endangered animals or even build a massive wildlife park."[11] One could pursue these things playfully online, and, according to the website, "feel good" afterward. In the process, the platform received much attention in the media, and more and more players started crowdsourcing for more and more projects (though by far not the ten million that Pifworld figured would be reached "in no time"). But Pifworld was never just about money. The platform, according to its founders, is "a tool to change the world—your way":

Everyone has so much to give. And so much more than only money. With Pifworld you can change the world—your way. You want to do something in a way you feel adds real value. You want to do it in a personal way. But you also want share it with your friends. You want to have impact, but in an easy way. We give you these tools. On Pifworld you will find all kind of projects and charities you can donate to. But it is very well possible that your value is in something completely different than money. So we created different roles so that everyone can take part. You can become a Volunteer for a charity. You can become a Reporter and blog about all kind of things relevant for a better world. You can become Fundraiser for a project or a charity. You can become Team Captain and set up a team of fundraisers. If you work for a charity, you can become Fieldworker and report from the ground. Or you just want to donate.[12]

While this basic idea remained, the platform changed drastically between 2010 and 2015. In the early days, a picture of the planet at the top of the page came forward on the screen if one pressed the "play with the planet" button. One could then move the planet around to see what projects were on offer and looking for support. The organization referred to itself as the "online charity platform for the new giving," and there seemed to be an atmosphere of being against the established order and having found a new method to do something for good causes and succeed where established conservation and development organizations had failed.[13]

Anno 2015, pifworld.com had changed dramatically. Its slogan became "global network for a better world" and it dropped the hashtag #DoGoodFeelGood. The idea of being new, against the established order, and having a key to success where others had failed had disappeared. There seemed to be a more realistic stance of what the organization could add. Under the heading "Change the world your way" it stated: "We can see current times—with real global challenges—as a barrier we cannot overcome. But at the same time, the Internet enables us all to take part. How to create a better world if you are on your own? PIF World enables you to do good in a powerful and easy way— together with others."[14] It seemed Pifworld had realized that it was simply occupying a niche rather than enabling world revolution. Other elements remained: Pifworld still believed that the internet enables "all of us to take part," reinforcing the ideal of "the liberating force of network technologies," where "old hierarchies seem to vanish—race, age, gender, class, education, nationality."[15] The activities and operations of Pifworld, like those of other "platforms for good," correspond with the political-economic model of platform capitalism, where the circulation of capital (including money, expertise, brands, knowledge, etc.) increasingly depends on the fluidity and integration of networks.[16] Online platforms as techno-cultural and socioeconomic constructs, as I argue, are central in this circulation and in turn highly influence how online users see or understand—in this case—(doing good for) nature online.[17] The case of the elephant corridor project illustrates this well.

THE ELEPHANT CORRIDOR

The elephant corridor was one of the most important and visible early projects on the Pifworld platform. This was not because it was necessarily more important to save elephants than to help poor children or mothers with HIV, but because of the people and organizations behind the initiative, and the way it was embedded in broader conservation and development projects in Southern Africa. First, the elephant corridor was square in the center of the massive Kavango Zambezi (KAZA) Transfrontier Conservation Area (TFCA) between Namibia, Angola, Zambia, Zimbabwe, and Botswana. This TFCA is the largest of such conservation areas in the region and according to the official KAZA website was "expected to span an area of approximately 287,132 km², almost the size of Italy (300,979 km²) and include no fewer than thirty six (36) formally proclaimed national parks, game reserves, forest reserves, game/wildlife management areas as well as intervening conservation and tourism concessions set aside for consumptive and non-consumptive uses of natural resources."[18] This meant that Pifworld was able to consistently market the elephant corridor project as the "first and key step" in building "the largest wildlife park in the world." According to the Pifworld site: "Let's build the largest wildlife park in the world starting with the Elephant Corridor to give room to 100,000 Elephants. So far, the project is crowd-funded by more than 500 supporters, 33 teams and 20 companies from all over the world. This is huge! What makes The Elephant Corridor so special? It is a unique and innovative project that enables the elephants in Botswana to roam freely across the border to Zambia. This project is the first and key step in the realisation of world's biggest wildlife park covering an area of 300,000 km2."[19]

A second key argument why this project was special is that it enabled Pifworld to link itself to the name of Nelson Mandela, one of the cofounders of the Peace Parks Foundation, the organization behind the elephant corridor initiative. "Pifworld realizes Nelson Mandela's dream," was one of the earlier news headlines in relation to the project.[20] "Nelson Mandela Dreams of Elephant Corridors" was the title of a blogpost soon after the project came online in 2010.[21] A picture with

Nelson Mandela in front of several elephants aimed to drive the point home and was circulated often.[22] Being able to tie oneself to Mandela's legacy and name recognition is any marketer's dream.

A third reason for the importance of the elephant corridor was that multibillionaire Richard Branson threw his weight behind the project. According to the website's introduction to the video that Branson taped in support for the project: "Sir Richard Branson is an ambassador of the Elephant Corridor campaign right here on Pifworld. In this video he tells you why and invites you to join him in realizing one of Mandela's dreams: Building an Elephant Corridor with people worldwide!"[23] Below I will discuss the content of the video, but, needless to say, all this was good for publicity: "Sir Richard Branson twitters for Dutch chari-entrepreneur," read a headline.[24]

The main reason that these links could be made was because the elephant corridor project was a project by the NGO Peace Parks Foundation (PPF). PPF is a well-resourced environmental NGO, dedicated to supporting the establishment of TFCAs in Southern Africa and beyond, and backed by some of the wealthiest individuals and companies in South Africa and globally, including Richard Branson.[25] The foundation was the brainchild of Anton Rupert, the wealthiest man in South Africa in his time, and was cofounded on Rupert's invitation by Nelson Mandela and Prince Bernhard of the Netherlands. Guided by the slogan "the global solution," the PPF has been an influential player in environmental discussions in Southern Africa and an astute marketer and fundraiser for peace parks.[26] The Netherlands has always been an important country for the foundation, as it gets consistent support from the Dutch Postcode lottery and Dutch elites. The link to pifworld.com and its largely Dutch audience therefore seemed no coincidence.

The PPF was an active "player" on the Pifworld website, urging players to donate to the elephant corridor. A figure posted on 31 March 2010 on Pifworld by the PPF shows what the corridor should look like.[27] It draws a straight arrow from Chobe national park in Botswana via the Namibian Caprivi strip to the Kafue National Park in Zambia. From the map, therefore, it appeared as though the corridor is a straightforward project that would enable "100,000 elephants running to freedom" in order to "boost eco-tourism in southern Zambia," according to the Dutch PPF director, who was also active on the site in late 2012.[28]

Like the PPF and Branson, many players were very enthusiastic about the project, and left comments to express their support. It seemed in mid-2012, especially after the major gift from the MAVA Foundation, that the corridor was set to happen and that we could see a hundred thousand elephants running to freedom soon thereafter. However, by April 2015, there was no elephant corridor, and there were no elephants running to freedom, certainly not to southern Zambia. The imaginations and ideas online did not correspond with the offline dynamics on the ground in the KAZA TFCA. What happened?

CONTRADICTIONS IN THE ELEPHANT CORRIDOR

Research on the ground in Botswana, Namibia, and Zambia quickly demonstrated that the corridor did not exist and, importantly, could and would not exist in the foreseeable future. My first interviews in Gaborone in January 2013 and in Kasane, Botswana, in July 2013, made this very clear. A senior civil servant at the Ministry of Environment, Wildlife and Tourism of Botswana responsible for communication about TFCAs, said she knew nothing about an elephant corridor project.[29] More dramatic was my interview with the director of a local Botswana NGO. This informant immediately started questioning me, as she thought I was involved with the elephant corridor project. For the first forty-five minutes of our meeting, the director was quite literally fuming about how unrealistic this project was and how it nearly got them into a fight with the Botswana government. In her words:

> Yes, someone at Department of Wildlife two years ago asked me whether this was our thing, and they were furious that someone else was fundraising for this and they didn't know anything about it. And nobody had contacted them, and so they inquired with us. And then I checked it out I was floored because it didn't exist—I was absolutely appalled. So I mentioned this to the KAZA office several times, but then they say the Peace Parks Foundation wants it. But I feel money needs to go to where it is needed most and hence they need to be advised where they can best put their money—not in this type of elephant corridor.[30]

While this director was most explicit, other interviewees confirmed that no plans for an elephant corridor like the one on Pifworld existed or were in development. Several staff officers of the KAZA secretariat in an interview did say that there were plans for an elephant corridor, but much further west, through Bwabwata National Park, and into a different part of Zambia.[31] On the ground, none of the people I spoke to were aware of or supported the idea of a corridor as proposed on the Pifworld website. In fact, they pointed toward the opposite: that much of the lands that were supposed to be part of the corridor are highly contested lands where many local people would not want to encounter elephants. The Pifworld elephant corridor project, to be sure, also regularly mentioned this point, although, arguably, it did not adequately convey the importance of the problem. As DeMotts and Hoon contend, for many actors involved in KAZA, including the Botswana government, "there is no consideration of what it is like to live with the anxiety and pressure of" wildlife damage and "*possible* wildlife damage." The Botswana state believes elephant damages can be compensated, but "compensation reasserts state control and ownership, masking inequalities in the name of a greater national good that hides costs of living with wildlife."[32]

If these issues are serious and contested in Botswana, they are even more so in Zambia. Whereas in Botswana the state heavily intervenes on behalf of conservation, this is much less so in Zambia, and hence there seems to be a much more contested politics between governmental, private, and communal players regarding land for conservation and alternative uses in southern Zambia, with the situation often changing rapidly as (funding) situations change for different actors.[33] Moreover, wildlife corridors were not new in Zambia. In a critical review about earlier corridor experiences, Metcalfe and Kepe argue: "Zambian landscape-level planning could undermine the KAZA TFCA objectives of biodiversity conservation and improved local livelihoods because its land policy encourages investment in communal land without ensuring good conservation or equitable returns for land access. Sectoral and state-dominated natural resource tenure policy is exacerbating the social–ecological scale mismatch produced by land policy. Inefficient community–public sector governance undermines the prospects for an equitable community–private sector relationship."[34]

The "scale mismatches" that Metcalfe and Kepe talk about, interestingly, are especially problematic in "the case in Inyambo and Sekute, where social and ecological issues cannot be adequately addressed because tenure is divided and land and natural resources are managed by governance systems that do not effectively combine public, community, and private interests."[35] Inyambo and Sekute are the two chiefdoms where the Simalaha Community Conservancy was being implemented, supported by the Pifworld elephant corridor project. In interviews and meetings in southern Zambia in February 2015, these sentiments were broadly supported, but also clear was that some community members benefitted from the intervention by receiving support for "conservation agriculture." Overall, however, the different interests involved in conservation in southern Zambia, as well as the role of the state, continued to be fragile and difficult, and hence whether this will lead to a land-tenure system conducive to massive elephant migration in the near future remains extremely doubtful.[36]

Finally, in Namibia, similar problems occurred—many elephant-human conflicts, with most residents not very keen to have (more) elephants on their doorstep.[37] But other tensions also seemed to brew under the surface in the Namibian Caprivi, as noted by Lieneke Eloff de Visser (LdV) in conversation with a researcher from the Namibia Nature Foundation (NNF). This researcher is complaining about the Peace Parks Foundation and their support for the Simalaha Community Conservancy on the Zambian side of the border, which he argues works *against* the corridor:

NNF Researcher: Across here (*points across the river to Zambia*), chief (*? Name unclear*) is on their board, and Peace Parks have provided him with a big game reserve there. Which is huge, all fenced off, and they are putting in game. But it is actually the wildlife corridor that KAZA is promoting! So it fenced off the corridor. We are trying to get the corridor between Kafue and Chobe reestablished, and Peace Parks puts a fence across! Completely fenced off. If you drive from here to Livingstone via Mwandi, there is this long, long game fence the whole way.

LdV: What is the purpose?

NNF Researcher: It is a private deal, they are keeping the chief happy by giving him his game reserve. You can see why they would do it, fences protect the wildlife from poachers, but it negates everything KAZA is trying to do.[38]

The reason for the fence, I was later told, is to protect the wildlife introduced into Simalaha and encourage them to breed, after which they will be released and the fences taken down. Yet whether this will have the desired effect in terms of more constructive human-wildlife relations remains to be seen. As members of the Sekute Community Development Trust indicated, if there would be no more support from the outside, chances are high that all gains would soon dissipate.[39] All this evidence shows that elephants were not "running to freedom" in southern Zambia. Often it was the opposite: due to poaching pressures, many elephants ran to the relative safety in Botswana and—to lesser degree—Namibia, where at the time shoot-to-kill anti-poaching policies had been introduced (Botswana) or were considered (Namibia).[40]

Clearly, the online nature 2.0 space of the elephant corridor on pifworld.com and the "on-the-ground" realities in Botswana, Namibia, and Zambia were worlds apart. This irony was further compounded by several other contradictions in the elephant corridor project. First, the organization behind the corridor, the PPF, has been consistently criticized for being an elitist organization that has turned peace parks into a top-down, neoliberal project that reinforces social inequalities and hides uncomfortable contradictions such as the fact that most, if not all, of PPFs funders are companies and individuals with extremely large environmental footprints.[41]

Second, Richard Branson—one of PPFs elite backers—is anything but a dedicated environmentalist.[42] His backing of the elephant corridor is thus a rather pyrrhic victory for Pifworld. Beyond his abysmal environmental record, however, the message that Branson recorded in support of the elephant corridor displays disturbing colonial discourses. When in the video Branson rhetorically asks the question, "What is Africa?" he answers: "Africa is its animals. That is the beauty of Africa. That's what makes it different from the rest of the world. And to lose those animals would be catastrophic." Branson squarely lays the blame for "dwindling wildlife numbers" on "Africa's increasing (human) populations" and argues that Africa should "increase the amount of land for the animals and by increasing the amount of land for the animals, that will help human beings."[43] Elsewhere, I have argued that this colonial view employs a strategy of "inverted commons": nature in Africa apparently belongs to the whole globe, but "only Africans pay the real price in terms of their conservation."[44]

A third and final contradiction behind the elephant corridor was that since 2010, Southern Africa has seen a militarization of conservation due to massive poaching of elephants and rhinos.[45] As mentioned above, Botswana took a lead in this by introducing a shoot-to-kill anti-poaching policy, which the then Botswana Environment Minister proudly defended at the World Parks Congress in Sydney in November 2014 by stating: "I have been criticized for saying this but will say it again: God will judge the poachers. It is up to us to arrange the meeting."[46] Clearly, these types of violent rhetoric and related violent and intimidating practices do not sit well with the idea that through the elephant corridor project, Pifworld players are contributing to a "peace park."[47] They also complicate any idea of the truth about nature, even though it is a fact that elephants, rhinos, and other African animals have been and continue to be under much poaching pressure.

All this begs the question whether Pifworld did not know that there were serious issues with the elephant corridor, and that the rhetoric around a corridor could well have been scrapped around late 2012, early 2013. In practice, the opposite happened: it stayed online, and players were encouraging each other to remain devoted to the project. A dedicated Pifworld group was even set up for the "ivory revolution," which argued that "by joining the Ivory Revolution you can help realize Nelson Mandela's dream: creating the biggest nature park on the planet. The first step is creating an Elephant Corridor than can help save the lives of 100,000 elephants."[48] Set up in December 2010, this group remained active until mid-2013, and neither here, nor any other group or site on Pifworld related to the elephant corridor ever mentioned any contradictions in the project.

This, to be sure, was not inevitable: a Pifworld executive in an interview in 2012 mentioned that if people wanted to, they could put local reports online and provide alternative accounts of what happens. Indeed, he encouraged me to do so.[49] The fact that no alternative voices or messages were recorded is interesting but does not necessarily mean that players thought that everything was perfect with the project. It does indicate that there is a large disconnect between online rhetoric and discourses and offline discourses and practices in Southern Africa and that these online discourses can be sustained for a long time despite social media's capabilities to broadcast counter-voices. How can we explain this disconnect, and how does this relate to saving nature under platform capitalist conditions?

THE POLITICS OF PLATFORMS AND CONTROL OVER "DOING GOOD" ONLINE

The elephant corridor project may sound like a familiar case: foreigners who want to help out and "do good" in a faraway context but who seem rather oblivious about the contradictions in the project they are supporting. They even—in the case of Botswana—complicate local politics through their support. While this is an important conclusion in itself, it is hardly surprising and not, I argue, the real (or only) significance of the case. Critical development and environmental studies research has long shown that interventions never work out as planned, that they are always more contradictory in practice than on paper. Likewise, as David Mosse has shown, contradictions and tensions in the field often do not influence the policies and discourses in donor contexts: "Policy goals come into contradiction with other institutional or 'system goals' such that policy models are poor guides to understanding the practices, events and effects of development actors, which are shaped by the relationships and interests and cultures of specific organizational settings."[50]

In the case of the elephant corridor, then, we have to delve deeper into the "relationships and interests and cultures" of Pifworld and related platforms. And to talk about an online new media platform is in many ways rather different from what Mosse talked about: carefully choreographed and thought-through interventions, backed up by a professional development apparatus. On Pifworld and related platforms for good this is not the case. International cooperation 2.0, as the 1% Club states, is about cocreation and two-way communication between all actors through the internet. In principle, everyone can start up a local initiative anywhere in the world and seek money for it, and Pifworld, 1% Club, and other platforms are explicit in encouraging people to do so. And just as traditional (non-2.0) development and conservation organizations compete(d) with each other for influence on the donor agenda and often lost sight of dynamics in the countries they wished to support, so online platforms also must compete with each other (and with traditional organizations).[51] Hence, building on the discussions in chapters 1 and 2, and following Van Dijck, the platform itself, and the online "ecosystem" of platforms in which it moves, become a prime focus of attention.[52]

In this section I delve deeper into the peculiarities and politics of online "platforms for good" to argue that behind the elephant corridor there is an intensification of familiar development and conservation intervention dynamics as well as several newer ones peculiar to nature 2.0. I will elaborate on the most important of these, though not all of them relate equally to the Pifworld platform. They are intensifications and consequences related more generally to the ecosystem of online platforms for good and, as such, form the context within which Pifworld and other platforms operate, but also the context that affects daily praxis and decisions by online netizens.

A first intensification is that the sheer abundance of good causes erodes "the basis for adjudicating between competing and multiplying narratives."[53] Whereas with pre-2.0 development cooperation it was often difficult to gauge the politics of the "noble causes" one wanted to support, this becomes even harder on web 2.0 platforms. All causes are presented as equally good, and the question is merely about what you want to support. In this vein, Pifworld's answer to the Frequently Asked Question "Does Pifworld screen nonprofits or projects before they launch?" is telling: "Pifworld screens nonprofits, although we do not investigate a nonprofit's ability to complete their projects. Supporters ultimately decide the validity and worthiness of a nonprofit by whether or not they decide to support it."[54] This is a market-based approach to validity and worthiness: if online players buy (into) it, validity and worthiness of a project are assumed.[55]

A second intensification relates to the earlier discussed nature of web 2.0 and how it influences online prosumers. With Pifworld and similar platforms, what is new is that they enable people to cocreate the kinds of natures they want to conserve and support. Yet, as argued by Andrejevic, "As users shifted from consuming mediated images to creating them, they gained a self-conscious, practice-based awareness about their constructed character."[56] This, one might argue, is a good thing: the "post-deferential attitude" might lead online netizens to not accept conservation and development projects at face value but to influence these, and even to start their own initiatives. This is highly encouraged by Pifworld and other platforms. The 1% Club states: "We enable you to raise funds and kick-start your initiative via your own network. We take care of administration and make sure you can effectively share your campaign with your network."[57] Yet this seeming politicization of doing good is, at the same time, a depoliticization in that the focus is now even more on local, individual projects in a development marketplace and even less on cooperative action.[58] In fact, a nature 2.0 post-deferential attitude about the production, performativity, and constructedness of conservation and development interventions might lead to a more general attitude that the only worthwhile project is one that "you" are involved in or support.

Third and related, the cocreative aspect of online nature 2.0 platforms also seems to intensify and encourage an understanding of the public and the common as the sum of individual interests, likes, and expressions of support. This, again, is not new and builds on a longer political trend already captured by Hannah Arendt in the 1950s and subsequently taken further through the neoliberal turn: "Public life takes on the deceptive aspect of a total of private interests as though these interests could create a new quality through sheer addition. All the so-called liberal concepts of politics (. . .)—such as unlimited competition regulated by a secret balance which comes mysteriously from the sum total of competing activities, the pursuit of 'enlightened self-interest' as an adequate political virtue, unlimited progress inherent in the mere succession of events—have this in common: they simply add up private lives and personal behavior patterns and present the sum as laws of history, or economics, or politics."[59]

Clearly, this quote has a direct connection to Arendt's emphasis on the importance of shared reality as a condition for the pursuit of truth. Yet Pifworld and similar platforms have taken these dynamics several steps further through their focus on what I call—inspired by Goldman and Papson—the "generic online you," which I conceptualize as the technologically mediated abstraction of a subject-object.[60] I use the term *subject-object* to indicate the tension between the importance attached to agency in target individuals and how technological mediation through web 2.0 techniques renders this agency a generic abstraction as part of a pool of objects (or "you's") seeking to "do-good." In turn, it is the sum of these subject-objects that online platforms see as a broader public or social force for good, which is quite different from Arendt's ideas about public life. This, I argue, is how one should understand the earlier above description of Pifworld's idea about *'playing it forward'* and its more recent explaining of the 'pif' part of Pifworld as *pay it forward*: "In the movie, *Pay It Forward*, a young boy discovers a system to do good for others. After doing a good deed, the recipient must then perform a good deed for someone else. In this way, good deeds multiply endlessly and can have enormous potential to change the world. From the movie came the idea for a platform that provides the tools for people to connect and make a positive impact. PIF World has taken this concept and brought it online. On the PIF World platform individuals, nonprofits and companies team up to bring about social change."[61]

The fourth and last difference is perhaps the one that truly sets nature 2.0 apart from older forms of conservation and development, namely the specific ways in which the above elements are technologically mediated. Nature 2.0 and the algorithmization of conservation (and development) that guide individual online philanthropic and altruistic engagements, are influenced and informed by and through digital algorithms. And depending on their specific modes of reasoning, algorithms may provide different answers to the same question asked by different people. Similarly, different platforms based on different algorithms or other calculative software may incorporate different ideas about the ideal natures to target for conservation and what to suggest to online players based, among other things, on their browsing history (enabled by cookies). It is in this way that I refer to the "technologically mediated" part of the technologically mediated abstraction of a subject-object that sets the politics of platforms for good apart from more traditional conservation and development dynamics.

These four elements—and arguably others not mentioned here—are the "elephant 2.0" in the room of new online charities. They build on, intensify, and change the older elephant in the room of development and conservation interventions—that policy does not lead to practice—to such a degree that, I argue, we are seeing quite a different beast emerge altogether, one that revolves around an online politics of platforms.[62] The politics of platforms is a metaphor for tapping into (online) ephemeral value circulation, for tapping into twenty-first-century online incarnations of capital. A platform is like an intersection, and the more actors, products, financial transactions, and good intentions pass through, the more this can be turned into material and immaterial wealth and capital. It also means that the platform must be continuously reinvented, cleaned, and updated. "Traffic" can be redirected at any point in time, and the use of one platform is never guaranteed, even for the most popular ones like Facebook or Twitter. Platforms are highly liquid forms of engagement, and their use for purposes of doing social or environmental good is therefore equally liquid. Consequently, the characteristics of new media within the contemporary capitalist context forces developers of platforms to focus, first and foremost, on the platform—regardless of good intentions and objectives. This means that doing good becomes more fleeting than it had arguably already become. Doing good has truly become a brand, an image, a lifestyle, or a piece of clothing, like so many other liquid tastes.[63]

It is here that (material) elephants start receding into the background and where their plight merges with other conservation and development causes to become the background against which platforms compete over the capital flows that determine possibilities for doing good online. The elephant 2.0 is a liquid elephant, one that morphs into a "mother with HIV" or a "child slave" depending on a combination of the tastes of the "generic you's," the workings of online algorithms, and the marketing capabilities of those behind online projects. As shown above, this latter element, especially, made the elephant corridor stand out on the Pifworld platform; it provided for effective public relations and marketing for Pifworld and hence a way to advertise their platform as "the crowdsourcing platform."[64] And this liquid project never ends. As of 2020, Pifworld was still working hard to get as many environmental nongovernmental organizations as possible on its platform so that online players could more clearly and quickly make a choice between them. This would further intensify the four elements outlined above, and hence intensify the politics of online platforms for good.

CONCLUSION

What can we conclude from this chapter about the elephant 2.0? What kind of beast is this and what are the consequences for conservation? I argued that the elephant 2.0—as a metaphor for trying to save nature through online platforms—is a rather *liquid* creature. At the same time, the elephant 2.0—as a manifestation of nature 2.0—is an increasingly *accidental* creature. It earned these associations due to two important nature 2.0 attributes signaled in this chapter: the fact that (material) elephants become the background against which the politics of platforms for good is being played out in the online realm, and the way in which this politics resembles a qualitative change in, and intensification of the elephant in the room of conservation and development interventions, that policy does not lead to practice. Together, these elements have repercussions for sharing truths and natures online. Based on the above analysis, I come to two important conclusions.

First, online platforms for good render do-gooding increasingly accidental; one's support for a particular good cause is increasingly likely to be based not (only) on personal preferences and a calculated politics of support but rather on the liquid vagaries of the politics of platforms. Subject-objects may think they are getting involved in natures that they are passionate about, but the increasing ease and fleetingness with which this happens—deliberately facilitated in this way by platforms— makes for a stark difference between online imaginations around these natures and their offline material attributes.[65] Second and following, the analysis moved beyond the argument that the truth about elephants on the platform had almost no semblance to offline realities; in the politics of platforms the question of whether there is a link between online and offline truth literally no longer matters. As such, this chapter empirically supports the point made in chapter 2 that online platforms, ultimately, do not care whether those who are active and leaving data online are honest, lying, or bullshitting, as long as they traverse the platform and leave behind data that can be used. The elephant 2.0 in this chapter, in short, is post-truth in action: an expression of the power of platform capitalism in the domain of doing good.

The accidental, liquid elephant 2.0, then, places the enthusiasm of online players and do-gooders in a different light. Doing good becomes synonymous with small, individual projects, supported by "generic you's" with little to no overt inclination to be concerned with broader ideas about the public sphere or the commons. Yet this very conclusion is difficult to see, as the new types of doing good online tend to become part of digital natureglut's spectacular environmentalisms, from texts to symbols, likes, shares, retweets and ultimately the numbers that show how popular something is (how often it is viewed, commented on, retweeted, etc.). Through this sheer or potential intensity, it is hard to see or understand the political economy that infuses and directs the politics of platforms that influences the sharing of truths and natures.

Whether this matters for online players is something that needs to be investigated. The positive, entrepreneurial forms of do-gooding on Pifworld and similar websites do not inspire much confidence that anything resembling structural change or political struggle might be on the mind of players as they engage platforms for good. For this to happen it seems that clearer lines need to be drawn in relation to the contemporary political economic realities of global capitalism and its social and environmental contradictions—a discussion we will come back to in the conclusion. More directly relevant for this chapter is that time, money, and energy spent online can be(come) greatly misguided. I am not saying that all online activism is necessarily misguided. But the fact that the political economy and politics of platform capitalism behind these initiatives are "black boxed" shows that the online sharing of "the truth about nature" for the purposes of conservation can undermine the idea of truth more generally when any link to truth is no longer necessary. Whether or not there was ever going to be an elephant corridor literally did not matter online: the project was great for the platform. In sum: post-truth in action.

CHAPTER 6

Kruger 2.0

The Politics of Distinction

#AfricanSafari
#Big5

INTRODUCTION

In chapter 2, I concluded that online, cocreated natures are not necessarily *shared*; that they are customized to individual preferences, subject to broader political, economic, and technological possibilities and
interests. In chapter 3 I concluded that platform capitalism may highly
influence but does not determine conservation in the new media era.
Instead, it intersects with many other different conditionalities of power
in important and sometimes surprising ways. In this chapter, these two
arguments will come together in (relation to) the empirical context of the
Kruger National Park (KNP or Kruger) in South Africa. This national
park supposedly represents nature that everybody shares, that signifies
the "real Africa," and that belongs to all in South Africa, if not the
world.[1] It is also a very popular nature, widely shared online by those
who visit it and work there. And for those who cannot visit, Google
enables people to share in the natures that Kruger boasts: "Now people
from all over the globe can have a safari experience from the comfort of
their own home, thanks to the latest Google Street View images."[2]

But just as cocreated natures are not necessarily shared, the sharing of Kruger natures is also problematic upon closer scrutiny. The
South African constitution may say that Kruger natures belong to all
in South Africa, in daily praxis this sharing is highly skewed, especially
across racial and class lines. Those visiting the Kruger park are still

overwhelmingly white, while the same goes for the sharing of Kruger's natures online. Indeed, the chapter shows that it is predominantly afflu-ent whites who use new media platforms and technologies such as Face-book groups, webcams, and mobile phone apps to share, celebrate, and spectacularize Kruger natures. What is more: they share Kruger natures as they like to see them: without context, history, or positionality. This, for many, represents a deep "truth about nature"—namely, that nature is at its best without (other) people.[3] Many also feel passionate about the truth about nature in the way I have been using it in the book: that Kruger natures are worthy of protection, especially in the face of poach-ing pressures.

While I strongly disagree with the former point, I am not going to argue that the latter point is untrue. What I will show is that this truth acquires particular connotations in South Africa's historical, political, and social contexts and that these greatly impact the racial and class dynamics and positionalities that influence how Kruger natures are shared. The main element in these contexts is the critical role of the Kruger in the development of apartheid and the ways in which it became a classic symbol of a white conservation fortress.[4] Since apartheid ended in 1994, there have been serious attempts to break through the fortress, though historical legacies continued to strongly influence the politics of access to and control over the Kruger. More recently, the massive "green militarization" triggered by rampant rhino poaching in the KNP (which I will discuss in more detail in the following chapter) has further undone much of the limited progress that had been achieved. The result is a return of "Fortress Kruger," a term actually used by those involved in protecting KNP from poaching incursions.[5]

The sharing of truths and natures about Kruger through new media intersects with and complicates these legacies and dynamics. In fact, the chapter argues that new media and how they are used to share Kruger truths and natures reinforce the unjust legacies of Fortress Kruger. The particular mechanism that effectuates this is a novel politics of distinc-tion triggered by new media in relation to the park and what it repre-sents socially. This politics of distinction functions in two integrated and mutually reinforcing ways: how new media offer individuals new tools to distinguish themselves *and* how it allows individuals to inscribe distinctions and boundaries into the social space. This leads to com-plex new ways in which the boundaries of Fortress Kruger are rendered (more) permeable to some and (more) restrictive for others. By focusing on mediatized dynamics of social distinction, I will not only show how the lines between inside and outside remain starkly racialized in the Kruger but also that it is precisely through rendering park boundaries more permeable that new media technologies may help to reinforce the racialized and unequal class hierarchies of the social order that fortress conservation was built on.

The chapter thus demonstrates in a powerful way how the widely shared and popular natures of the Kruger park—and the particular truths attached to these—are deeply embedded in broader social, political-economic, and technological contexts, histories, and positionalities. In what follows, I will first give some historical and recent background to the (new) mediation and green militarization of the KNP, after which I discuss different new media dynamics and how these are changing access to and control over the park through a politics of distinction. In the conclusion I return to the tension between the sharing of Kruger truths and natures and the distinctions that they reinforce and hide.

MEDIATING KRUGER NATURES

The Kruger is South Africa's most famous park. Visited by over 1.8 million tourists annually, it boasts all the familiar wildlife that visitors generally want to see in Africa.[6] The Kruger has also long been a highly developed and highly mediated park.[7] Social media and web 2.0 technologies are now taking these dynamics to new levels, leading to new virtual-material interactions in (relation to) the park, and to new value articulations generated by the park for different actors. As the analysis of several prominent new media forums will show, intense mediation has led to changed experiences and expectations of the park, but also changing material dynamics in the park. To contextualize these changes, I briefly discuss the history of "Kruger mediations" in relation to KNPs fortress characteristics and the specific truths about nature it helped to develop.

Jane Carruthers shows that mediation played a crucial role in the development of the KNP. In the 1920s and 1930s, dedicating an enormous tract of land to wildlife did not sit well with Afrikaner lower classes who could not see the value in "unproductive" conservation.[8] Support was ultimately garnered by the symbolism that the KNP acquired through adopting the name of Transvaal president Paul Kruger and its role in bringing together English and Afrikaans interests in the developing nation. By the 1920s, "all the daily newspapers in the country welcomed the formation of a national park and even vied with each other to be the scheme's greatest supporter, stressing the common heritage and values that wildlife represented for whites and how these could strengthen national unity."[9] This symbolism was attuned to and significant within the emerging apartheid political economy. Through the KNP, whites were able to bond with an Edenic Africa, filled with "unspoiled" nature and wildlife, and simultaneously control African peoples.[10] As narrated by Carruthers:

> In exploring the idea that whites romanticized their past through the natural landscape and its wildlife, it is imperative to take cognizance of the fact that whites chose to disregard the role that Africans had played in that past. African attitudes and interests were ignored or over-ridden. One can, however, argue in this respect that what the national parks did accomplish as far as Africans were concerned was to deny them access to a large portion of the Transvaal. . . . In South Africa it appears that the considerable African resistance to the game reserves may actually have accelerated the formation of the national park precisely because tighter central administration was considered to be a deterrent to African occupation of the area under consideration. The new park must therefore be seen as a means of providing more effective control over both neighbouring Africans and the few who still resided within the park.[11]

The symbolic importance of Kruger as a romanticized white fortress was reflected in iconic mediations of the park geared toward the developing tourist industry.[12] Waterhole photography, especially, helped to capture "African wilderness," which in turn, as argued by Bunn, provided ways to make sense of larger political-economic and social changes. Building on Walter Benjamin's critique of industrial modernity, he argues that Kruger was "a typically modernist form of symbolically enclosed space" that was to provide protection from "the destructive force of early twentieth-century industrialisation, mechanisation, and shocking new experiences of time." Rapid political economic, cultural, social and war developments between the 1920s and the 1950s were believed to have "widespread negative effects" on people, with a main threat being the "numbing of the senses." In response, "Wilderness experience would simply restore the deadened, instinctual power of the sense, and the beautiful, mirroring semblance of the waterhole photo was designed to achieve just that sort of sympathetic reawakening."[13]

These basic tendencies—the romanticization of the land, control over black Africans, and the idea of Kruger as a "modernist form of symbolically enclosed space" of deeply truthful natures (seemingly) separate from the destructive forces of global capitalism—were reinforced during the apartheid regime and continued to influence Kruger mediations. Carruthers shows that after the 1920s Kruger was firmly cemented into the Afrikaans nationalist project that combined apartheid white supremacy and religious fundamentalism into a fortress park that "became increasingly controlled by a growing team of scientists and efficient bureaucrats."[14] This, then, was the specifically South African form in which mediation of Kruger natures developed. As we will see in more detail in the next chapter, science and related ideas regarding "the truth about nature" in Kruger and South Africa were deeply implicated in broader narratives and stories that fit the apartheid political economy.

Some of this changed with the demise of apartheid in 1994, though the idea of the park as Edenic Africa, unspoiled by (black) people, and the emphasis on top-down bureaucracy and science continue to influence practices and representations of the KNP.[15] Still, after 1994, KNP's fortress properties loosened somewhat, culminating in several community-based programs and one case of successful land restitution.[16] Official representations of the park also changed, and the notion that Kruger was a heritage shared by all South Africans became a leading theme for parastatal South African National Parks (SANParks). Instead of communicating Kruger as a fortress protecting nature from outside influences, mediation revolved around a policy focused on making "National Parks accessible (at affordable prices) to communities that were previously excluded to the biodiversity, cultural-heritage and other experiences that South Africa's national parks can offer."[17]

Since 2008, however, breaking down the fortress and letting local communities benefit from the KNP has come under strain due to the rhino-poaching crisis in South Africa, which is centered on Kruger, the park with the largest population of rhinos globally.[18] For example, in December 2013, a flagship community-based resource-harvesting project was canceled.[19] Meanwhile, more general fortress tendencies are making a violent return. Since the start of the crisis, the KNP has seen massive investments in "green militarization," with the former military commander in charge of anti-poaching stating in an interview that he planned to establish a Fortress Kruger: an "Intensive Protection Zone, which will be a sanctuary within a sanctuary."[20] As a result, mediation of the park also changed dramatically. Next to the "standard" images of the park as an unspoiled African Eden, the Kruger became increasingly portrayed as a war zone.[21] These starkly contradictory images both find expression in the "new mediation" of Kruger 2.0.

FORTRESS KRUGER'S "NEW MEDIATION"

Like nature 2.0 more generally, Kruger is cocreated through many online forums, including Facebook groups, Twitter, tourism websites, discussion groups, YouTube channels, wildlife-cams, mobile apps, and more, in effect creating a "Kruger 2.0." This online cocreation changes the politics of control over and access to parks and their resources, though some platforms obviously have more effects on park dynamics than others. To be sure: traditional (pre-2.0) media also influenced control over and access to parks, especially by influencing representations and selecting what information would become public.[22] New media, as argued, present a qualitative change because of their ability to let anybody with internet access not only represent or mediate the park, but actively influence, modify or contest representations on potentially large scales. This has impacted conservation authorities as it makes it harder for them to control information and representations. One example concerns rhino poaching statistics. While poaching statistics were officially released by the Department of Environmental Affairs (DEA), it was checked and challenged by online activist groups like the Outraged South African Citizens Against Poaching (OSCAP) and Save Our Rhino Facebook groups that made it a sport to be ahead of official statistics and be a more trustworthy source. Both their Facebook group banners showed poaching statistics numbers, which were updated very frequently.[23]

There are many ways in which new media impact protected areas. Important to emphasize is that these changes can strengthen *and* challenge ideas and practices of fortress conservation, sometimes simultaneously. Take, for example, the "Battle at Kruger" YouTube video.[24] According to the *Mail&Guardian*, "This is the ultimate Kruger video, and, with over 72m views on YouTube, it's certainly the most famous. Professional camera crews would kill to have witnessed a scene such as this one—in which a herd of cape buffalo, a pride of lions, and some crocodiles go head to head."[25] What makes the video interesting for so many viewers is not just that it "compresses what is often seen on TV wildlife documentaries as staple iconic fare" but that it was made by tourists. The video's shaky images and fairly low resolution add "to the aesthetic authenticity of the event" and hence the idea is that "anyone who happens to be in the right place at the right time can distribute what professionals produce over much lengthier periods of time at a cost of millions of dollars."[26]

Rijsdijk argues that "Battle at Kruger maintains a precarious balance between the sober, scientific observations of wildlife typical of wildlife filmmaking in the mid- to late-20th century, and more recent forms of radical individual accounts of wildlife captured in a more reflexive and personal manner."[27] And it is precisely this precarious balance between the truth about nature as revealed by science and nature 2.0 that strengthens *and* challenges the idea of parks as pristine wildlife fortresses. On the one hand, documentaries normally made by authorized "experts" are "real": Battle at Kruger affirms that spectacular Wild Africa scenes occur in everyday life as well. On the other hand, because amateurs shot the scene, everybody can—in principle—access and share these spectacular sights normally only disclosed to authorized experts. Thus, Battle at Kruger reinforces and challenges certain hierarchies associated with the fortress model.

This example, however, is still rather indirectly related to the tension between sharing and boundary making that is central to this chapter. New media offer far greater possibilities to influence the politics of access to and control over fortress conservation spaces. Conceptualizing a "politics of distinction" will help explicate these new media possibilities and how, by dramatically amplifying the sharing of Kruger natures, they transgress and reconstitute social and political hierarchies and boundaries.

NEW MEDIA AND THE POLITICS OF DISTINCTION

For the South African state and SANParks, Kruger is a profitable asset through which South Africa brands itself as a prime tourist destination for spectacular wilderness. This renders certain representations of the KNP highly valuable, visible, and political.[28] With the great majority of KNPs visitors being (South African and foreign) whites, the Edenic, unspoiled fortress image has remained a crucial part of KNPs' representation, irrespective of the need to ensure the park's social viability toward neighboring communities and South Africa's black majority.[29] It is in relation to these representations that new media offer individuals new tools to distinguish themselves *and* make new distinctions. They can support or disrupt certain representations, make them go viral, or completely ignore them. Through individual and mass actions on new media—based on complex individually and socially mediated tastes and preferences—certain elements may be emphasized or placed in a particular light. This follows Bourdieu's argument that "social subjects, classified by their classifications, distinguish themselves by the distinctions they make."[30] A politics of distinction, therefore, refers to two meanings of distinction: setting oneself apart from others and inscribing boundaries or differences into the social space.

According to Bourdieu, these practices of distinction are not performed in isolation. They take place in reference to social orders that are already "progressively inscribed in people's minds" through such dynamics as "the hierarchies and classifications inscribed in objects (especially cultural products), in institutions . . . , or simply in language," among others.[31] Hence, it is important to again emphasize that "fortress conservation" is the outcome of a particular social order associated with certain hierarchies, classifications, institutions, and language. When actors therefore advocate for reinforcing "Fortress Kruger" or for reinstating the hierarchies, classifications, institutions, and language associated with fortress conservation, they—purposely or inadvertently—reinforce (the legitimacy of) a particular social order or political economy of power. This, in turn, has consequences for other actors that I will come back to in the conclusion of this chapter.

At the same time, Bourdieu shows that distinctions are not linear or one-sided: there are numerous social forms/axes that overlap and compete.[32] New media are not simply added onto myriad other forms of distinction; they extend, change, and widen the differential spaces through which distinctions are practiced and operate. Hence, following chapter 1, a focus on new media is not to say that there were no politics of distinction in relation to older media. New media enable different forms of distinction, and analyzing them illuminates what actually happens in terms of the changing politics of access to and control over fortress spaces that lurks behind the online sharing of Kruger natures.

One important change was already noted: the (further) erosion of a form of authority whereby official organs—usually the state—control most information about parks and how they are represented. Another key change builds on Andrejevic's point about the generational shift toward the "fragmentation and 'nichification' of audiences in the contemporary media landscape." He argues that this was not simply an outcome of the proliferation of (new) media outlets but also "a reconceptualization of news as a customizable commodity subject to the vagaries of taste that govern other forms of consumption."[33] New media have contributed to this reconceptualization in a major way by allowing people to customize their preferred representations of the KNP. These representations, especially in relation to fortress ideas and practices, help some actors to place themselves in a privileged position with respect to the park, while shutting out or bypassing others. The next sections analyze four important new media forums that are changing the dynamics of access to and control over Fortress Kruger: wildlife cams, Facebook groups, the SANParks forums, and an app called Latest Sightings. All these may, I will argue, strengthen *and* challenge fortress dynamics in their transgression of park boundaries, though they do so differentially, with each successive forum tipping the balance more decidedly toward strengthening Fortress Kruger.

WILDLIFE CAMS

Wildlife cameras—webcams that allow viewers to see wild nature 24/7—have become very popular.[34] The world's first wildlife cam was www .africam.com. This was "the first company to broadcast live refresh images from the African bush back in 1999 and in 2006 it again was the first to stream a live 24/7 feed from Nkorho Pan," located in a private reserve next to Kruger.[35] In an interview, the former director of Africam stated that his philosophy "is being passive, a Zen-type approach; animals must come to us; it is about peace, tranquility, ambience, etcetera. That is what we are trying to create."[36] Because they do not do post-production, he reckoned that they have a particular viewing-demographic, which in 2014 came to "probably two hundred thousand unique visitors per month." He estimated that "70 percent of our viewers are women over thirty-five–forty and older" and that "there are also lots of older people in old-age homes" watching wildlife cams, especially in the US and Europe as they cannot (afford to) travel to South Africa.[37]

This may sound as though wildlife cams are passive only: they allow people to access parks from a distance but do not give them any control. But this is not entirely correct. According to the director, many people are very active in discussion forums around the webcams and regularly try to intervene after watching events: "They ask us to interfere; even people from US calling to say we must bring in SPCA to shoot an elephant that seemed injured but was actually pregnant." The same thing also happened with an "example of a lion that got hurt." He argues that "people react with their emotions and say that if we don't do anything about it they [will] make our lives difficult; and they do!"[38] While these attempts are perhaps laughable to some, webcams can trigger people to attempt to influence park governance.

The founder and former owner of Africam, who currently owns a private game reserve next to KNP and also hosts wildlife cams, corroborated these comments.[39] He said that people are very active on discussion groups, that they know the animals better than he does, and that they track all their daily movements on the cameras. A more intimate group of people controls the webcams, and does so 24/7, in rotating shifts in different time zones. He mentions that people also tried to force him, on two occasions, to intervene in his reserve, after they had seen dynamics that seemingly warranted intervention. Ultimately, he did not, but in the meantime, he was threatened with legal action, typecast in a negative way in various media, and put under pressure in other ways.[40]

This goes to show that even though wildlife cameras do not allow *direct* access or control, they do influence the way in which those who grow emotionally attached to what they see on the cameras are able to assert pressure on conservation governance.[41] It does *not* mean that this limited influence necessarily promotes parks as fortresses; the relations that people develop with animals through webcams and their resultant (emotional or other) responses are simply too complex.[42] Even though wildlife cams do not convey much of the social and political context and surroundings of Kruger natures and as such can be seen as conveyors of typical fortress natures, the direct influence that viewers have on conservation is limited. This changes, however, with Facebook groups.

FACEBOOK GROUPS

Facebook has become one of the most important social media platforms and a prime organizing platform for many social, political, economic, and other interests, including through Facebook groups.[43] It therefore has the potential to quite significantly influence issues of access to and control over Kruger, particularly because social media are taken very seriously by SANParks: All South African parks have their own Facebook pages; many have their own Facebook groups; and SANParks has staff working full-time on engaging the public through Facebook and other social media.[44] In an interview, a SANParks media and communication officer remarked that due to the rise of social media, "we are now forced to listen to the public's opinion on a daily basis. Now we cannot ignore them anymore; we have given them a platform where they can express themselves, and they can share their views—good, bad, or ugly—and we take them very seriously."[45] The Kruger is well represented in different Facebook groups and it is interesting to see how they represent the park and how members distinguish themselves in relation to Fortress Kruger. These dynamics, again, are complex and multidimensional, but two distinct and prominent uses of these groups stick out.

The first relates to the general prominence of the rhino-poaching crisis on Kruger- or SANParks-related Facebook groups. On the "official" SANParks Kruger Facebook Group managed by the SANParks Web Forum and Online Stakeholder Practitioner, for example, over one hundred forty-one thousand members discuss a variety of topics.[46] Many are related to sightings, but issues such as the rhino-poaching crisis, the way SANParks is run, or the use of social media in parks—inter alia—are also discussed. In an interview, SANParks social media staff mentioned that they were struggling with the rhino issue in particular. From 2010 onward, conservation supporters have put increasing pressure on SANParks to communicate information on the crisis through social media. The staff mentioned that if they do not respond the same day, or sometimes within two hours, people think they have something to hide and start rumors, which can lead to uncomfortable situations.[47] Another example is the aforementioned OSCAP and related rhino-poaching groups, which exert influence by constantly pushing SANParks and the South African government on the rhino-poaching issue. Not only do they follow and broadcast everything that happens in relation to the crisis, close observations also show that they influence more mainstream media, thus increasing pressure on SANParks to pursue the "green militarization" of Kruger. In these ways, online netizens distinguish themselves and pressurize the management of parks in a fortress direction. The next chapter will develop these issues in the links between the rhino-poaching crisis and new media in more depth.

But netizens also distinguish themselves by the distinctions they make, especially in how they represent the park. Of particular importance in this respect is the fact that several of the largest groups exist solely to appreciate KNP. One group with over seventy thousand members is "Kruger National Park—Best Place on Earth." Its introductory message states: "The intention of this site is for members to post and share their wonderful experiences in the Greater Kruger National Park and to support these with photos, videos and comments. The good news, and good feel, of the Group needs to be maintained and no amount of negativity or commentary on this site will produce any action or activity from SANParks, as this Group is NOT affiliated to SANParks."[48] Browsing through the group's wall shows that most posts are indeed dedicated to this feel-good aim. It focuses on the Kruger as though it does not function in context, but solely on animal sightings, camp facilities, and the like. KNP, in this and many similar sites, is consumed as a depoliticized, decontextualized, ahistorical entity. Here, political issues such as the rhino-poaching crisis are seen as negative and could provoke a moderator comment such as the following:

> The original intention of this site was for members to post and share their wonderful experiences in the Greater Kruger National Park, and to support these with photos, videos and comments. The good news, and good feel, of the Group has transgressed into negativity around the activities of Poachers. Whilst we do not condone the death of one single Rhino, no amount of commentary on this site will produce any action or activity. . . . We have therefore decided that the site will revert back into line with the original intentions of being a positive, good feeling and good news, site for all Kruger National Park lovers.[49]

Similar discussions and warnings have been aired on the Kruger Appreciation Society Facebook group.[50] Several others have the same policy, clearly with an aim to create an online space of controlled representations of the Edenic Africa kind. This is what *positive* and *good* refer to here, obviously leaving out the many "negative" and "bad" aspects of Kruger as a fortress space to those who do not have the same feelings toward the park as the group's members. Much governance (and disciplining) goes into maintaining a focus on the positive, feel-good essence of Kruger that fits neatly with fortress conservation truths of people-free, wild nature.

All these examples come from prominent and visible Facebook groups, and a distinctive feature of all of them is that their membership is overwhelmingly white. This is clear from screening the members' sections of these groups and is in line with KNP visitors' profiles.[51] While not surprising, it does say something about the potential influence of one segment of the public over SANParks in relation to others. Since SANParks takes social media very seriously as part of their corporate outreach, disproportionate weight is given to the types of discussions and images that appear on these Facebook groups vis-à-vis other voices, for example, black Soweto township residents surveyed by Butler and Richardson.[52] Hence, forms of distinction are created simply by the proportionality of social media users and their preoccupations. This imbalance is reinforced by SANParks' dependence on tourism income, which, for a substantial part, is generated precisely by those active on the above Facebook groups (and other social media). A rapidly increasing amount of tourism bookings is generated through online e-business, which a

SANParks senior manager believes has a close link with the organization's activities and presence on social media.[53] In this way, fortress conservation–oriented publics are able to foreground their outlook on nature by their distinctive use of social media.

The extent to which this has an effect is hard to gauge but should not be over- or underestimated. It should not be underestimated exactly because prominent uses of Kruger-related Facebook groups directly promote Kruger in its fortress form. It should also not be overestimated because even if SANParks takes social media seriously, the relations of Facebook group members to animals and the park are more complex than these two prominent uses suggest, while many of them are not very active and stand quite far from SANParks. This is different with the SANParks forums.

SANPARKS FORUMS

The SANParks website has its own discussion platform: the SANParks Forums.[54] As of July 2020, the Forums had over 35,900 users ("forumites" or "mites") and many hundreds of discussion threads under thirty-four primary topics. This web 2.0 space differs from Facebook groups in that it is integrated into SANParks and that the core active community is more tightly knit and more involved in the organization than most Facebook group moderators, though all of them seem to spend much time online in these capacities.[55] According to one Forums moderator in an interview, she spends over forty hours per week online, "whether in the weekend or at night."[56] Forum moderators are like honorary SANParks employees without a contract, although they occasionally get costs associated with their volunteer work reimbursed.

The Forums have an elaborate code of conduct and set of rules for online behavior and the work involved in managing this is considerable. According to a former moderator, "SANParks wants moderators online 24/7 to catch drunk, or racist comments. Basically, to patrol and to clean—those are the two main tasks of the moderators."[57] In return, the moderators, but also other active members, distinguish themselves in relation to the organization and get rewarded for this. Since May 2010, the long-standing SANParks "honorary rangers" organization added the "virtual region."[58] This introduces itself as follows: "We are located in cyberspace, with members in all parts of the country and even as far as the Netherlands. The SANParks Forums is our home park where we promote the South African National Parks."[59] "Virtual

Honorary Rangers" (VHRs) from this "region" can distinguish them-. selves through their contributions (posts and otherwise) and so move up from junior to senior, distinguished, and even "legendary" VHR.

A major difference between the virtual and other honorary ranger regions is that the SANParks forums are accessible to everyone with an internet connection, and hence many people come there for information about South African parks.[60] Thus, according to a moderator, "forum assistants," moderators, and other distinguished VHRs play an important role in giving people information, fundraising, etcetera.[61] In return for this labor, the most active members get special access to Kruger and SANParks, such as an invitation for an annual braai in Kruger, "which is a chance for forumites to meet with SANParks personnel" to play cricket and do joint fundraising.[62] A corollary is that forumites distinguish themselves from other visitors to the park. Forumites are for instance supposed to put yellow ribbons on their cars so that they can identify each other and "meet and greet" in the park. But this is not easy, according to one:

> By the time I see forum members yellow ribbons while driving its normally
> to late to say hi because we have already passed each other so an idea I
> have is what about selling those yellow wrist bands to forum members with
> say "SANParks Forum Member" written on it and that way when you are
> relaxed and in the camp you will be able to meet fellow forum members. . . .
> If it takes off then extra colors could be added to identify the members
> "rank" as a forum member, say yellow for a regular, green for a Virtual
> Ranger, red for a Moderator etc.[63]

Other members liked the idea, and one of the moderators replied, "We (as in the forum members led by a committee who are working with the VHRs and SANParks) are in the process of determining a logo specifically for the online community and the idea is to then sell branded merchandise to raise funds for anti poaching etc."[64]

Through these and other distinctions, SANParks Forums VHRs distinguish themselves and influence access to and control over the park. It is therefore important to see who (active) forumites are. According to a former moderator, they are "mostly white."[65] Another moderator stated: "We don't have black members on the forum, which is a big challenge for me." Referring to a talk by a prominent SANParks employee, she argues that Kruger

> was dominated, or owned by a certain group, which is the Afrikaans com-
> munity—it was like a pilgrimage; to go to the Kruger every year. And we see
> a large group of people battling with the fact that it is not like that anymore,

that they have to share the park with the rest of South Africa and the world. I cannot understand that this group doesn't change—and they are the most negative group and they use social media to vent that. But they don't realize things have to change. And also the communities around the park, if they don't benefit, they would want to farm the area, claim the land, etcetera. If they feel they benefit they will fight for it—and if they don't benefit there is no Kruger. . . . The forum is mainly white, it is not a true reflection of the clientele and stakeholders of SANParks.[66]

In effect, there is still a "fortress conservation" mentality among a large segment of white South Africans who were used to having the park for themselves. And they actively use new media to counter any transformation agenda that SANParks embarks on. One issue brought this out especially well: the plan to build a luxury hotel to attract the emerging black middle class to the park, which led to a "heated race row," as reported in the *Mail&Guardian* on 1 July 2011:

SANParks chief executive David Mabunda this week lashed out at the "racial slurs" expressed by members of a vocal lobby group set up in May to oppose the proposed hotels. Called Aikona (Against Interference in Kruger Our Nature Asset), the group says it has a membership of more than 250. Its criticisms on social media have been particularly vociferous. "The racial slurs expressed by some members of the public professing to be supporters of Aikona have not only surfaced in the Lowveld media but also in various newspaper letters, blogs, SANParks forum, Facebook and Twitter. It has become one of Aikona's hallmarks," Mabunda wrote.[67]

This meant that also on the SANParks Forums, drastic action was needed in response to this issue, according to a moderator: "We have strict rules, and got rid of a lot of people who posted racist comments, and we have flushed out the majority—some of whom started their own groups. The issue of the hotel is a good example: complete and utter negativity— they stir passions, have contact in the *Die Beeld* newspaper. People even started lawsuit against SANParks; they cannot accept that SANParks has to change and it is no longer the pristine park they can visit."[68]

In other words, an influential and vocal group of whites that think they "own the park" ferociously defends a particular social order in the Kruger, associated with racialized and unequal hierarchies, classifications, institutions, and language. A luxury hotel does not fit in there, but as Bunn notes, a traditional-looking African thatch rondavel hut does.[69] Though some of these are very luxurious, they at once signal "native" dwellings through "which the white presence is able to stage itself as though adapted to the African environment," and something to be left behind for blacks, as argued by SANParks staff.[70] Years later, still no decision on the hotels had been made, which testifies to the powers behind trying to maintain a Fortress Kruger that resembles a former (but still influential) social order.[71]

The official policy on the SANParks Forums is one of transformation of the old social order. Many active forumites, especially the moderators, are not against transformation and try to represent the organization as best as possible. They are therefore quite different from the "influential and vocal group of whites who think they own the park" and whom they had to "flush out" of the Forums. In this sense their actions undermine the fortress mentality. At the same time, the Forums still reflect the old social order in terms of racial composition and a particular outlook on a romanticized African Wilderness. Thus, while moderators and active forumites officially promote transformation, there is also a certain ambiguity in their trying to be "closer" to a transforming SANParks while vying for privileged access to Kruger. The latter ambition is why some of the most active members joined the Forums in the first place, and how they distinguish themselves vis-à-vis other visitors. The Forums therefore show that there are major ambiguities and important degrees in kind when it comes to promoting fortress conservation.

LATEST SIGHTINGS

Latest Sightings is an animal sighting service where Kruger visitors are able to share sightings through their mobile devices over an app, Twitter, Facebook, or a dedicated Whatsapp group.[72] A young teenager from South Africa, Nadav Ossendryver, started it because he was bored driving around the park "seeing nothing." In many online interviews, like this one from 2012, he relates how the idea got started: "'Whenever we came here I used to beg my parents to stop every car passing and ask them what they'd seen,'" remembers Nadav, who is currently a grade 10 student. 'After a while they got irritated, so I was thinking, what's an easy way of getting people to share their sightings without having to stop every car?'"[73]

He started a blog and a YouTube channel for Kruger videos, which became so popular that he developed a smartphone app. The commercialization of his adventure started when he became a YouTube partner, which earned him advertising income and allowed him to start employing people. With success—Latest Sightings has become one of the best-viewed South African YouTube Channels (see figure 7)—rhetoric

FIGURE 7. Nadav Ossendryver receives award for "passing 1,000,000 subscribers."
Credit: Latest Sightings.

around Latest Sightings also changed. Nadav was branded by *South African Entrepreneur Magazine* as a role model "young entrepreneur."[74] He also won several other entrepreneurial awards.[75] Facebook, Google, and others courted him, and Latestsightings.com later started introducing Nadav as follows:

> Nadav Ossendryver is one of those teenagers you just hope your child is going to be like. Part techno-boffin, part drummer, big part tennis player, A-grade Matric scholar! He was just 15 years old when he established Latest Sightings and never imagined that it would be a fulltime business before he even finished school. He also couldn't have imagined that it would lead him to meeting Barack Obama or Kingsley Holgate, or gracing the boardrooms of Microsoft and Nokia. Despite his profile he remains a conservationist and the bush is definitely his place to be. He's far more at home in a tent and next to the campfire than at his desk studying for his next maths distinction! He gets his biggest kicks from spotting wild dogs or meeting community members to chat about what they have seen![76]

Never mind the failed attempt to balance idolatry and modesty, with Nadav's rapidly changing fortunes, his rhetoric also changed. In an interview from October 2014 he elaborates again on the Kruger beginnings: "People go and they hate it because they see nothing and they think it's so boring. I got a friend who went just from the gate to the camp and saw nothing and he left that day, he couldn't handle it. And I hated that. I hated listening to people because when I go, you know, we always have a latest sighting that I am thinking I wish if these people just saw a lion . . . they would enjoy it. That is one of the reasons why I created Latest sightings, to make people enjoy the Kruger; to create a love for wildlife."[77]

Once just a boy frustrated about not seeing wildlife, Nadav now aims to help people "create a love for wildlife." This idea was developed further over time, leading the company to proclaim in 2018 that they "educate its followers about wildlife, nature and its behavior" and "that rangers and vets can now attend to injured animals that would have otherwise gone unnoticed like they did before the Latest Sightings community."[78] All of this is meant to stimulate "safari tourism" and help develop a (new) sense of appreciation for Kruger's natures. This new sense, then, is clearly different from simply driving around the park and enjoying whatever comes one's way. Through new media, people are able to not only share sightings but also "chase" sightings by others; the company boasts that they "help people maximize their safari by helping app-users see more animals through members sharing their wildlife sightings in real-time."[79] This can change dynamics in parks considerably, as I have noticed myself while using Latest Sightings on several research trips to the KNP between 2014 and 2017. The types of spectacular sightings (of lions, cheetahs, etc.) seemed to attract more people more quickly than before, something that many have been complaining about, including SANParks Forum members.[80] Complaints noted often were that it leads to speeding to catch a sighting in time and that it devalues an appreciation for the park as a whole by focusing only on spectacular sightings.

More generally, Latest Sightings has led to a dramatic intensification and extension of an older politics of distinction in the park, namely, around animal sightings. In Kruger tours and drives, sightings are everything and visitors spend countless hours discussing and comparing them. I was reminded of this when I joined a "safari tour" late February, early March 2014 in Kruger. The first and main distinction for every tourist is having seen the #Big5: lion, elephant, leopard, rhino, and buffalo. After that, the gradations are endless: how many times have you seen the big 5? Were they doing anything spectacular like hunting? How close to the road were they? How long have you been able to see them? And so forth. From there, distinctions are built up around a more intimate knowledge of the park, how many times and how long one goes to Kruger, what the good spots and strategies are for sightings, and so on.

These politics of distinction are now taken to a new level through Latest Sightings and similar initiatives. They enable people visiting KNP to broadcast their sighting distinctions into the World Wide Web and for others to vicariously enjoy sightings from a distance. This is another way in which the boundaries of Kruger are transgressed and (literally) mediated. But the idea of access to and control over Fortress Kruger has changed in another important way through Latest Sightings and the intensified politics of distinction it has brought. It has, I argue, further "spectacularized" the park in its fortress form. That is, Latest Sightings helps to transform the relations between humans and nature by further turning it into spectacular environmentalisms.

By focusing exclusively on individual and preferably on spectacular sightings (of the more charismatic animals doing "cool" things) and sending these in ever greater numbers into cyberspace, Latest Sightings helps people to consume fortress conservation images of timeless nature without people or context. In turn, Andrejevic's argument about online content as "a customizable commodity subject to the vagaries of taste that govern other forms of consumption" further enables fragmented and "nichified" audiences to focus on building this spectacular relationship with the kind of nature they love. Hence, this argument includes but also moves beyond Andrejevic's point of "the commercial logic of customization in which marketers seek to manage consumers by tapping into a dominant feeling-tone or 'sentiment.'"[81]

It is clear that young entrepreneur Nadav has become a successful commercial marketer of customized images that tap into a particular sentiment dependent on fortress parks as "quintessential landscapes of consumption."[82] But the hallmark of new media, as mentioned, is cocreation, and hence, he has helped to allow an entire community to market, share, and tap into these sentiments. So when Nadav in a TV interview says that what makes Latest Sightings so successful is that it promotes a community of like-minded individuals interested to share sightings, he is exactly right.[83] He does not, however, add that this community is mainly white and to a great degree still invested in a fortress conservation social order in which the KNP plays a vital symbolic role.[84] With this in mind, the following conversation between TV host Bruce Whitfield and Nadav becomes revealing:

Bruce: You love the bush and you don't mind sitting out there but you don't have to do it all yourself because it is about creating that community of interest and what latestsightings.com has done is created a destination for nature-lovers to go to, to share the content.

Nadav: And that's I think the key to getting the most unbelievable content because, you know, as you said, one camera man goes and waits a whole year to get like maybe an hour worth of unbelievable footage but when you expand that to over a hundred thousand people going, one of them are bound to see something unbelievable every single day. And you know that is basically what happens. And when they are part of this community and share that with the rest of the world, the rest of the world watches and I think that's what really has been able to grow our . . .

Bruce: OK, I want to see some cool content.[85]

The segment makes it seem as though "the community" is the whole world, whereas in reality, it is a highly racially skewed community. Later in the interview, Nadav explains that he wants to start paying "members of the community," hoping that "if you can go to the Kruger and get paid, you would send in the most unbelievable videos and also sightings and it also kind of locks you into the community." This has indeed since transpired. Latest Sightings now has a "film and earn" program where you can "earn cash monthly by uploading your wildlife photos & videos."[86] Photo and videos that have gone viral have "earned some members over $15,000 already." Latest Sightings also provides hints as to "what goes viral," namely: "Videos and photos that tell a story; Cute, funny, heartwarming videos and pics; Straight out rare sightings and experiences," and "Action packed hunts and fights."[87] All this—accompanied by fitting images on the website combining social media and money signifiers—render Kruger's nature 2.0 capital as spectacular environmentalisms, which are supposedly valuable for members, Latest Sightings, Kruger, and wildlife.

Because these spectacular environmentalisms lock people into the community, I argue, they also help to lock the community further into the social order that they are already invested in, while locking out those who seek to change this order. This, however, is not inevitable, nor do I argue that all Latest Sightings community members are "fortress minded." The realities of mediated relations between people and nonhuman natures are simply too complex. The point here, however, is that on the platform there is hardly space for more nuanced discussions around the politics of access to and control over Kruger as a contested space. The very format of focusing on sightings ensures a singularity that neatly fits the fortress narrative while shutting out other, more complex narratives. It is in this specific sense that I am arguing that Latest Sightings strengthens the fortress mentality of KNP visitors. Kruger park management insists that Latest Sightings does not influence park management.[88] But it is clear that strengthening the fortress mentality among those that bring in most of the much-needed tourism income for the park could "further undermine alternative ways of understanding and connecting to the environment."[89] It also further obfuscates the way in which Kruger functions in a larger political economic context and, as such, makes more radically democratic options involving black neighboring communities more difficult.

CONCLUSION

This chapter has sought to understand how the sharing of Kruger's natures through new media relates to and influences the legacies of the social order the park was founded on. Studying four new media forums gave insight into the differential ways in which new media platforms change control over and access to fortress conservation spaces. Wildlife cams allow people to cross the boundaries of parks virtually, while the virtual possibilities offered by Latest Sightings allow those in the park to help mediate their and other's relationships with Kruger in a highly focused, yet spectacular manner. What the chapter shows is that these forms of sharing nature across fortress boundaries may actually reinforce rather than weaken the class and racial hierarchies that these boundaries represent.

In other words, through the transgressions of social media, several basic tendencies of fortress conservation and the truths and natures this is built on are being strengthened rather than weakened. New media have allowed a particular community of actors to find new ways to distinguish themselves in relation to Fortress Kruger and to enhance the power of distinctive representations and truth discourses regarding the KNP. Both this community and the distinctions they promote are still largely steeped in a social order associated with particular hierarchies, classifications, institutions, and language. What is more, as I have shown, these distinctions are backed up by and mediated through particular political economies of power—in this case, the class and purchasing power of whites. And with neoliberalized park governance and Kruger depending almost exclusively on tourist income, this has significant effects.

This also goes a long way to explain why "local communities" hardly played any role in the analysis. It is not because they are not on new media. Rather, they are simply not nearly as invested in the new media spaces that influence representations of the Kruger as SAN-Parks might like them to be.[90] New media around the park reflects the political economy of the park, which is still steeped in a fortress social order. The nichification and fragmentation of audiences through new media, in turn, might account for the fact that I encountered little resistance to these images on the platforms discussed. As the cases showed, there was dissent and disagreement—sometimes hectic and sharp—but mostly between whites, rarely between blacks and whites.[91] This adds another layer of complexity to Maguranyanga's conclusion that the "'deracialization' or 'Africanization' of park management does not necessarily ensure the 'transformation' of park management practices."[92] This added layer relates to a new politics of distinction that enables certain people to garner access to the park in new ways.

As I have shown, particularly through the SANParks Forums, people distinguish themselves by resisting *and* supporting the transformation agenda, but the very racial composition of those active in new media platforms and their own desires regarding access to the park render even their actions in favor of transformation ambiguous. In this way, the forums neither strengthen nor challenge still-dominant fortress conservation ideas. These ambiguities may also be present under the surface of the case of Latest Sightings, yet I argued that this platform's format hinders these from appearing openly. Focused on utterly atomized and random sightings of wildlife, Latest Sightings fits the fortress framework extremely well and leaves little space for contexts around the park such as claims by communities living on the edge of Kruger.[93] Hence the Kruger case shows that new media and conservation boundaries interact counterintuitively: as the lines around fortress parks are ever more frequently and intensely transgressed and reconstructed through new media, they may equally strengthen rather than weaken the racialized and unequal hierarchies these parks were built on.[94]

How does this conclusion relate to broader political economies of platform capitalism and conservation? Conservation organizations, but also companies like Google, Facebook, and others, mostly seem to support the particular truths and natures espoused by the new media forums discussed in this chapter, not only because they elicit support for conservation but also because they are highly profitable. Latest Sightings exemplifies this most clearly. For several years now, Latest Sightings has been one of the most viewed YouTube channels in South Africa, and its online popularity and profitability might make the natures it displays seem legitimate. But as I have shown, this legitimacy is highly racialized and therefore fragile, certainly in the South African political context. YouTube's algorithms may not care about this, but most of South African society certainly does. This discrepancy not only says something about the power of platform capitalism and how it reinforces a racialized Kruger 2.0. It also says something about the limits of platform capitalism. By allowing its algorithms to popularize very specific and racialized truths and natures as well as the fortress distinctions they reinforce, the platforms might (help to) undermine the possibilities of sharing—*in all its connotations*—Kruger's natures with those constituencies that will ultimately decide on their fate. This, too, is part of the politics of distinction of the Kruger 2.0.

CHAPTER 7

Rhino 2.0

The Politics of Hysteria

#IAm4Rhinos
#WhoseSideAreYouOn

INTRODUCTION

Rhino poaching has risen sharply in Southern Africa since 2007 due to the massive increase in the value and illegal trade of rhino horn. The result has been a major poaching war between poachers and conservation agencies in and around many parks and reserves, especially the Kruger National Park in South Africa, as we saw in the previous chapter. This poaching war and the highly emotive discourses and imageries that accompany it have deeply affected the politics of conservation in the country. Yet when the South African Department of Environmental Affairs in January 2014 officially confirmed that 1,004 rhinos had been killed the year prior, a certain emotional threshold seemed to have been surpassed.[1] The outcry on social media and the amount of voices saying that rhino poaching was "out of control," reached epic proportions.[2] For most environmentalists, this was a "truth about nature" of dramatic clarity and proportion, leading to a sense of crisis that has propelled rhino poaching to become the preeminent conservation issue in South Africa over the last decade and one of the main conservation issues worldwide.

Since the beginning of the poaching crisis in 2008, a massive response by governments, private rhino owners, the conservation sector, and the general public has erupted, in South Africa and globally. This response has been exceptionally diverse and creative—accompanied by heated discussions about the best solutions for the crisis.[3] Often, however, the proposed solutions ultimately focus on fundraising for (military) counter-poaching initiatives or information and awareness campaigns. The great majority of these ideas depend heavily on online communication, social media, and new media platforms; indeed, one could say that the rhino is increasingly "saved" online as much as offline.

This chapter investigates dominant online responses to the rhino-poaching crisis and argues that these should be understood as part of a politics of hysteria, though one that has nothing to do with historical, gender-biased ideas about hysteria.[4] *Hysteria* is here defined as a situation in which emotions run so high that it leads to exaggerated, extreme, or uncontrolled behavior.[5] What exactly constitutes exaggerated, extreme, or uncontrolled is a difficult question, and I will not conceptualize these terms on the individual level. The chapter focuses on how those involved in my research—and online anti-rhino poaching activists more generally—deal with this "out-of-control" situation and how it relates to dominant online and offline actions, discourses, and imageries. Given the massive volume of online commentary and activities, this is necessarily a partial exercise. Moreover, given the high emotions triggered by the poaching crisis and their intricate links to broader racial, political, and social dynamics in South Africa and globally, formulating generalizations about these emotions runs the risk of making individuals feel unfairly categorized or stereotyped, which could lead to (personalized) online reprisals—something that, as we shall see, occurs regularly.

Yet, after closely following and analyzing the rhino-poaching saga for over seven years, I believe that a "politics of hysteria" is an appropriate description of some of the dominant online expressions in response to the crisis. Two expressions, I argue, are particularly prominent, those of heroism and violence. As the chapter will show, many online commentators and discourses heavily depend on showing how certain groups or individuals go out of their way to counter rhino poaching. In the process, vilification and heroization go hand in hand: because those slaughtering rhinos are often considered "evildoers," those going out to protect rhinos are easily rendered "heroes." At the same time, both poaching and anti-poaching activities, discourses, and imageries are drenched in violence. Material forms of violence, especially the "green militarization" of parks, together with myriad social and discursive forms of violence often, as we will see, lead to exaggerated, extreme, or uncontrolled behavior.[6]

Expressions of violence and heroism allow people to believe they are taking control of a problem that affects them deeply, a belief that, in turn, acquires specific connotations in the South African context and its complex histories of the connections between race, nature, capital, and control. Indeed, a central argument is that the poaching crisis unleashes deeper emotions about (the fear of losing) control that haunt many whites in South Africa and beyond, and that new media help to air. Paradoxically, then, new media give people more control over the sharing of emotions that are perhaps not as easily expressed through other channels or in person, only to foster a loss of this control in the online expression of these emotions. Important to emphasize, however, is that this politics of hysteria has two sides. One side is how online emotions are moving out of generally accepted bounds or control. The other side refers to how the workings of platform capitalism are innately bound up with other conditionalities of power and often intensify and exaggerate these.

So, while in the last chapter the racial and class contradictions of new media around Kruger seem—on the surface—to be glossed over by the park's popularity and profitability, this is no longer the case with the rhino-poaching crisis. In this chapter, the "truth about nature" that nature is not doing well but can be saved through appropriate action is rendered acute through the fear of the rhino's extinction and the role it plays in broader histories of conservation in South Africa. The subsequent sharing of this truth online becomes exaggerated in a peculiar way: as a powerful and consequential truth discourse where villains and heroes are supposedly easy to distinguish and where the evil of rhino poaching becomes divorced from the historical circumstances that have greatly contributed to the poaching crisis in the first place. Here, post-truth as an expression of power under platform capitalism gains another connotation. It employs a conservation crisis to fuel and intensify an unequal, racial, and unsustainable political economy, with a deeply contradictory consequence: undermining the possibility for addressing some of the roots of the rhino-poaching crisis. In order to make this argument and understand the dramatic online (and offline) responses to the rhino-poaching crisis, we first need to delve deeper into historical and recent contexts around the connections between race, nature, capital, and control that the last chapter touched on.

RACE, NATURE, CAPITAL, CONTROL

Central in these contexts is the interconnectedness between histories of (white) belonging through the environment and (black) dispossession through conservation. As many authors have convincingly shown,

European, white imaginaries about pristine African wilderness were directly responsible for the forced removal of many African communities from their land to create "fortress conservation" spaces.[7] Brooks even refers to "a brutal geography of forced removal" when describing the history of the famous Hluhluwe game reserve that played a pivotal role in the conservation of the white rhino.[8] Indeed, conservation more generally, we can argue with Moore, was a central strategy for whites to ground "racialized rule in spatial practices."[9]

But beyond dispossessing many Africans in order to create wilderness spaces, "by writing themselves so single-mindedly into the landscape, many whites wrote themselves out of the society."[10] David Hughes, in his book *Whiteness in Zimbabwe*, forcefully argues that white belonging in Africa through the environment was tied both to their *exclusion* from black societies and their *control* of land and people. Building on the work of Dyer, he argues more generally that many whites explicitly value "the control of self and the control of others," including territory."[11] This renders what he calls "post-mastery whiteness" a difficult and complex positionality. Giving up control, as has happened in all parts of Africa, but very late in Zimbabwe and South Africa, was (and still is) not easy, clear-cut, or one-dimensional, and in many areas whites have tried to hold on to privilege and power, especially economically but also through entitlements to nature, land, and territory.[12]

The loss of state power in South Africa, then, was not only a loss of control but also a loss of a vehicle for belonging for many whites. Yet, while whites may have lost control over the state, they have de facto retained much control over conservation spaces, another prime vehicle for belonging.[13] This concerns not only private wilderness estates that have seen rapid growth in numbers over the last decade but also public protected areas now administered by the black post-apartheid government.[14] It is here that the importance of capital becomes apparent. Whites still occupy a dominant position in the South African economy, and they, as well as foreign whites, are by far the majority of visitors to South Africa's national parks.[15] And since these parks have been thoroughly neoliberalized, they depend on tourist income and thus must appease, at least to some degree, their (white) clientele (as argued in the previous chapter). Moreover, the tourism industry is in overwhelmingly white hands, and hence it is white (South African) tourism capital that habitually employs the typical wilderness imageries that aim to attract white European or American tourists. These confluent dynamics have ensured that conservation spaces, and especially the Kruger National

Park as one of the prime symbols of African wilderness, become even more important in relation to white feelings of belonging and control.

But there is another important element to this focus on conservation spaces and the animals they contain. A quote from an insightful essay by Gérard Wajcman helps to explain:

> Humanity passes its time watching the animals. We've invented all kinds of devices expressly for the purpose. We never grow tired of it. No doubt they represent for us a perfect world. Something strange, different from our own, from our uncertain screwed up chaotic mess of a world. All of which makes the animal world look that much better. Sometimes it seems so foreign that we stand before their perfection and we are stupefied and stricken mute, and despite our sincere wishes, we wonder whether we could ever be like them, ever become so marvellous a society as have the ants and the penguins, where everyone has a place, where everyone is in his place, and where everyone knows and does exactly as he must so that everything can keep on in its proper place, so that society can perpetuate itself, unchanged, indefinitely the same and infinitely perfect. We've had a hard time of it, finding our places. After the disasters of the 20th century the animal societies seem to have become the ideal.[16]

Slavoj Žižek, interpreting this quote, believes that this longing for animal utopia speaks to two contemporary cultural phenomena: "First, the popularity of Darwinist reductions of human societies to animal ones, with their explanations of human achievements in terms of evolutionary adaptation."[17] Second, "we can also explain why we obviously find it so pleasurable to watch endless animal documentaries on specialized channels (*Nature*, *Animal Kingdom*, *National Geographic*): they provide a glimpse into a utopian world where no language or training are needed, in other words, into a 'harmonious society' in which everyone spontaneously knows his or her role."[18] While Žižek does not make the connection, this also has obvious links with the historical and contemporary situation in South(ern) Africa. Apartheid was an attempt at a society "where everyone is in his place, and where everyone knows and does exactly as he must so that everything can keep on in its proper place."[19] Kruger was an intrinsic element of this (imagined) society, and symbolized not only a perfect world of animals, but also a perfect separation between a controlled space where everything "has its place" and the chaotic world outside where so much seems "out of place" and "out of control."[20]

With the rhino-poaching crisis, this out of place, out of control, outside world has wrested itself onto conservation spaces, and especially the Kruger, to a degree that has thoroughly shaken up the conservation world and broader (especially white) publics. This is not to say that in reality conservation spaces were somehow separate from the rest of society, nor that "white publics" is a homogenous, undifferentiated entity.[21] Yet despite the many differences of opinion, stances, and responses, the public outcry to the rhino-poaching crisis is predominantly white, something that was acknowledged and indeed lamented by many (white) informants during my research. The Kruger Park for many South African whites resembles not merely a protected area with beautiful animals, but a social space where their belonging to the continent and the country can be expressed more fully. According to one informant, many whites think they still "own the park," and long for the old days when they did not have to share the park with blacks and foreigners.[22]

These elements of race, control, and belonging are tightly connected to capital: conservation and wildlife are important in the broader political economy of South Africa, and particularly, again, for white South Africans who dominate the tourism industry.[23] An "attack" on the Kruger such as through rhino poaching, therefore, for many, comes close to an attack on white belonging *and* white capital and hence legitimizes violent counterstrategies.[24] One of these has been a wholesale "green militarization" of the Kruger that has led to many suspected poachers' deaths.[25] To be sure, violence in the name of conservation is not new; neither is the legitimation of this violence in name of the "higher" cause of conservation. As Neumann argues, "Certain ways of treating humans that are widely recognized as immoral, such as shooting them on-sight and executing them without trial, become normalized and accepted within the boundaries of some national parks and justifiable in the name of biodiversity protection."[26]

What is new is the scale and intensity of public outpouring in relation to the rhino-poaching crisis and the way new online media facilitate this. Many people concerned with or enraged about the poaching crisis express their feelings and opinions online and so air their emotions. Yet expressing emotions in online spaces through these new technologies influences them in peculiar ways, something that only recently has started being addressed in scholarly writing.[27] Crucially, whereas Steyn and Foster found that more private (daily) "white talk" enables whites to express deeper emotions and opinions in a subdued, implicit manner, the internet seems to have become a space where many of these inhibitions often do not apply.[28] To the contrary, social media spaces appear to encourage more extreme or exaggerated behavior, which seems further exacerbated with issues like the rhino-poaching crisis that many believe are out of control.

SAVING THE RHINO ONLINE

The rhino-poaching crisis, as mentioned, has become one of the main conservation issues worldwide. Hence it is no surprise that most major conservation organizations have prominent online rhino spaces dedicated to #StopPoaching. Rhinos are one of WWFs "critical species" and the poaching crisis is a prominent feature on their rhino page.[29] The African Wildlife Foundation has a dedicated rhino page using various celebrities, among others, to inform people about poaching.[30] Some other organizations are dedicated wholly to the rhino, like Save the Rhino, and it is no surprise that their websites focus heavily on the poaching crisis.[31]

All these and many other websites give general information about rhino poaching. Much of this is centered on the main reason for the crisis—namely, "the increasing demand and very high prices being paid for rhino horn, which fuels escalating poaching."[32] They show how this demand comes mainly from China and Vietnam's emerging middle and upper classes, fueled by a widespread believe that rhino horn has medicinal properties and can enhance status, luck, wealth, and so forth.[33] Also documented is how the high price of rhino horn has led to ever more sophisticated poaching methods, including the use of helicopters, and the involvement of well-organized international crime syndicates, and how the crisis is centered on South Africa as the home to over 80 percent of the global rhino population.[34] Included on many websites is the dire warning that if poaching trends continue to increase, the rhino will soon be extinct in the wild.

These websites, however, are the "old-fashioned" way in which the web is used to inform people about the by now familiar and fairly standard explanations for the poaching crisis and solutions for saving the rhino. They are still important but have increasingly given way to 2.0 cocreative online technologies and platforms as an important way to reach audiences and for concerned citizens to "take action." As the most dominant social media, Twitter and Facebook have been especially important in communicating the rhino-poaching crisis. For example, in September 2013, a veritable "rhino twitter storm" was launched through the hashtag #IAm4Rhinos.[35] Organized by WWF South Africa, the goal was to get one million tweets using the hashtag before World Rhino Day on 22 September 2013 and so raise awareness for the poaching crisis.[36] More generally, being active on Twitter or Facebook seems an accepted way to do something for rhinos, as suggested by South African wildlife veterinarian Dr. Will Fowlds. During the time of my fieldwork, a photo of a rhino accompanied by the text "Make a commitment to do one thing every day for rhinos, even if it is just a tweet or a post—if not a day then a week—Dr Will Fowlds" was shared often on Facebook and Twitter.[37]

Precisely what the tweets or posts should be directed toward, and how they impact rhinos in practice often remains unclear—a problem that also concerned the twitter storm initiators.[38] Yet, in line with chapter 3, this is not to say that they cannot or do not have (political, social, environmental) impacts. Lovink's argument that "online discussion tends to take place within 'echo chambers' where groups of like-minded individuals, consciously or not, avoid debate with their cultural or political adversaries," is true in many instances, but not always.[39] A case in point is the many rhino Facebook groups that have sprung up during the early years of the poaching crisis. During my research, I became a member of some of the biggest and most vocal of these. When following discussions, it was clear that many members share certain passions and beliefs or react to certain posts quite similarly. But this does not mean there are no contestations or that these groups are mere "echo chambers."

One group in particular, the Outraged South African Citizens Against Poaching (OSCAP) Facebook group, rapidly grew into an active political force in the South African and even international conservation landscape. It has over nineteen thousand group members, developed into a full-fledged, registered nongovernmental organization (NGO) and has a satellite organization in the UK.[40] In 2014, it organized an international conference on risk assessment of rhino horn trade" and so became the leading organization behind the—until then rather subdued—anti-trade camp in the South African rhino horn trade debate.[41] Its (leading) members write letters to politicians, do street demonstrations, and visit bail hearings of suspected rhino poachers to protest their (potential) release on bail. According to the organization's facilitator in an interview, it is important to do things "on the ground," next to raising awareness on social media, otherwise you end up as a "yapping dog, which doesn't really help."[42] At the same time, it is clear that the Facebook group page remains the core of the organization, and also what gives it legitimacy.[43]

Several other Facebook groups have been able to organize people around the rhino-poaching crisis, while there are many hundreds of individual Facebook pages dedicated to the cause. Besides Twitter and

Facebook, other platforms also serve to rally support for anti-poaching measures, including blogs, YouTube channels, Google+, Instagram, Pinterest, and many more. The blog http://fightforrhinos.com/, like OSCAP, turned into a registered NGO in the United States, and partnered with another volunteer organization from Britain, Helping Rhinos, in order "to save rhinos from extinction by creating awareness and providing support for rhino conservation projects."[44] Yet another interactive platform employed to raise awareness and funds for rhino conservation is online gaming, such as the WWF South Africa sponsored Rhino Raid game mentioned in chapter 3. Popular games, such as RuneScape, "have added virtual rhino sidekicks to their medieval playing field" to "raise awareness about the threats facing these iconic animals" and so help gamers "game for good."[45]

One could go on, but it should be clear from this small selection that many online tools are being used to #SaveTheRhino. And when studying and analyzing the breadth of online responses to the rhino-poaching crisis, it is easy to start seeing how "hysteria" could be an appropriate banner to describe many online discourses and imageries. This relates, initially, to the first part of the above definition of hysteria as "a situation where emotions run high." So, for example, the OSCAP Facebook group for some time used a banner with a screaming, agonized face, shouting "stop the poaching," accompanied by a number that represented the current "rhino death toll" for a specific year.[46]

More generally, rhino-poaching discussions on Facebook groups, Twitter, and other online platforms are often highly emotional. When Facebook groups such as OSCAP or Save Our Rhino update their poaching statistics, many of their members react with outrage, grief, and sadness, often supported by emoticons to express their feelings. Dr. William Fowlds, mentioned above, became famous for showing his emotions on video after two rhinos were poached on the Kariega Game Reserve in South Africa's Eastern Cape province. One survived, the other did not. The video that was shot of Dr. Fowlds weeping over the deceased rhino went viral, subsequently inspiring others to take up the cause.[47] Organizations responsible for protecting rhinos, like the South African conservation parastatal SANParks have also realized how emotional the rhino issue can be on social media. In an interview, several SANParks social media staff mentioned that conservation supporters have put increasing pressure on them to communicate information on and solutions for the crisis through social media. They stated that because of the emotions involved, people get suspicious if the organization does not respond the same day, or sometimes within two hours, leading them to start rumors that are sometimes uncomfortable for the organization.[48]

All this is not surprising: animal welfare issues have long been known to lead to situations where emotions run high.[49] The more interesting part of hysteria is how these heated emotions lead to forms of "exaggerated, extreme, or uncontrolled behavior." In the next two sections, I will analyze two emotive expressions that I argue are particularly dominant in online rhino-poaching discourses and imageries, heroism and violence: the online (self-)representations of actors and their actions as critical for the animal's survival and the overwhelming presence of discourses and images of violence and rage. These expressions often overlap, and focusing on these is not to say that they are the only or even the most prominent ones. Love and care for rhinos and wildlife, for example, is also prominent online and expressed in manifold ways. In fact—following Lorimer and Whatmore—violence and care/concern seem to often go together remarkably well in online discourses, as we shall see.[50]

RHINO HEROISM

Rhinos, as one of the charismatic African megafauna, arouse strong global emotions, and doing something for rhino conservation is therefore often seen as something that is apolitical and innately good. Add to this the fact that rhinos are poached in violent and often cruel ways (hacking off horns while they are still alive) and it is no wonder that many see this as a classic good-versus-evil story where "the truth" is plain for all to see. One prominent example comes from Great Britain's Prince William and Prince Harry. They founded United For Wildlife, which "has brought together the world's leading wildlife charities under a common purpose; to create a global movement for change. Whilst animals continue to be killed by criminals, whilst whole species are hunted to extinction, we will join together to ask one simple question: Whose side are you on?"[51] United for Wildlife organized an international conference on the illegal wildlife trade in February 2014 and launched a major social media campaign under the banner #WhoseSideAreYouOn.[52] According to Prince William, the choice is easy: either you are with the critically endangered species or with "the criminals who kill them for money."[53] This is a strong framing, based on a powerful truth discourse, and it has had equally powerful effect. Since the campaign started around 2013, it has convened several conferences, brought together some of the activities of the major global conservation organizations, and been able to gain much (media and other) attention for this cause, among others, by enlisting many celebrities, politicians, and other well-known figures, including soccer player David Beckham.

The fact that this hero-versus-villain truth discourse is a dramatic oversimplification of very complex and contradictory realities is evident, and the point here is not to show the dangers of this oversimplification and their possible effects. In this section I am more interested in the felt need to portray "rhino rescuers" as heroes and the "truth work" that this does. A first thing to note in this respect is that there are many degrees of heroism in the online rhino realm. Some are straightforward, like the people behind Rocking for Rhinos, who introduce themselves as follows:

> 2012 sees the dawn of a new era as a new breed of Conservation Heroes emerge from the bloodied battlefields of the bushveld, they have been sent to Earth for one purpose . . . To protect South Africa's Wildlife from the poacher scum that rapes and pillages the land on a daily basis. They are known around these parts as "Rocking For Rhinos"! No longer will South Africa's threatened Wildlife be left alone to fend for itself, for as long as poacher scum invades the land, Rocking For Rhinos will be there in full force to CONSERVE, PRESERVE and PROTECT![54]

These new, all-white "conservation heroes" portray themselves as Rambo-style warriors, fully equipped with semi-automatic rifles and army outfits, and many others do likewise.[55] In a *Sunday Times* insert called "Rhino Rambo" of 2 October 2011, the focus is on Australian former special forces commando Damien Mander. Mander "honed his warrior skills in the deadly crucible of Baghdad," and now "the former soldier is using them to protect Africa's Rhino," according to the article.[56] Mander founded the International Anti-Poaching Foundation based on a para-military style of conservation and hopes to enroll people into a "green army" that aims to "protect wildlife in volatile regions."[57]

Many more have been drawn by the lure to become a "conservation Rambo," including several US former elite soldiers in Animal Planet's *Battleground: Rhino Wars*.[58] Indeed, according to an experienced ranger trainer at the Southern African Wildlife College, he regularly receives requests from former elite soldiers to come and "shoot poachers"— something he "obviously cannot accommodate."[59] Clearly, the lure to become a "rhino hero" appeals to many, though those that try do not always get recognized as such. When Tom Hardy, an English actor, tried to save rhinos in a documentary *The Poaching Wars with Tom*

Hardy, he faced wide criticism for failing to live up to expectations. One reviewer noted: "What a shame that Tom Hardy seemed more interested in playing Rambo than actually gripping the issues at hand."[60]

Other examples of highly visible and violent (wannabe) rhino heroes abound, but of interest here are also the subtler heroizations on daily social media interactions. Since the start of the rhino-poaching crisis in 2007, many people have been stepping up to organize anti-poaching activities, raise awareness and funding, or do other work. In contrast to the "conservation Rambos," these are often not the violent heroes but, for example, nurturing heroes, such as those behind the Rhino Orphanage, who take care of orphaned rhino calves after their mothers have been poached.[61] On their Facebook page and other Facebook and social media discussions during my research, they were regularly referred to as heroes in the poaching-crisis.[62]

Another such hero is one mentioned already, wildlife veterinarian William Fowlds. Dr. Fowlds became well known in South African rhino circles after he took care of two surviving poached rhinos on Kariega Game Reserve in the Eastern Cape in March 2012.[63] One of these, named Themba, succumbed to injuries after two weeks, but the other one, Thandi, survived and became an inspiration for many to undertake action: a woman from Scotland who volunteered at Kariega, founded an NGO, Thandi's Fund Raiser; a man from the Eastern Cape was inspired to start The Rhino Run; and so on.[64] Their websites and Facebook pages regularly refer to Dr. Fowlds with adoration. Emboldened by these and other showings of support and his video going viral, Dr. Fowlds had become somewhat of a (social) media star and clearly positioned himself as such at the 2014 Annual South African Veterinary Association meeting on 6 March in Pretoria, attended by the author. He referred back to the video often and said that vets and people must show how much they care about rhinos and that this emotional attachment was what was going to make the difference, as long as the (social) media storytelling becomes more organized.[65]

Other, different forms of heroization can be mentioned, like the work done by documentary maker Rian van Der Walt, who interviews "the heroes of the rhino war."[66] But important here is that most of the heroes and those doing the heroization are whites (South African or otherwise). This, however, does not mean that only whites can be heroes, or are heroized in relation to the rhino-poaching crisis. One important category of heroes is the rangers working in parks, the majority of whom are black. One organization explicitly dedicated to rangers is the Thin Green Line Foundation, whose founder, Sean Wil-more, argues that "these guys dedicate their lives to their jobs and to our planet and should be treated like heroes."[67] United for Wildlife also put up a video on their website, so we can all "hear from the unsung heroes of conservation."[68] On many rhino Facebook groups, such as the OSCAP group, there is regular attention for rangers in the field, like this message on Christmas Day 2014: "Over the next couple of days while you are with friends and family celebrating and having a great holiday I would like you to keep the Rangers that are out in the field protect-ing our wildlife in your thoughts. They not only put their lives on the line daily but they are also deprived of spending this time with their family and friends."[69] In the many comments that followed, rangers are highly praised, and there is much heroization going on. Over the course of my research from 2012 to 2015, I saw an increasing amount of these comments, which testifies to the felt need to sing the praises of those who are out in the field protecting the rhinos and wildlife that many are so passionate and emotional about. One US veterinarian even started a foundation, the Silent Heroes Foundation, dedicated to these heroes: "To us, the 'Silent Heroes' are all of those individuals working on the front lines and/or quietly behind the scenes of conservation . . . in Africa. Additionally it includes all of those heroes who support our work and allow us to make a small but viable impact on those things for which we are passionate about in the world."[70]

Clearly, from this discussion, heroism and the active heroization of people and organizations in everyday praxis is an important emotive expression in "saving the rhino online." At the same time, heroization is also an important truth discourse in the Foucauldian sense: it produces a politics of truth that "induces regular effects of power," in this case a powerful good-versus-evil or hero-versus-villain discourse whereby anybody active in stopping poaching is a hero, someone that needs to be admired and whose work is (innately) good.[71] So while heroization is perhaps not much of an extreme or uncontrolled expression, it lays an important basis for a particular truth discourse. This discourse becomes more disturbing when connected to the other main emotion online, that of violence.

RHINO VIOLENCE

The rhino-poaching crisis is steeped in many forms of violence—that much is clear from the emerging literature on this topic. Duffy argues that in the war to save biodiversity "militarized forms of anti-poaching are increasingly justified by conservation NGOs keen to protect wild-life."[72] Lunstrum refers to the "striking" and "lethal" "green militariza-tion" taking place in the Kruger Park and indeed in many conservation areas around the world.[73] Humphreys and Smith write that "the inten-sification of the counter-poaching strategy is clearly part of a trend that has witnessed the increasing militarization of wildlife management, the physical manifestation of this approach also bears resemblance to some notable developments in late-modern warfare. These develop-ments have seen an emphasis on the close targeting of individuals or groups, broadly identified in the current military argot as 'man-hunting' or 'targeted killings.' The combative language suggests that a policy of enhanced confrontation with the poachers is being ramped up."[74]

My colleague Maano Ramutsindela and I, finally, argue that various forms of "green violence" are taking place in the rhino-poaching crisis, including material, social, and discursive forms.[75] In all, it is clear that violence is one of the—if not *the*—prime expression in both offline and online discourses and activities against rhino poaching. What I will show is that in the online realm, these violent expressions become extreme, exaggerated, even uncontrolled or uncontrollable, and that this has important consequences for the truth discourse produced around the rhino-poaching crisis.

One of the most frequent forms of online violence is what I started calling "celebrating the death of poachers." Especially on Facebook groups, but also on other social media, news reports about poachers being caught or killed are habitually greeted with enthusiasm and often extreme forms of discursive violence. For example, when a news item is shared on a rhino Facebook group with the title "two suspected poach-ers killed in Kruger shoot out," a bare three hours later there are over seventy "likes" and many comments, including: "yay—two less to worry about!!"; "Good, kill more!!!"; "Yippie"; "Good riddance to bad rub-bish", "great work, kill them all", and so forth.[76] Another comment in response to a similar news story is more extensive: "Yay!!!—Best news I have heard today—well done—Photograph their dead bodies and make a few million leaflets—then drop them over every bloody village in Mozambique and around the park in SA—talk about Big rewards for tip offs and let every poacher know they WILL DIE"[77]

Over the course of my research I collected hundreds of screen shots of these types of responses, with an overwhelming majority of whites—predominantly South African—cheering the death or injury of *suspected* poachers. What is more, many add graphics to their comments. One that I saw often showed several bullets, accompanied by the following text: "microchip implant allows animal poachers to talk directly to God. Specifically designed to be injected into the forehead. When properly installed, it will allow the Poacher to speak to God!! Available sizes from .223 to .50 cal." Another one showed a rhino with an electric saw who had just cut off the nose of a black male, accompanied by the text: "And? Do you like it?"[78]

Many similar examples could be given. The next example, however, is important, as it demonstrates that commenters are willing to push their arguments very far. The following was part of a discussion that ensued after news was shared that buffalo had killed a *suspected* poacher:

Commenter 1: Poachers deserve to die! Thats final—and besides, this was divine intervention! The Universe got rid of a cruel poacher who kills for a living, so why should poachers live? So they can kill and maim our wildlife?

Commenter 2: Not all human life is worthy of respect, in my opinion. Some humans really are just a waste of skin and oxygen thieves. Society is enriched when they are no longer dwelling amongst us.

Commenter 3: aha yes totally agree . . . but then if I follow that through there would be very few humans left on earth—which would be a good thing for the earth of course. but I am not the judge. rapists and killers of other humans are tried and then sentenced (and yes, I think we should have the death penalty back).

Commenter 2: Nah. I don't even respect their right to life. They do not begin to display the faintest smattering of RESPECT and therefore will not receive mine. If we are going to respect their right to life it simply means we agree that poachers should not be shot on sight. And I certainly do not agree with that!!

What is extreme or exaggerated is that poachers here are placed in an Agambian "state of exception," where their right to life no longer applies.[79] Poachers are seen as evil monsters that rupture the apolitical "dream spaces" that conservation areas represent for many whites, and hence killing them is seen as legitimate.[80] This, then, goes beyond the "mere" cheering of the death of *suspected* poachers; these are extreme expressions of hate against *suspected* poachers though sadly fairly common in online social media spaces.[81]

Despite the large majority of comments condoning and cheering violence, there is resistance as well, and occasionally some commenters do make the point that online discursive violence might be extreme or unhelpful. These comments, however, were often immediately attacked by others, as in the below exchange after the sharing of the news that rangers wounded a *suspected* poacher:

Commenter 1: Cruelty to animals is totally unacceptable, but cruelty to a human being is just fine? And we call ourselves civilised . . .

Commenter 2: Oh [*name of commenter one*] get over yourself—this is certainly not cruelty to a human being—he is NOT DEAD, like so many of our Rhino !!! I would prefer to actually see 1 DEAD poacher and save 10 Rhino !! Grow up and see the big picture here—people like you make me want to puke !!

Here is another example after a similar news story was shared on Facebook:

Commenter 1: It's easy to say, shoot them. who of us had to aim at another human to kill, it's not easy, trust me.

Commenter 2: Yes [*name of commenter one*] not easy but then they aim at magnificent beings that are totally innocent of any such evil deeds, so they deserve to be taken out of society as alive they are a menace and a very serious threat, not only to the animals teetering on the brink of extinction, but to the rest of humanity as we need the same animals for our own preservation. And anyhow, there are far too many humans on this planet we are heading for some disaster so low scum humans not really a loss.

And a final example relates to the news of a shooting of a *suspected* rhino and elephant poacher in the buttocks:

Commenter 1: Um . . . They're still people . . . Legal to shoot them? People, lease STOP blind hating . . . At least try. . . . You don't know their reasons.

Commenter 2: [*name of commenter one*]—whatever planet did you come from? Haven't you seen the photo of the elephant who HAS NO FACE ? The poachers left her there on a road WITH A HOLE where she used to have eyes, mouth and TUSKS ! . . . so don't post rubbish comments about poachers 'still being people' . . . Because THEY ARE NOT HUMAN !

Commenter 3: [*name of commenter one*], you are on a group to
support rhino poaching, yet it shows you are in this group to
defend the poaches . . . of course it's not legal to shoot people,
BUT NOR IS RHINO POACHING the ONLY difference is these
poor animals have NO Defense beside US!!!!!

Commenter 4: [*name of commenter one*] . . . try caring for the
younge left behind or the animals that dont die imm and have to
be doctored . . . are you awake???Fuck their reasons . . . they are
and never will be good enough . . . this is murder . . . cold bloody
murder,i would have shot him in the face,twice for good measure.

Interestingly (and disturbingly), not only do commenters lose control
when espousing extreme language and the condoning of death, even
those that try to control others are often viciously, and sometimes even
personally attacked. All this makes the job of online moderators of
Facebook groups, discussions forums, or other platforms difficult and
demanding. In interviews, several of them expressed frustration at the
violence online and stated that they have a hard time controlling discussions and have to keep repeating themselves to people.[82] On 23 July
2018, The OSCAP Facebook group moderator felt the need to put up
the following announcement that is always visible on top of the page:
"Please note that this group does not condone racist, hate or comments
calling for death of poachers. We understand that this is an extremely
emotive subject but admin will delete these comments. We need to follow the laws of this country even if others do not."[83]

THE POLITICS OF HYSTERIA

The foregoing showed that, for many, the rhino-poaching crisis is "out
of control" and that heroized and violent discourses are ways to (discur-
sively) regain control. New online media play a crucial and contradictory role in these dynamics. For starters, control over what is happening
to rhinos is exactly what is lacking online—most online activists do
not have any control over whether poachers decide to poach, or how
game farmers or parks protect their rhinos. And despite the regular
nods toward all the work done to halt the crisis, many still see poaching
numbers going up or not down fast enough and despair. Some use this
feeling to come up with solutions themselves, such as the NGO Rhino
Rescue Project, which promotes the poisoning of horns as "an out-of-the

box solution to an out-of-control problem."[84] But most others use new media to raise awareness or funding and voice their frustrations.

In other words, new media have given people more control to show and give voice/image to their emotive expressions though often in ways that can themselves be seen as "out of control." The control over a technology of expression then—paradoxically—engenders more general feelings of losing control. It is therefore perhaps not coincidental that two dominant expressions online are about (re)gaining control: heroes are, of course, always (supposed to be) in control and violence is a way of responding to a lack of control by finding a singular focus in dealing with a problem (though both expressions and their related practices habitually increase rather than decrease further violence).[85]

In turn, and following Kepe, it is important to emphasize that the great majority of people on new media doing the heroization and cheering or calling for violence, are whites.[86] Obviously, there are exceptions, but in my research on this issue from 2011 to 2019, these have been rare (though sometimes very vocal). This is in line with broader laments of many respondents regarding the general dominance of whites in (online) conservation and anti-poaching discussions and activities, and does not actually say much about heroization or violence in general.[87] The question that arises is not why so many whites feel the apparent need for heroes or violence, but what "truth work" these particular emotions do for them.

From the "rhino hero" discussion, one type of work stands out, one related to the etymology of hero as protector or defender. Many whites are so emotional about the rhino-poaching crisis that they strongly feel the need for someone to protect rhinos against evil, against "poacher scum," as Rocking for Rhinos has it. This protector or defender should be the state, but online discourses make it clear that many whites feel that the state fails miserably in this role.[88] Hence they look for other protectors, someone who takes control of a situation out of control. This, I argue, is a key reason for the hero expression. In turn, the severity and import of this reason increases when linked to expressions of violence: a good-versus-evil story more easily condones or legitimates violence. After all, we *must* choose: #WhoseSideAreYouOn.

All this is significant in the South African context of shifting racial political-economic power balances, where whites have lost most of the control they felt they had a God-given right to for generations.[89] Since the end of apartheid, there has been a simmering (and sometimes quite

overt) sense of hysteria among parts of the white population in South
Africa that try to retain control over their lives, culture, language, education, businesses, and more vis-á-vis the black majority.[90] Conservation remains one of the main bastions of white control and—because
of their history as spaces of (black) displacement and dispossession—
important in relation to belonging for many (South African) whites.
In turn, this is further strengthened by the idea of animal kingdoms as
places that are perfect and where everything is "in place," as mentioned
in the previous chapter.[91]

The online politics of hysteria, I argue, is a response to this sense of
loss of control and belonging. A politics of hysteria indicates a dialectic
between a (sense) of a (structural, social) situation or context out of control and individual types of extreme or uncontrolled violent responses on
new media focused on the agency or actions of certain groups of "evildoers" (especially the poachers and crime syndicates, but also the state
and others). These extreme emotions, in turn, not only represent particular (political) interests focused on the safeguarding of certain conservation spaces as places of white belonging and control, they also drown
out broader political-economic power structures that historically privileged, and continue to privilege, these interests. Yet the broader political
economy within which rhino-poaching occurs and within which whites
still hold a special place rarely gets discussed, save perhaps for occasional
debates in relation to the rhino-horn trade. But, even here, important
contradictions are rarely acknowledged, such as one Humphreys and
Smith pointed to: "The intense focus on rhinos in South Africa stems
from the ever-expanding 'commodification' of the animals, lying at the
heart not only of illegal horn-selling networks but also of the tourist
industry, whether for 'sport hunting' or wildlife viewing, on which parts
of the South African economy are heavily dependent."[92]

These parts, as mentioned, are highly dominated by whites, yet the
online hysteria around the rhino-poaching crisis obscures these and
other fundamental political economic structures that continue to rest on
and reinforce white privilege.[93] It is here, also, that social media come
to play an important role, as it makes hysterical expressions seem more
intense due to the speed, reach, and (potential) volume of expressions,
something that, as we saw in the previous chapter, can directly influence
(offline) institutional politics. Sarah Ahmed poignantly articulates one
element in how this works. She argues that "emotions work as a form
of capital: affect does not reside positively in the sign or commodity,
but is produced as an effect of its circulation."[94] Kuntsman—further

quoting Ahmed—ads that "emotions accumulate strength as they move between subjects and texts, and are 'not contained within the contours of a subject.'"[95] This, I argue, is also the role that social media play in increasing the political potency of affective expressions: they enable the hyper-circulation of affects and emotions that help to increase the pressure on organizations and people, as the earlier referred interview with SANParks media officers showed. As such, the politics of hysteria through new media becomes a potent force for political mobilization and intervention that not only emanates from historical and contemporary political-economic connections between race, nature, affect, and control, but also reinforces these.

CONCLUSION

What this chapter has shown is that hysteria becomes part of a politics and discourse of truth and, as such, also a conduit with important political effects. Exaggeration works: it helps to gain control over a situation "out of control" and it helps to emphasize "the truth" about rhinos. Yet it also makes the (online) rhino 2.0 quite different from the offline rhino: for example, it renders the rhino 2.0 more threatened than the offline rhino actually is. This, ironically, has been good for conservation in so far that it generated attention and donations. But it also makes the online rhino 2.0 a more hysteric animal in interesting ways. It is the historical and contemporary context around race, nature, capital, and control that laid the basis for the current emotional connotations attached to the rhino-poaching crisis. But in their expression online, these emotions are divorced from this same historical context; instead a simplistic good-versus-evil or hero-versus-villain truth discourse predominates. Not only does it strengthen fortress Kruger dynamics, as we saw in the previous chapter, it also intervenes in the public domain in a powerful way, as this chapter has shown.

If we step out of the specific context of this chapter, we can see that all of this takes place in a broader context where "the truth about nature" as I have used it in this book is ramped up to forms of hysteria more generally: either we do something now, or the world will perish. In the introduction I quoted the Nature Needs Half or Half Earth movement that truly believes, following the subtitle of E. O Wilson's (2016) book, that our planet is "fighting for life." Other, similar types of rhetoric have become expressed around the current sixth extinction crisis, for example, the reference to "biological annihilation."[96] All this becomes a threat: if we do not do conservation forcefully right now, we will lose such-and-such species or life on earth in its entirety.[97]

Some proponents of harsher—even violent—forms of environmentalism make this point very explicitly. McCann argues that the narrative advanced by critics of green violence "perhaps most worryingly, does not appear to grasp that wildlife—such as lions, elephants, and rhinos—must be protected today or there will be none left for the future."[98] He concludes his essay by arguing: "Now is not the time to roll back on our efforts to stop the slaughter, now is the time to do all we possibly can to prevent this ecological and moral catastrophe: the destruction of the living planet and the extinction of species."[99] And McCann is not a lone voice. Mogomotsi and Madigele have the following to say to those who would critique their support of Botswana's (former) shoot-to-kill anti-poaching policy: "To the moralists, such a position is very difficult to accept; however, we argue that it is a necessary evil, considering the obligation to protect rhinos from extinction. It appears that poachers will do anything to ensure that they kill these animals, unless they are made aware of the possibility of their own death in the process."[100]

These types of hysteric expressions have also increasingly become part of accepted truth discourses around nature and conservation. And they are not new. As Crawford argued earlier: "When environmental questions are posed within the context of threat, they also invoke issues of security, risk, and necessity. It is in this frame that environmental politics can appear to operate as a unifying political imperative—this is what must be done to preserve lives, to preserve the planet, to preserve animals, plants, and all nonhuman others."[101] Social media, and specifically platform capitalism, give more urgency and circulation to this politics of hysteria and the truth discourses it espouses. Hysteria thus becomes part of a broader, societal politics of truth that is again beyond context and narrowly focused on the "truth about (threatened) nature" in isolated form.

This chapter has shown that the ability of new media to facilitate hysteria not only enables potent political interventions but contributes to changing the very nature of environmental politics altogether. This is an environmental politics increasingly steeped in a conviction of truth as urgent, immediate, and unambiguous—a tendency now reinforced by environmentalists' desire to counter post-truth. A search for deeper, situated understanding becomes impossible: then it would be "too late." The ironic corollary is that truth itself becomes impossible; not in the literal sense, but by its dissipation in the hysterical urgency of the defense of truth.

Conclusion

Speaking Truth to Power

#TheTruthAboutNature
#NatureNow

Faced with the post-truth conundrum and multiple environmental crises, but equally out of a passion and love for biodiversity, many environmentalists are trying hard to conserve, communicate, and share #TheTruthAboutNature. They are convinced that the global state of the environment is deeply worrying but that appropriate action can (still) be taken to mediate the situation. I mentioned in the introduction that I, too, believe that there is truthfulness to our environmental predicament. And that, following Harry Frankfurt, we should not be indifferent to truth and acknowledge the high stakes that this particular truth is concerned with. At the same time, I have argued that these truths are meaningless outside of context and history and in relation to different positionalities. Throughout the chapters in part 3, I have tried to give meaning to these contexts, and so also to many connotations and different interpretations of this truth.

As the journey progressed, it may have seemed that I could—perhaps *should*—have ditched the term altogether. Given the fact that I have only started scratching the surface regarding the many connotations and interpretations in one particular region of the world, what use is there for the idea of truth? Would it not be simpler to agree with Latour that the word *truth* adds only little weight to discursive power plays? Especially when I had already agreed with Foucault that truth is always power? Can we, after all this, still conserve an idea of truth? The answer to this question is not merely affirmative. This book argues that, in fact, it is critically important to do so, and that the way to do so is to rekindle the art of speaking truth to power. I will use the conclusion to explicate this point and the stakes involved. Along the way, I rehearse the book's main arguments and interventions.

WHY CONSERVE TRUTH?

The more straightforward answer to this question is that deconstructing truth claims—including claims related to "the truth about nature"—can actually help us get closer to truth. To a good degree, I have followed this line of thinking in the book and I would argue that many other scholars do the same in their work. They may not believe in the utility of truth as a productive concept, but still interrogate, deconstruct, and challenge consequential truth claims in order to acquire a more truthful understanding of the world. From this perspective, I argue that it is precisely by interrogating the details of (socio-)environmental crises in specific places and the connotations or different interpretations of this truth that we should come to a deeper appreciation of its importance and a more realistic idea about how to address, share, and conserve it. It allows us, for example, to understand that the importance of the conservation of megafauna in (Southern) Africa cannot be seen outside the region's deeply unjust conservation histories and contexts, and the racial, gender, class, and other inequalities and positionalities they have shaped and been part of. Not taking into account the latter is foolish and bigoted and would risk (further) delegitimization of conservation.[1]

This understanding, to be sure, does not equal "(the) truth." But it does arise out of and is embedded in a quest where truth is seen as legitimate and as something more than *just* a discursive tactic or an expression of power. It is, in other words, fundamentally embedded in a metaphysics of truth tensions, which indicates a need to *always* be critical of any truth claim and the powers behind them while at the same time *always* continuing to search for truth. Contemporary social theory finds this difficult and indeed has for a long time.[2] If, as Foucault taught us, truth is power; and if power is dispersed, complex, and scattered, as posthumanist Braidotti argues, then it seems truth must be also. The idea is that truth will always be caught in the shifting sands of everyday (material and intellectual) praxis and thus likely change with every (theoretical or experiential) "turn."[3] In fact: not only could truth not obtain solid form; trying to search for this would be suspicious, an indication for a need for power.

Yet Foucault himself famously argued that power can be positive and productive; that it does something in the world; it is not just negative.[4] What if truth could equally be productive? What if it can be positive in the meaning that Foucault ascribed to it: that it facilitates, not just represses; that it affords; and that it provides meaning. Truth tensions relate to how searching for truth inevitably leads one to confront tensions between how truth can repress but also enable; how it muddles but also clarifies, and how it nuances but also sharpens, how it blurs and fortifies distinctions *simultaneously*. Chapter 6 illustrated this point: the shifting sand of blurred new media boundaries was precisely the hinge that enabled the solidification of the racialized borders of a national park.

The single most important way to make truth productive, I argue, is by speaking it to power; to make explicit how *understanding* speaks truth to power and aims to make a difference. Speaking truth to power entails finding meaning in things we have in common that go against structural power and those who legitimate and (aim to) expand this power. This, in short, is why we need to conserve truth: to enable a deeper understanding of power *and to confront and transcend power at the same time*. This, at least, is how I understand Foucault's point about "detaching the power of truth from the forms of hegemony, social, economic and cultural, within which it operates at the present time."[5] This does not mean that truth becomes objective or beyond power *in general*; rather that it transcends specific forms of hegemonic power at particular points in time. These moments are precisely what can make a difference and show that structural change is possible.

But the reason I call for rekindling the art of speaking truth to power is not just so that we can know that *structural* change is possible but because structural change is *necessary*. Here is a second important reason to conserve truth and how this is wrapped up in a *political ecology of truth*: to acknowledge and act on the truthfulness of our environmental predicament and how it intersects with the truthfulness of the obscene inequalities in the world today. This truth makes it necessary to challenge and transcend hegemonic forms of power and hence to challenge post-truth. The latter is especially important because it makes this transcending more difficult by hollowing out the sharing of truth from the inside. We can understand this better, I argued, when post-truth is conceptualized as an expression of power under platform capitalism.

THE NATURE OF POST-TRUTH

Post-truth is not about people in power who do not care about the truth. It is also not, in the words of Conservation International, about "people in charge of important sh*t who don't believe in science."[6] Individual people do not "do" post-truth. They certainly lie and bullshit. But as I explained based on Harry Frankfurt's work, these are different from post-truth. No matter how important it is to challenge and confront individual liars and bullshitters—especially those in power!—conceptualizing post-truth solely in relation to the behavior of individuals is highly problematic. First, it provides an excuse for saying that "bad apples" produce post-truth. The more structural dynamics that induce post-truth are thereby left undetected and unchallenged, which makes any solution to address it shallow and ineffective. Second, it is ahistorical: focusing solely on individuals does not help to understand the broader historical contexts that have led to this particular juncture where post-truth has become such a conundrum.[7] To get to the nature of post-truth, therefore, part 2 of the book attended to the more structural and historical dynamics that have brought us to this juncture. This led to what I argue is the most appropriate way to conceptualize post-truth: as an expression of power under platform capitalism.

What is the broader significance of this conceptualization? It means that post-truth is not a Foucauldian truth discourse. It is, literally, *beyond* truth. And the way to understand this is to appreciate the rise of platform capitalism. Here, I built on Nick Srnicek's work, which demonstrates that platforms have become the quintessential capitalist organizations of our time since they allow companies to position themselves between users and "the ground upon which their activities occur." This gives them privileged access to record the data that users leave behind and use these to balance users' cocreative possibilities with commercially directed forms of information provision and ordering.[8] Underlying this is the logic of algorithmic relationships and calculations, where "correlation takes the place of correspondence (between symbolic representation and that which is represented) and effective intensity comes to stand in for and displace referential 'truth,' authenticity, and factual evidence."[9] The algorithms that enable platform capitalism literally produce "knowledge without truth."[10]

To be clear, the point about post-truth is not that information generated by algorithms cannot be true, interesting, or lively. As we have seen, it is often even more so, leading to intensified spectacular environmentalisms. Rather, it is that *whether something is true or not does not matter for algorithms or the (commercial) success of platforms.* And hence, to a good degree, this influences what people get exposed to online, what knowledge is available to them, and how they understand this. Most fundamentally, it means that understandings and experiences of reality are less and less *shared.* People can build their own realities online; platforms and algorithms duly enable and manipulate this. Still, one could ask: what is the problem? Realities have historically rarely been shared, especially since large parts of humanity have either not been very connected or have been connected in fragmented, haphazard ways.[11] Historically, "reality," and the "truths" they encapsulated, may therefore always have had more purchase within specific (social, religious, cultural, and other) communities. But perhaps this is precisely the point: community is not the same as connection.[12] Platforms and algorithms do build community; yet they simultaneously "hypermodulate" the connections that enable these communities into "countless dispersed micro-experiences."[13]

The commercial exploitation of this fundamental, "cocreative" tension between how realities are simultaneously shared and deeply individuated through online new media is the core of platform power and why it hollows out truth. It means that the sharing of truths and natures online contributes to and strengthens platform capitalism, with two major, problematic consequences. The first is to reinforce logics of capital and capitalism more generally, which does little to alleviate the dynamics that have led to our current environmental predicament. The second is an undermining of any idea of truth, including "the truth about nature," by stimulating post-truth. A critical intervention of the book has been to integrate these two consequences into a conceptualization of post-truth. Post-truth, therefore, *is* our contemporary shared reality. Countering post-truth by sharing truth more widely, vehemently, and passionately through new media amounts to a fundamental contradiction caught up in a vicious circle that could undermine attempts to alleviate environmental crises.

THE TENSION-RIDDEN SPACE

Another critical intervention of the book has been to argue that while this threat is very real, it is not one-dimensional or all-determining. To illustrate this, I complemented the analysis of the political economy of platform capitalism in part 2 with empirical illustrations of saving and sharing nature in the new media age in part 3 of the book. One reason for this is that for conservation—contra the dominant tenor in social media studies—a sharp distinction between online and offline animals and ecosystems is obvious and crucial. Hence, platform capitalism may highly influence nature and conservation; it does not determine them. It takes shape in and through different contexts, histories, and positionalities and intersects with many other conditionalities of power, including those of race, class, gender, and more, in important and sometimes surprising ways. To gauge this influence more accurately, I studied the politics and everyday praxis of saving nature in the era of post-truth and platform capitalism in a variety of empirical settings.

For example, in chapter 4, I showed that many conservation actors are aware of platform contradictions and that they try to mediate this through a politics of cocreation. The other chapters moved even deeper into the specifics of environmentalism 2.0, mainly in Southern Africa, to show how sharing the truth about nature on elephant corridors, the Kruger National Park, and in response to rhino poaching does not make sense outside of very specific historical, racial, social, and other contexts, histories, and positionalities. Certainly, the book would have looked very different when another region had taken center stage empirically. There are, for example, no (wild) rhinos in Latin America, and a focus on this continent might thus have had a very different discussion of the relations between political economy, certain animals, and race. A focus on Asia could have included rhinos, but a discussion on the same relations would again have been very different. These differences are critical and reemphasize why any search for truth needs to delve deep into history, positionalities, and context.

But to a good degree, I am convinced that, even if another region had been foregrounded empirically, the book would have been very similar and made the same overarching interventions. I would have still made the point that the platform capitalist mechanisms and issues unearthed in part 2 are global and generic while the way that they work out in regional or local contexts are not. I would also have continued to emphasize that in between these two is the space of politics, the space where the tension between difference and equivalence is "articulated" and mediated in daily life.[14] And lastly, I would have remained convinced that this politics takes many forms. The specific focus in this book showed that in the 2.0 era the politics of cocreation, platforms, distinction, and hysteria are worthy of special attention. Whether they are equally important in other regions or contexts needs to be empirically verified.

The broader point is this: these forms of politics are among the concrete ways in which truth tensions take shape. They respond to, interpret, and come out of different ways in which "the truth about nature" as I defined it in the introduction is connected to histories, contexts, and positionalities within—and acted on by employing—platform possibilities. It is these contexts, histories, and positionalities that give deeper *meaning* to the ways in which nature 2.0 is employed to save offline natures and, hence, following Hannah Arendt, enable us to move from knowledge to understanding. A central (methodological, philosophical) premise hereby is that combining attention to political-economic power and daily praxis is critical to move from knowledge to understanding. Only in this way, I argue, can we meaningfully approach the question of truth, namely by situating ourselves on *the tension and mutual co-constitution between solid rock and shifting sand.*[15] It is this tension-ridden space that conservation needs to acknowledge and occupy in order to construct a meaningful politics moving forward.

No doubt, this is uncomfortable. The tension-ridden space is decisively equivocal—yet this is precisely the point of *understanding*. Remember Hannah Arendt: "Understanding, as distinguished from having correct information and scientific knowledge, is a complicated process which never produces unequivocal results."[16] In a sense, this is what part 3 of the book tried to do in relation to part 2. Popular language and common sense are important for Arendt; they refer to the societal context within which truth gets interpreted and becomes meaningful (in the way in which "natural capital" becomes meaningful in the context of the *capitalist* interpretation of capitalist crisis). Thus, to be meaningful, (material) nature needs to be acknowledged *and* transcended, which can never be done through science alone. Surely a scientist could find "solid rock" in concluding that the (material) natures in Kruger Park are of universal importance and should be conserved. But how do you render Kruger's conservation meaningful within the everyday shifting sands of dealing with historical dispossession, racial tension, poaching violence, and more? Certainly not by simply insisting on the former outside of context. Hence, the question of "the truth about nature" must always be approached through the tension-ridden space between solid rock and shifting sand.

In many ways, this already happens in practice. As mentioned above, the forms of politics identified in part 3 are among the concrete ways in which truth tensions take shape between the abstract political economy of structural power *and* how this political economy is co-constituted through everyday life with its specific contexts, histories, and positionalities. The point is that these empirical forms of politics shape truth tensions *within*—or without explicitly questioning—hegemonic power. The politics of truth tensions that I proposed in part 1 is different because it presupposes a politics explicitly aimed at challenging hegemony by speaking truth to power. The remainder of this conclusion reflects on what this might look like.

THE POLITICS OF TRUTH TENSIONS

A politics of truth tensions is different from a politics of *truth wars*.[17] Truth wars are waged, for example, by those who claim to know an absolute, solid truth and fight to get this accepted. In this book, these were often (though not exclusively!) the environmentalists and biologists who base their truth on science, facts, and evidence. Truth wars are also fought by those who relentlessly and passionately deconstruct any idea of truth as an attempt to challenge power. These are often (though not exclusively!) critical academics attempting to do justice to the shifting sands of everyday relationalities and positionalities that shape and are shaped by power. Both sides are important but ultimately limited. The first do not take seriously that truth is always power and the second do not take seriously that truth is also more than power. A politics of truth tensions differs from a politics of truth wars by transcending both of these. This makes it a more appropriate basis for speaking truth to power.[18] Truth tensions also transcend the truism that being "right" or "having" the truth and being acknowledged for this are two different things. Under post-truth and platform capitalism, not being right and getting away with it—even profiting from it—increasingly becomes the norm. The question then becomes what to do about post-truth if sharing the truth about nature does get this truth acknowledged but could also undermine it. In other words, what is a politics of truth tensions in the era of post-truth politics and platform capitalism?

Conceptually, I answer this question by combining Chantal Mouffe and Hannah Arendt. This combination may appear strange, since Mouffe sees her project opposed to that of Arendt: "Some theorists such as Hannah Arendt envisage the political as a space of freedom and public deliberation, while others see it as a space of power, conflict and antagonism. My understanding of 'the political' clearly belongs to the second perspective." While Mouffe has a point in that Arendt sometimes espouses an idealist model of the political, I argue that there is space for a tension-ridden yet productive combination between the two perspectives.[19] As stated in chapter 1, two central elements in Mouffe's project are also central to my own idea of politics—namely, that it is about (dealing with) conflict, power, and antagonism and that it takes place within the framework of hegemony. Mouffe argues that a democratic politics should aim to transform an antagonistic we/they relation between "enemies" into an agonistic relation between opponents that are adversaries. At the same time, "what is at stake in the agonistic struggle . . . is the very configuration of power relations around which a given society is structured: it is a struggle between opposing hegemonic projects which can never be reconciled rationally."[20]

What I believe Hannah Arendt can add to this is the importance of understanding—of giving meaning to knowledge—as the basic fuel for conflicting positions within hegemonic struggle. And although Arendt kept the idea of a common world and common sense alive (which is not the same as a world without conflict) she was also critical of capitalist ways of thinking and doing. In fact, she argued in the early 1950s: "Since the beginning of this century, the growth of meaninglessness has been accompanied by loss of common sense. In many respects, this has appeared simply as an increasing stupidity. We know of no civilization before ours in which people were gullible enough to form their buying habits in accordance with the maxim that 'self-praise is the highest recommendation,' the assumption of all advertising."[21] If she were alive today, Arendt would probably say that post-truth, and those contemporary actors who express it most fully, have helped to elevate stupidity to heights even she could not have foreseen. As an expression of *hegemonic* power, post-truth from this perspective simply intensified forms of meaninglessness and stupidity (and, Arendt may add, forms of totalitarianism) that have a much longer history. At the same time, we need to acknowledge the way hegemonic power changes in unprecedented ways.[22] The power of analysis is to build a narrative that allows us to see how and why contemporary commonsense concepts and ideas such as natural capital, post-truth, or sharing nature become meaningful within a context of the intensification and inability of capitalist power to deal with its negative environmental contradictions. It is this narrative (part 2) and the histories, contexts, and positionalities that complicate it (part 3) that we need to understand to allow for agonistic politics and hegemonic struggle in the Mouffian sense. This is what the book has aimed to do: to elevate the knowledge about "the truth about nature" under contemporary platform capitalism into a journey of *understanding* that may give meaning to the hegemonic struggle to deal with our environmental predicament.[23]

How does this conceptual understanding translate into a more concrete, earthly politics? What does a politics of solid rock and shifting sand look like for environmentalism in the twenty-first century? A detailed answer is beyond the scope of this book but is the central concern of a related project.[24] There, Robert Fletcher and I reflect on recent developments and conflicts within the conservation community that indicate a growing realization among many actors that there is a fundamental contradiction between long-term sustainable conservation and hegemonic capitalist power. It finds hope in how certain conservationists are moving toward more hegemonic forms of struggle. They increasingly realize, in other words, that "the truth about nature" as conservation sees it may be related to a bigger truth—though they mostly do not do this justice, precisely (and ironically) in the name of the urgency of the truth about nature as described in chapters 2 and 7.

This book closes by arguing that any concrete, earthly politics of truth tensions must always come together in and take inspiration from the art of speaking truth to power. This means, following Mouffe, that we need to clarify and open up differences and to situate these vis-à-vis hegemonic power. It means to name and resist hegemonic power but also to develop truth-discourses that transcend it, that create new, shared realities.[25] This links with Nealon's account of Foucault's politics: "As Foucault insists, the critical project is not one where individual intellectuals judge problems, but a more collective procedure organized around naming and responding to the problems themselves."[26] After this, he quotes Foucault as follows: "I concern myself with determining problems, unleashing them, revealing them within the framework of such complexity as to shut the mouths of prophets and legislators: all those who speak for others and above others. It is at that moment that the complexity of the problem will be able to appear in its connection with people's lives; and consequently, the legitimacy of a common enterprise will be able to appear through concrete questions, difficult cases, revolutionary movements, reflections, and evidence. . . . It is all a social enterprise."[27] An earthly politics of truth tensions is a common, social enterprise: it searches for truthful understandings of specific problems and puzzles—such as the post-truth conundrum in relation to environmental crises—and situates this in relation to hegemonic power such that it enables change and transcendence. Both of these come together in the art of speaking truth to power.

SPEAKING TRUTH TO POWER

I finally return to a core problem identified at the end of chapter 1: If truth is, as I have argued, caught between solid rock and shifting sand, and if it can only be approached by going on a journey to find it, how can we ever hope to speak it? Let alone speak it to power? In this book, we have traveled a great journey to get here. I have compiled and presented many facts, stories, discourses, and other forms of data to bring to light the complexities of environmentalism in the era of post-truth and platform capitalism. Yet this does not mean that this book automatically speaks truth to power, and certainly not that truth to power can only be spoken in lengthy and weighty academic volumes that grind through contexts, histories, and positionalities. In actual, earthly politics, these are necessarily brought down to essences, key points, and narratives that become the kernels of more holistic understandings that take seriously the tension between solid rock and shifting sand.

In fact, this is what much theory actually does. So why is that not being used more often to speak truth to power? One reason, I speculate, is that critical theory has partially lost itself in turns, trends, and other sectarian debates.[28] And while I do not argue that these cannot hold important and relevant insights and cues for politics, I do hold that they are limited and limiting. They reflect, increasingly, a platform capitalist model, with many niches where intellectuals stick to bounded discourses rather than attempt to speak truth to power in a holistic sense. Again, there are plenty of exceptions, and given the deep pains that neoliberal ideology has inflicted on academia by forcing scholars to increasingly focus on niche debates to get published, cited, and so forth, this may be logical. But breaking out of it is imperative, and can only be done by challenging hegemonic power, or, in Neil Smith's words, reinvigorating the "revolutionary imperative."[29] Scholars' own experiences within the contexts, histories, and positionalities of their institutions should aid them in this. But only if they are willing to distill their experiences into forms that speak truth to power.

Speaking truth to power, in essence, is about the art of compressing the understanding that is the basis of truth into commonsense kernels that challenge hegemony. These kernels reflect the building blocks of any journey toward understanding: the facts, evidence, and data that allow for the construction of knowledge related to histories, contexts, positionalities, and more. Speaking truth to power therefore relies on and can be expressed through these kernels of data and knowledge, though at the same time also always needs to transcend them. But here we come back to the problem identified above: can only those who have written long books that succeed in understanding speak truth to power? Evidently not. Hannah Arendt, in relation to totalitarianism, gives a clue on how to deal with this: "Many people say that one cannot fight totalitarianism without understanding it. Fortunately, this is not true; if it were, our case would be hopeless. Understanding, as distinguished from having correct information and scientific knowledge, is a complicated process which never produces unequivocal results. It is an unending activity by which, in constant change and variation, we come to terms with and reconcile ourselves to reality."[30] Similarly, and fortunately, we do not all have to understand post-truth to fight it. But we do have to come to terms with and reconcile ourselves to the reality that post-truth is a part of our world. Post-truth, in other words, is our *shared reality*, one that has become part of the hegemonic common sense, even if it is premised on the very shattering of the idea of a shared reality. As I showed in the beginning of the introduction, environmental actors have clearly accepted this reality and started to fight it.

Enter the importance of narrative. To a degree, this tension between understanding and politics can be mediated through narratives that conjoin elements of commons and context into something that makes (common) sense. And while chapter 2 concluded that narratives have fragmented online, this does not necessarily mean that users do not understand them. Precisely because narratives try to build (on) *common* sense, they often do not need to be watched (or read) in full for people to understand where they are going or what the central message is. Hence the importance for conservation narratives to play into dominant cultural, social, or other tropes that people tend to recognize. One of the dominant conservation narratives that I highlighted is that of natural capital, which is a "truth discourse" that signifies the continued strength of our contemporary capitalist political economy. But it is a truth discourse and narrative of power that is deeply contradictory; it is both an acknowledgment that capitalism is at the root of our environmental problems and a caustic reinforcement of capitalist ways of being and thinking.

Narratives, in short, are necessary; they essentialize context and show what we (could) have in common. Narratives are also problematic, as they come to direct what we see and recognize as truth. Algorithms and platforms, in turn, conflate and reshuffle all of these. Indeed, they do so deliberately to enable commercially attractive spectacles. To move beyond this conundrum, this book has also built a narrative; one that tackles hegemonic power head-on but also accepts its tension-ridden connection with contexts, histories, and positionalities. How, then, can we translate this narrative into the kernels that speak truth to power? For this there is no generic answer or magic formula: it is, in fact, an *art*. And the moment one tries to rationally explain how to produce art, it forfeits the purpose. If, however, we get back to the metatheoretical bearings around truth tensions that have guided this book, one particular politics aimed at transcending post-truth stands out—namely, moving from platform capitalism to post-capitalist platforms.

FROM PLATFORM CAPITALISM
TO POST-CAPITALIST PLATFORMS

Clearly, new media are not the key to "saving" nature, and my research has not shown me any glimpses of an effective "digital conservation movement" or "vast green army" online. In fact, the opposite: new media make it more difficult to see—because of the density of the digital natureglut—that the workings of platform capitalism might rather undermine any long-term effective conservation movement or "green army."[31] Speaking truth to power, therefore, necessitates confronting capitalism. Capitalism is a solid political economic rock, if ever there was one. Yet it is also always shifting sand. Like any power formation, it is a highly complicated vortex of solid rocks and shifting sands that has gelled into particular (yet changing) institutionalized and ideological forms over time. This is the hegemony that conservation politics must confront. Hence, to conserve truth in a time of meaning-poor platform capitalist post-truth, in the final analysis, means building meaning-rich post-capitalist platforms. It means building different narratives that allow not just for the building of knowledge around conserving biodiversity in between platforms, post-truth, and power; it means building platforms that allow for understanding and the emergence of alternative truths to become common sense. These are truths that do not make sense to power; and that is precisely how they challenge power.

Does this mean abandoning algorithms and social media platforms altogether? Not necessarily. But to the extent that they are focused on capital accumulation, yes, they will need to be abandoned. Algorithms, after all, do as their creators tell them to do and, hence, they could perhaps be used for different, post-capitalist ends.[32] At the moment, this may seem far-fetched in a context where conservation is eager to speak the language of capitalist power; where it employs specific truth discourses to speak nature to power. And while I believe this is a futile exercise, the natural capital example does show why paying attention to environmental conservation is so important within broader hegemonic struggles. This is because the basis for its truth claims are (supposed to be) different from those in power: they need to arise from facts, evidence, and science, rather than an ideology of growth and accumulation. And the facts, evidence, and science, conservation says, are clear: the environment is going from bad to worse under capitalism, and we need to act. The question, then, is how long conservation will believe those in power who proclaim that the logic of capital will be the logic to get us out of this capitalist crisis?

If the recent Anthropocene conservation debates are anything to go by, it seems that this belief is breaking down.[33] Environmentalists are experimenting with more radical, even post-capitalist forms of politics, even on online platforms. And to be sure: just because these online platforms are capitalist does not mean that "truth to power" cannot be communicated on or through them, including through kernels that aim to condense a bigger truth. Indeed, several of the various hashtags I have used throughout the book represent precisely these types of kernels. #NatureNow is another one designed to signal a basic truth. It was launched in September 2019 in a joint video by Swedish environmental youth activist Greta Thunberg and British climate activist George Monbiot. The latter, especially, has made it clear that capitalism needs to be transcended, while the former, through her very being and arguments, seems to present a threat to, especially white male, capitalist actors.[34] Together, they are promoting natural climate solutions whereby nature becomes the basis for tackling climate. They urge all of us to take this seriously and, of course, to share the video on social media.[35]

It is here that we are right back at the beginning of the book. Yet this book is only one possible journey of understanding, offered as a way to not get trapped in a vicious cycle of sharing truths and natures under current forms of hegemonic power. Sharing truths and natures with an eye to tackling the environmental crisis we still must, and they begin with kernels. As long as we remember that any truth kernel is meaningless and sloganesque outside of a concomitant journey to understand and transcend the solid rock of hegemonic power in order to affect actual transformation and differences that open new modes of being and perspectives of other worlds.[36] Truth kernels should not be individuated marketing gimmicks but must be linked to broader narratives that speak truth to hegemonic power and allow for understanding. The difference is this: they now become part of a new shared reality; a commonsense post-capitalist platform.

Notes

INTRODUCTION: THE TRUTH ABOUT NATURE?

1. Although some are certainly trying, see the "conservation optimism summit" in 2017: https://www.conservationoptimism.org/, accessed 17 May 2017.

2. High-profile publications that make this point include Newbold et al. (2016); Watson et al. (2016); Ceballos et al. (2017), and the IPBES (2019) report. It must be added that there is a lively debate on this, with some scholars insisting we look more at those indicators that are positive (Thomas, 2017).

3. Keyes, 2004.

4. See https://www.conservation.org/Pages/default.aspx and https://www.youtube.com/watch?v=h6bTR0Y45Rw&feature=youtu.be, accessed 24 March 2018.

5. http://www.latimes.com/opinion/op-ed/la-oe-barnett-nature-alternative-facts-20170210-story.html, accessed 3 January 2018.

6. This point follows from a much longer debate about the (social) construction of nature that has riled up conservationists for a long time, see Soulé and Lease (1995); Castree and Braun (2001), and the "science wars" more generally (Ward, 1996).

7. Noss et al., 2015.

8. Locke, 2014; McKibben, 2017.

9. https://rebellion.earth/the-truth/demands/, accessed 23 September 2019; Extinction Rebellion (2019).

10. Wilson, 2016; Dinerstein et al, 2017.

11. http://natureneedshalf.org/, accessed 18 May 2017.

12. http://www.jamesborrell.com/a-post-post-truth-world-evidence-and-conservation-in-2017/, accessed 3 January 2017. See also Sutherland and Wordley (2017: 2): "If we do not make concerted efforts to hold ourselves

and each other to account when we fail to use evidence, we are complicit in the perpetuation of a post-truth world."

13. As the author of the quoted text told me in person during a conversation in Cambridge on 11 December 2018.

14. Among others: biodiversity, ecosystems, and landscapes are under severe pressure in many parts of the world (CBD, 2014; UNEP, 2014), further worsened by climate change (Klein, 2014); a tremendous intensification of resource extraction efforts after the financial crisis is, according to Muradian et al. (2012: 562) "driving the expansion of the extraction frontier into even more ecologically and socially vulnerable areas"; wildlife crime has risen rapidly (again) in many biodiverse areas (Brashares et al., 2014), resulting in the slaughter of charismatic species like elephants and rhinos and subsequent forms of "green militarization" or "green violence" (Duffy, 2014; Lunstrum, 2014; Büscher and Ramutsindela, 2016); the sixth great extinction event in the history of earth is now fully underway, which some biologists refer to as a wholesale "biological annihilation" (Kolbert, 2014; Ceballos et al. 2017); and finally, a recent reassessment of the famous 1972 *Limits to Growth* report from the Club of Rome (Meadows et al., 1972) concludes that "historical data" align well with the report's original "business-as-usual" scenario and argues that the "potential global collapse" predicted in *Limits to Growth* is "perhaps more imminent than generally recognised" (Turner, 2014: 5). Midway through 2020, the evidence suggests that the COVID-19 pandemic has not fundamentally changed this dire picture. See https://t2sresearch.org/output/close-the-tap-covid-19-and-the-need-for-convivial-conservation/, accessed 20 July 2020.

15. Ceballos et al., 2017.

16. Clearly, as Ursula Heise (2016: 20) argues, this truth is also part of a particular narrative or "story template," "according to which nature in general and biodiversity in particular has done nothing but deteriorate under the impact of modern societies." This story, she argues, "is mostly taken for granted and details that do not unambiguously fit into this narrative tend to be underemphasized or left out." It should be made clear that even though I worry about our nonhuman environment, I do not buy into the story template of continuous, linear, or unambiguous decline across all environmental indicators.

17. See Lepore, 2018: 636.

18. Latour, 1988: 227; Ward, 1996.

19. See, for example, Paige West's (2016) otherwise excellent book *Dispossession and the Environment*. On page 7 she mentions "truth" twice (in between quotation marks), in order to spend the rest of the book deconstructing environmental discourses and rhetoric about Papua New Guinea without mentioning the word once more.

20. Frankfurt, 2017: 6.

21. I will be referring to this phrase regularly throughout the book, the generic meaning of which is as indicated at the start of this section: that nature is not doing well but can be saved through appropriate ("evidence-based") action. I use the phrase for two reasons: to show that truth claims are always about power and embedded within particular histories, contexts, and positionalities,

but can still be used to search for deeper understanding; and because it continues to be the main driving force behind many environmental actions.

22. I want to emphasize that what is unprecedented is the way this power works, not the problems it responds to or how people have been understanding the latter. This important distinction follows Giraud and Aghassi-Isfahani's (2020) critique of Latour's use of the term which "runs the risk of consecrating the marginalization of precisely the perspectives that are most under attack in the contemporary political moment." Whether this also means completely discarding any search for "common worlds," as they argue, is a more complicated matter, dependent on one's ontological position and definition of commons. As I will later argue, following Arendt, I do believe that commons can be built across ontological differences but, following Giraud and Aghassi-Isfahani, only if we take political economy and its historical marginalization of indigenous and other worldviews seriously.

23. Zuboff, 2019: 515–516. Byung-Chul Han (2017: 11–12) argues that with the rise of big data, "we are entering the age of digital psychopolitics. It means passing from passive surveillance to active steering."

24. Zuboff, 2019: 8.

25. https://www.nature.org/en-us/what-we-do/our-insights/perspectives/we-need-a-technology-revolution-for-nature/, accessed 29 September 2019.

26. Berger-Tal and Lahoz-Monfort, 2018.

27. This argument is in line with Wendy Brown's (2019: 44–45) brilliant exposition of how neoliberalism destroyed the ideas of the social and society whereby a naked notion of "freedom without society" becomes "a pure instrument of power, shorn of concern for others, the world, or the future."

28. Han (2017: 59) likens Big Data to a totalitarian ideology ("Dataism"), which he argues is nihilistic because "it gives up on any and all meaning." Importantly, he adds: "Data and numbers are not narrative; they are additive. Meaning, on the other hand, is based on narration," See also Kitchin (2014).

CHAPTER 1. TRUTH TENSIONS

1. Ward, 1996.

2. Ibid., 143.

3. Ibid., 111, also 137, 143.

4. Lee, 2015: 7.

5. Sismondo, 2017.

6. Fujimura and Holmes, 2019: 1.

7. Angermuller, 2018: 4.

8. Palliser and Dodson, 2019.

9. Oreskes, 2019: back cover.

10. Marres, 2018: 423, 435, 438.

11. Giraud and Aghassi-Isfahana, 2020: 1.

12. Although it is not just about this gap in STS. The problem is broader, in that currently fashionable social theory has moved increasingly back into the realm of idealism, where process-oriented ontologies have led to an infinite

extension of agency in all directions and the forgoing of a material politics that can retain some solidity or permanence. There has been some backlash to this by the "new materialism" but this, too, is deeply problematic and cannot be the way forward. See Malm (2018), for a critique.

13. Which now should include nonhumans without the need for their representation (Latour, 2005: 225–234).

14. According to Latour "the last thing we need is for someone to compose in our stead the world to come" (Latour, 2005: 225). Because he writes "we" in this sentence (instead of "I"), Latour does precisely what he believes is not possible: compose a world for others who are apparently unable to understand that their world is only composed of themselves, nothing more.

15. Foucault, 1980: 131.

16. Ibid.: 133; see also 2008: 356.

17. Ibid.: 356.

18. Sullivan, 2019.

19. Merrifield, 2011: 18.

20. Medina and Wood, 2005; Frankfurt, 2017.

21. Büscher, 2013; Loftus, 2012; Harvey, 2014.

22. Svarstad et al. 2018: 352. See also Cavanagh, 2018.

23. Castree 2003; Carolan, 2005. There is a major debate about this co-constitution where authors like Malm (2018) have argued that new materialist and ontological approaches are dangerous due to their concept of the innate ontological entanglement of socionatures, and authors like Giraud (2019) argue that the problem with an overt focus on entanglement is that it lacks an ethics of exclusion.

24. Carolan, 2005: 400, 409. Castree (2014: 10) argues that there are four "principal meanings of the word nature in contemporary Anglophone societies": external, universal, intrinsic and super-ordinate natures. I will not go into these here.

25. See also Marazzi's poignant description: "Nature, as Einstein noted, is not the univocal text theorized by the scientists belonging to the Newtonian tradition, who thought that the observation of Nature and the deduction of its internal laws was sufficient to find the scientific legality of the physical world. The experience of theoretical inquiry has actually shown that Nature is, rather, an *equivocal* text that can be read according to *alternative modalities*" (Marazzi, 2011: 43, italics in original).

26. Frankfurt, 2017: 10.

27. Lorimer, 2015; Purdy, 2015; Turnhout, 2018.

28. Poovey, 1998: 29, backflap. Which might explain the rise of what Han (2015) refers to as the "Transparency Society."

29. See Jasanoff, 2006.

30. Shapin, 1994.

31. Frankfurt, 2017: 11, emphasis in original.

32. Most forcefully expressed in the chapters collected in Soulé and Lease (1995).

33. Proctor, 2001: 226, italics in original.

34. Arendt, 1994: 307–308.

35. No matter how sophisticated, important and sometimes exciting the contributions of these and other turns (see Green, 2013), they ultimately still seem to reflect particular academic trends that cater to specific epistemic communities or interests rather than trying to transcend these to allow for more holistic understanding. I suspect that the sacrifice of a productive search for truth might have something do to with this.

36. Arendt, 1994: 311.

37. Harvey, 2006.

38. Arendt is famous for saying that "the chances of factual truth surviving the onslaught of power are very slim indeed," suggesting that truth and power are separate, which indeed is sometimes what she is suggesting. At the same time, her work is deeply concerned with the mutual constitution of power/politics and truth, while the meaning of how she uses factual truth and power here, are different from how I understand them in this section.

39. As cited in Young-Bruehl, 2006: 28.

40. Though never impossible, as I will emphasize in further chapters and the conclusion.

41. Watson et al., 2016.

42. Büscher, 2016.

43. Arts et al., 2015; Gabrys, 2016; Bakker and Ritts, 2018.

44. Cf. Castree, 2014.

45. This is important, as it leads the book into media studies and allows for its infusion with political ecology (and vice versa). This infusion challenges a central trope in new media studies, namely that it is no longer meaningful to distinguish between online and offline, or between virtual and actual. In political ecology generally, and especially in relation to conservation, I hold that this distinction remains critical. Saving a virtual elephant is not the same thing as saving an elephant offline. See Büscher (2016) where I have elaborated in detail on this point. Some typical quotes in this respect are the following: according to Deuze (2007: xii) meaningful distinctions between "lived and mediated reality are fading"; Arvidsson (2006: 13) argues that the "complete integration of Media Culture and everyday life means that it no longer makes much sense to maintain a distinction between the two"; Farman (2012: 6) believes that "eventually, the collaboration between virtual space and what might be called 'actual' space becomes so intertwined that it is no longer useful to think of them as distinct categories"; and as a final example, Pettman (2017: 15, 126) states that there has been a "decisive erosion of the online/offline distinction" and that "the line between online and offline has been practically erased."

46. Harvey, 2006; Moore, 2015. The workings of this mode of embedding are highly complex and uneven but do not concern me here.

47. Srnicek, 2017; see also Langley and Leyshon, 2016. I do not use *surveillance capitalism*, as proposed by Zuboff (2019) as the main term to capture the rising forms of power. The simple reason for this is that the first drafts of this text were written before Zuboff's book came out in May 2019. More substantially, I believe the term *platform* better captures the organizational structure of this form of capitalism. I agree with Zuboff that it depends fully on surveillance and takes human experience as the basis for its mode of profit. Yet surveillance

as a mechanism and activity is integrated and part of platforms as structures organizing this form of capitalism, and not vice versa.

48. Srnicek, 2017; Sadowski, 2019. This is not to say that platforms now completely dominate the workings of global capitalism. The precise nature of platform capitalism in relation to other forms of capital accumulation, however, is beyond this book.

49. Jasanoff and Simmet, 2017.

50. Which, to be sure, does not imply they do not have agency, but rather that this agency is always dialectically constituted within and related to larger structural dynamics and forces.

51. This relates to a long debate about structure and agency; see Fletcher and Büscher, 2017; and Büscher and Fletcher, 2020, for elaborations of my and Robert Fletcher's position in this debate.

52. Mouffe differentiates between politics and "the political." For her, building on Heidegger, "politics refers to the 'ontic' level while 'the political' has to do with the 'ontological' one. This means that the ontic has to do with the manifold practices of conventional politics, while the ontological concerns the very way in which society is instituted" (Mouffe, 2005: 8–9). The forms of politics in the cases refer to the former, while speaking truth to power, for me, is part of the latter. I follow Mouffe in this distinction but will not consistently employ her terminology. I also do not equate the way society is instituted with the term *ontological*. To me, the latter denotes the very nature of being, with which I am not concerned here, while my conceptualization of how society is instituted relates more to historical political economic power.

53. Srnicek, 2017: 39

54. Sadowski, 2019; Han, 2017: 9.

55. Pasqual, 2015.

56. Rouvroy, 2013; cf. Marres, 2018.

57. Platforms do, increasingly, screen for certain types of content, such as explicit violence or pornography, which shows that they too cannot escape certain societal norms. Whether they are good (enough) at this is subject to intense debate.

58. Massumi, 2018.

59. Pettman, 2016; Igoe, 2017: 6.

60. Pettman, 2016: backflap.

61. In this sense, following West (2016), the dispossession of the possibility for a search for truth in order to be part of meaningful shared realities—which, as I noted, is increasingly reflected in a turn-obsessed critical theory—may be the ultimate form of dispossession under contemporary capitalism.

62. Hannan, 2018.

CHAPTER 2. SHARING TRUTHS AND NATURES

1. The links between conservation and new media are overanalyzed and under-researched at the same time. Overanalyzed because there are myriad online commentaries, discussions, and debates on this link, while many conservation organizations have very quickly had to make this one of their central

strategic priorities simply because, as several informants noted, this was the way to reach new people or target groups (Interviews with staff conservation organizations, October 2012, the Netherlands, April 2013, United States). The link is under-researched because so far there has been a dearth of academic work on the topic. On the one hand, the social science disciplines studying conservation and environmentalism, especially political ecology, geography, anthropology, and sociology, have so far paid scarce attention to new media. On the other hand, the booming field of new media studies has so far almost completely neglected environmental and conservation issues (Büscher, 2016).

2. As corroborated by interviews with large conservation organizations in Europe, Africa, and the United States between 2011 and 2015. See chapter 4.

3. http://rhinoypointerns.com/2014/02/26/a-digital-conservation-movement -the-holy-grail-for-wildlife/. Last viewed: 18 March 2014.

4. Fraser, 2011; Hawken, 2007: 6.

5. Observations from participating in relevant sessions focused on new media at the World Parks Congress, 12–19 November 2014, Sydney, Australia.

6. Another such project was WilderQuest, "a program incorporating an online environment and in-nature experiences . . . to encourage children and their families to spend time in nature" (http://wilderquest.nsw.gov.au /aboriginal/#/site/info/general, accessed 5 December 2014); Another online initiative heralded as game changer was the Virtual Ecotourism project www .vEcotourism.org, which "uses interactive on-line tours to connect the general public with conservation projects and local communities in ecologically and culturally sensitive areas worldwide" (http://www.vecotourism.org/news/about -vecotourism/, accessed 5 December 2014). See http://wpc2014.eventranet.com .au/presentations-topics/8 for an overview, accessed 5 December 2014.

7. http://www.bbc.com/news/science-environment-21655918 and http:// www.geog.ox.ac.uk/research/biodiversity/governance/, accessed 5 December 2014.

8. Klein, 2014: 466.

9. See, for example, http://www.bbc.com/news/science-environment-1367 2600, accessed 19 May 2017.

10. See several chapters in Schurman and Kelso (2003), especially the first two, for a history of how the famous Chakrabarthi court case in 1980 led to the possibility of privately owning *and* profiting from nature. See also Cooper (2008) and Carolan (2009) for broader discussions about biotechnology and patents in the neoliberal age.

11. See long-standing debates in political ecology: Neumann (2005), Bryant (2015), Perrault et al. (2015).

12. Moore, 2015.

13. Castree, 2003; Harvey, 2006.

14. CBD, 2014; WWF, 2016; IPBES, 2019.

15. Which, to be sure, is not to argue that sharing nature does not exist under capitalism, as it obviously does. The work by Nobel Prize–winner Elinor Ostrom and many colleagues showed precisely this (Ostrom 1990). Moreover, the same dynamics also happen over enlarged spaces of nature, such as trans-frontier conservation areas (Ramutsindela, 2007; Büscher, 2013) and many

conservationists these days work hard to establish corridors between pockets of conserved nature (Goldman, 2009).

16. Büscher, 2013; Büscher et al., 2014; Büscher and Fletcher, 2015.

17. This is a sentiment I consistently picked up in my research over the last fifteen years (Büscher, 2013) although I would at the same time argue that it is changing, as there is strategic interest on behalf of the powerful in the question of conservation. See Büscher and Fletcher (2015).

18. http://europa.eu/rapid/press-release_IP-09-1710_en.htm, accessed 19 May 2017.

19. http://www.teebweb.org/, accessed 19 May 2017.

20. http://europa.eu/rapid/press-release_IP-09-1710_en.htm, accessed 18 May 2017.

21. https://portals.iucn.org/library/sites/library/files/resrecfiles/WCC_2016 _RES_058_EN.pdf, accessed 19 May 2017.

22. https://naturalcapitalcoalition.org/who/history-vision-mission/

23. Robertson, 2007; Sullivan, 2013.

24. McAfee, 1999; Corson et al., 2013; Büscher et al., 2014.

25. https://www.theguardian.com/sustainable-business/2015/jan/29/businesses -learn-language-of-natural-capital-2015, accessed 19 May 2017.

26. Fletcher, 2014.

27. http://hawaiipublicradio.org/post/natural-capital-seeing-true-cost-business, accessed 19 May 2017.

28. http://naturalcapitalforum.com/about/, accessed 19 May 2017.

29. Turnhout et al., 2014.

30. Participatory observation with private rhino owners, Hoedspruit Area, Limpopo Province, South Africa, 2017–2018.

31. Player, 2013.

32. See http://www.telegraph.co.uk/news/uknews/prince-william/12194995 /Duke-of-Cambridge-I-can-see-George-being-a-bit-of-a-bum-in-the-conservation -world.html, last viewed: 15 December 2017. Together with several major conservation organizations, Prince William and the UK royal family started a massive campaign against wildlife crime, including on social media, asking the public, among others, #WhoseSideAreYouOn? While there are those of us who can share the rhino, there are also the "criminals" who want to destroy the species, and hence, Prince William argues, we must choose sides.

33. Cronon, 1995.

34. Descola and Pálsson, 1996; Nustad, 2015: 37–41.

35. Gitelman, 2008: 7; 158.

36. Castree, 2014: 64.

37. This can include nature itself, as it is obvious that nonhuman nature has agency, though not, importantly *political agency* (Swyngedouw and Ernston, 2018).

38. It is clear from this statement that I do not agree with those theoretical traditions that wish to impart the same type of agency to everything around us and in particular to constellations such as hybrids or "assemblages." See Bakker and Bridge (2006); Malm (2018).

39. Hinting back at Carolan's (2005: 400, 409) distinctions between Nature, nature, and "nature," I reiterate that the mediation of nature always becomes part of particular stories, imaginations, and truths: the use of language to "make sense of nature" (Castree, 2014), including through (employing) science, myth, discourse, narrative, technology, and so forth.

40. Again the "new conservation" debate is very relevant here; see Wapner, 2010; Lorimer, 2015.

41. See Brockington, 2008; Sandbrook, Adams et al., 2013.

42. My aim is not to give an overview of this history—see Elliot (2006) for an extensive treatment.

43. Gitelman, 2008: 10.

44. Ibid. William Beinart and Lotte Hughes (2007: 214–215), in their book on environment and empire, argue, for example, that visual images were highly important for British people in order to imagine the empire and therefore also "an inescapable element in the imagining of imperial nature" and the possibilities for its "possession, exploitation, and conservation." Yet Beinart and Hughes (2007: 231–232) emphasize that empirical realities under colonialism were not clear-cut and that "the natural environments of conquered territories were recorded and presented for a range of purposes," including by indigenous artists and in ways that destabilized rather than reinforced colonial stereotypes. Having said this, Beinart and Hughes conclude that "in certain respects, the multiplicity of images about nature and animals in the colonial era were important in stimulating conservationist impulses."

45. Carruthers, 1995; Brooks, 2005; Chris, 2006; Beinart and McKeown, 2009.

46. Adams 2004: 58.

47. Gitelman, 2008.

48. Mitman, 1999; Chris, 2006: 13.

49. Beinart and McKeown, 2009: 436.

50. Bousé, 2000; Scott, 2003.

51. Bagust, 2008: 220–221.

52. Though it is important to add that very early nature films, including *King Kong*, were highly spectacular and that the "realistic" phase was in many ways a response to the disgust at these early spectacular mediations (Mitman, 1999; Bousé, 2000).

53. Bousé, 2000: 36. Lejano et al. (2013) even extend "the power of networks" to environmental networks and movements more generally, though online media are not a specific focus of attention for them.

54. Bagust, 2008: 218, based on Bousé, 2000: 126.

55. Bousé, 2000: 91. See here also Donna Haraway's (1989) book *Primate Visions*.

56. Jeffries, 2003: 528–529, 533). This is still ongoing, and indeed intensifying, most notably through the Planet Earth film series, see: https://www.theguardian.com/commentisfree/2017/jan/01/bbc-planet-earth-not-help-natural-world, accessed 30 May 2017. See Brockington (2009) for a broader exposé on the role of celebrity in environmental politics, including people like Attenborough.

57. Weeks, 1999: 20.

58. Bousé, 2000: 95.

59. Louw, 2006: 160. See https://www.youtube.com/watch?v=Cc2Lxu6HjtQ, accessed 30 May 2017.

60. Cf. Chris, 2006: 79–121; Brockington, 2009: chap. 4.

61. Goodman et al., 2016: 681, 678. I want to emphasize both the power of capitalism and "its disruption," as this is something we will also see in later chapters. Hence, I agree with Goodman et al. (2016: 680) when they argue: "We are not disputing the power of mediated spectacle to distort and de-politicize, but rather are also working to draw attention to the critical need to not just understand the processes by which spectacular environmentalisms distract and de-politicize but also how some of their various forms might contain conditions for more radical critique."

62. Papacharrisi, 2010: 9.

63. I am fully aware that we are in times where new versions of the same (3.0; 4.0; no: 5.0!) tumble over each other to signify and intensify newness, so 2.0 sounds almost archaic. Yet the basic idea of all these iterations is the cocreative element, which is at the core of my theorization in this and the next chapter and why I stick to 2.0.

64. Dean, 2010: 39.

65. Email, The Nature Conservancy, 1 December 2014, 16:15.

66. The actual URLs are: http://support.nature.org/site/R?i=rbnDAr7BXE hvRuBqCYTjgw, and http://www.nature.org/membership-giving/more-ways -to-give/everyday-ways-to-help/index.htm?src=e.give&lu=3939922, accessed 3 December 2014.

67. Srnicek, 2017: 99.

68. This "new conservation" debate has caused quite a rift in the conservation biology community; see Marvier et al. (2011) and Marris (2011) for manifestos on "Saving Nature in a Post-Wild World" and Soulé (2014) and Miller et al. (2014) for critiques. For broader discussions, see Wapner (2010); Lorimer (2015); Büscher and Fletcher (2020).

69. Andrejevic, 2013: back cover.

70. Ibid.: 48–49

71. For some commentators, this is the essence of post-truth communication (Waisbord, 2018).

72. Of course, whether and how these natures exist offline and what would be needed for their effective conservation in highly complex, political environments is, like in the Nature Conservancy example, not always immediately clear. I will come back to this point in later chapters.

73. Büscher and Igoe, 2013.

74. Ritzer and Jurgenson, 2010.

75. Ibid.; Barassi and Treré, 2012.

76. Biersack, 2006: 14. Nature 2.0, for me therefore is not the same as virtual reality or virtual environments in Hillis's (1999: xvii, xxxii) sense of "immersive virtual environments," even though at times they come close in that web 2.0 equally allows for "extreme polyvalency and polyvocality."

77. http://my.nature.org/nature/, accessed 7 November 2013.

78. Andrejevic, 2013: 13.

79. Igoe, 2010.

80. Gabrys, 2013; Gehl, 2011.

81. Igoe, 2013; Nustad, 2015.

82. White and Wilbert, 2009: 6.

83. Bousé, 2000: 16–20; Candea, 2010.

84. Pettman, 2017.

85. Bousé (2000: 127–151, 130–131), building on Campbell, speaks of the "classic model of wildlife film": "its archetypal pattern traces the story of an individual animal from birth, through the perils of youth, the trials of adolescence, and finally to the time when he (and in some cases *she*) enters society as an adult, often after a victory of some sort."

86. Sullivan, 2016.

87. Poster, 2001: 16.

88. Which is something we can even all do ourselves, see: https://storify.com/, accessed 2 June 2017.

89. Kang, 2014: 30.

90. Lovink, 2012; Pettman, 2017.

91. Papacharissi, 2010: 19.

92. Van Dijck, 2013; Dean, 2010.

93. Igoe, 2017.

94. Mitman, 1999: 20.

95. Nealon, 2008.

CHAPTER 3. BETWEEN PLATFORMS, POST-TRUTH, AND POWER

1. http://endangeredemoji.com/faqs/, accessed 31 December 2017.

2. Another, similar campaign is the development of climoji's, which, according to its developers "serve as signifiers to amplify climate change and as a new signs with which to express despair, hope, and solidarity." See https://climoji.org/, accessed 28 March 2018.

3. https://www.facebook.com/socialmediaweeklondon/videos/975237629205353/, accessed 31 December 2017.

4. http://www.justforthis.com/, accessed 31 December 2017.

5. Ibid.

6. Ibid.

7. This clearly harks back to a central argument by one of the most influential media theorists, Marshall McLuhan (1964).

8. Igoe, 2010: 378.

9. Debord, 1967.

10. Bottici (2011: 67) argues that besides a quantitative increase in the amount of images around us all the time, there has been "an intrinsic *qualitative* change in the nature of images, a change that is likely to deeply affect the link between the political and the imaginal. Behind the virtual revolution there is indeed a deep change in the nature of images: not only have images become commodities, which are therefore subjected to the laws and treatment of all other commodities, but they are now also malleable in a way that has never

been the case. Images are not only *reproducible* in series, but they are also *modifiable* up to a point where they can be completely falsified. In other words, images have completely lost their link with the 'here' and 'now.'"

11. Coté and Pybus, 2007: 103. On the same page, they argue for web 2.0 developments more generally: "It is the variability of possible valorization processes that holds the secret abodes of surplus value for capital."

12. Igoe, 2010, 2013, 2017.

13. Büscher and Igoe, 2013: 290.

14. Igoe, 2010: 377.

15. Interview Dr. Ian Player, former KZN Wildlife, 9 January 2014, Karkloof, South Africa.

16. Geert Lovink (2011: 2) argues that "rather than foster new public engagements, online discussion tends to take place within 'echo chambers' where groups of like-minded individuals, consciously or not, avoid debate with their cultural or political adversaries."

17. Srnicek, 2017: 39.

18. Although there is a careful balance to be managed here. The news, at the beginning of 2018, that the average time spent on Facebook went down for the first time was met with some anxiety by investors, though Facebook responded by saying it wants to focus more on the quality of time spent, rather than the quantity of time spent on the network. See https://techcrunch.com/2018/01/11/facebook-time-well-spent/, accessed 26 February 2018.

19. Wajcman, 2015: 179.

20. Gillespie, 2014: 168.

21. Andrejevic, 2013: 140.

22. Rouvroy, 2013. This is not entirely so, as platforms do screen for certain types of content, such as explicit violence and pornography. How they do so and whether they are good at this is subject to intense debate.

23. Gillespie, 2014. Interestingly, following the #BlackLivesMatter protests in the United States in May 2020, this stance seemed to be shifting somewhat, with Twitter factchecking several of President Trump's tweets and Facebook. CEO Mark Zuckerberg subsequently argued that "Facebook shouldn't be the arbiter of truth of everything that people say online," thus reverting back to their preferred antipolitical positionality. https://www.theguardian.com/technology/2020/may/28/zuckerberg-facebook-police-online-speech-trump, accessed 22 July 2020.

24. See http://www.newsweek.com/coal-roller-257884, accessed 7 June 2017.

25. Rouvroy, 2013.

26. Ibid. Andrejevic (2013: 144) speaks in this vein of the "triumph of the algorithm as an organizing social principle": "one in which the rhythms of our daily lives create patterns beyond our comprehension and our predictive abilities (but not that of the database)—patterns that are turned back upon us for the purposes of sorting, exclusion, management and modulation. We fuel the algorithmic assemblage—we even create the algorithms (or at least the parameters according to which they develop)—only to face the prospect of finding ourselves at its mercy: subject to distributed and unaccountable decisions that affect our life chances and access to goods and services."

27. Rouvroy and Stiegler, 2016: 7. Nowhere is this clearer than with the idea of "Big Data," which, according to Boyd and Crawford (2012: 663), rely on "the widespread belief that large data sets offer a higher form of intelligence and knowledge that can generate insights that were previously impossible, with the aura of truth, objectivity, and accuracy."

28. Horkheimer and Adorno, 2002: 4. Obviously, this equivalence is no straightforward process and requires, as argued by Sian Sullivan, (2014: 5–6), several crucial shifts: first, a *discursive shift* "that has reframed both conservation practice and understandings of nonhuman natures in economic and financial terms"; second, an *institutional shift* that facilitates the organizational and network operationalization of regarding the world as natural capital; third, a *calculative and accounting shift* "that is enabling relatively untransformed and restored nonhuman natures to become technically inscribed as numerical signifiers of capital, such that these can be added to and offset against other forms of accounted capital and in economic models more generally"; and fourth, a *material shift* "through which 'external nature' is being calculated as if 'it' literally is, and can be leveraged as, money capital, thus becoming able to act as a financial asset that multiplies financial accumulation." I would add to this a fifth one, namely, a *political shift* that offers the political strategies to render the other shifts credible, believable, and legitimate (Büscher, 2013). It needs to be added that this political shift, like the other shifts, are precarious, unstable, and never complete or without resistance.

29. Horkheimer and Adorno, 2002: 4.

30. Arsel and Büscher, 2012: 62.

31. Merchant, 1983: 193.

32. Srnicek, 2017: 43.

33. Srnicek, 2017: 40–41.

34. Srnicek, 2017: 44. This explanation for the platform model obviously leans on a much longer, more complex history of capitalist development(s) that I cannot get into in detail here. One important element of this history concerns the intensification of a "political economy of the sign." To explain this, I follow Goldman (1994), who argues that in the historical process of overcoming barriers to capitalist commodity circulation, the commodity form had to annex "the semiotic universe" (186) in order to stimulate a consumption that can keep up with production. Starting in the early twentieth century, it became increasingly clear that consumption had to be stimulated through both material (especially higher wages) and discursive tactics (especially advertising). The latter are referred to as signs: myriad discursive symbols, communications or images that function to signal something—in this case, the need for consumers to play their part in the development of (an emerging) consumer capitalism, and so "realize" the value embodied in the production of goods and services.

Signs—particularly those urging all of us to consume more—have by now become nearly omnipresent. This leads to a problem: according to Goldman, we must "observe how the mechanisms by which a political economy of sign value reproduces itself also undermine and *contradict* the motivations for engaging in sign consumption or sign valorization" (1994: 188; see also Goldman and Papson, 2011: 187). In other words, over the last hundred years, consumers have had to gradually do more "realization labor" in terms of interpreting (and, ideally, taking appropriate action on) the ever-intensifying and increasing number of commodity signs thrown at them on a daily basis. Commodity signs, after all, do not reach their producer's desired effects all by themselves. Consumers need to respond to signs in particular ways and through this "labor" help realize the sign's material value. This sheds different light on web 2.0 and the dynamics of prosumption. If consumers have for long had to do increasing amounts of realization labor due to the ever-increasing velocity of commodity sign circulation (cf. Goldman and Papson, 2011: 187) then prosumption—the *blurring of production and consumption*—holds a long pedigree. Cocreation or prosumption through the web 2.0 from this angle is symptomatic, I argue, of the intensification of the production and circulation of commodity-sign values. This angle to the platform capitalist model forms the basis for the analysis I did with Jim Igoe in Büscher and Igoe (2013).

35. Zuboff, 2019: 154. According to Zuboff, "Google wants to be your copilot for life itself."

36. Srnicek, 2017: 44–45. Han (2017: 12) argues that "Facebook is the church—the global synagogue (literally 'assembly') of the Digital."

37. Foucault, 1980: 131.

38. As was aptly illustrated in early 2018 by the scandal around Cambridge Analytica, the company that (ab)used Facebook data to influence elections.

39. Shapin, 1994: 9–10.

40. Montaigne, in Shapin, 1994: 10.

41. Andrejevic, 2013: 13.

42. Ibid.: 8.

43. Ibid.: 9.

44. Oreskes and Conway, 2010. This is also facing resistance; see, for instance, the website https://www.desmog.uk/, which aims to "clear the PR pollution" by developing a "climate disinformation database." According to their "About Us" section: "DeSmog UK was launched in September 2014 as an investigative media outlet dedicated to cutting through the spin clouding the debate on energy and environment in Britain. Since then, our team of journalists and researchers has become a go-to source for accurate, fact-based information regarding misinformation campaigns on climate science in the UK" (https://www.desmog.uk/about-us, accessed 20 December 2017). While this is certainly a valuable initiative, it will take more to defeat post-truth, as I will show in this book.

45. Dean, 2005: 53.

46. Ibid.: 54.

47. Srnicek, 2017: 43, 5.

48. Gabrys, 2016; Bakker and Ritts, 2018. See http://smartconservationtools .org/, which aims to "Measure, evaluate and improve the effectiveness of your wildlife law enforcement patrols and site-based conservation activities." Accessed 25 May 2017.

49. http://www.huffingtonpost.com/natural-capital-coalition-/when-it-comes -to-natural_b_12043244.html, accessed 25 May 2017; emphasis added.

50. Marx, 1976. David Harvey (2010: 40–41) also emphasizes that "capital is not a thing but a process in which money is perpetually sent in search of more money" and "continuity of flow in the circulation of capital is very important. The process cannot be interrupted without incurring losses. There are also strong incentives to accelerate the speed of circulation. Those who can move faster through the various phases of capital circulation accrue higher profits than their competitors." Nitzan and Bichler (2009) have gone furthest in emphasizing that capital itself is a "symbolic quantification of power."

51. See, for example, for Facebook: https://www.theguardian.com/world/2015/jan/12/mark-zuckerberg-freedom-speech-facebook, accessed 20 December 2017. This clearly also has its limits, as Facebook has been pressurized more and more to halt the publication and circulation of generally unacceptable utterances or sights (racism, murder, etc.). See also http://wgntv.com/2017/06/22/mark-zuckerberg-launches-first-ever-facebook-community-summit-in-chicago/, accessed 31 December 2017, where Facebook's chief products officer, Chris Cox, explains the "countermeasures" they have put into place to ensure violence cannot be broadcast live.

52. Frank Pasquale (2015: 3, 14) speaks, in this regard, of the "black box society," where platforms encourage us to open all of our lives on the internet but they themselves aggressively deploy "strategies of obfuscation and secrecy to consolidate power and wealth."

53. Ibid.: 8–9.

54. Srnicek, 2017: 63. Although this obviously does not apply to a great many people in the world still. Which is precisely why Facebook set up an initiative called "internet.org" to bring "internet access and the benefits of connectivity to the portion of the world that doesn't have them." Interestingly, they end by saying, "The more we connect, the better it gets"—which I cannot help but think is really meant to apply to Facebook's profits, https://info.internet.org/en/mission/, accessed 20 December 2017.

55. Pasquale, 2015: 6, 79.

56. Frankfurt, 2005: 56.

57. Zuboff (2019: 211–212) captures this point by referring to the platform industry's trope of "dark data," where any behavior or action that is not offered as knowable data becomes suspect. She argues: "The message is that surveillance capitalism's new instruments will render the entire world's actions and conditions as behavioral flows. Each rendered bit is liberated from its life in the social, no longer inconveniently encumbered by moral reasoning, politics, social norms, rights, values, relationships, feelings, contexts, and situations. In the flatness of this flow, data is data, and behavior is behavior. The body is simply a set of coordinates in time and space where sensation and action are translated as data. All things animate and inanimate share the same existential status in this blended confection, each reborn as an objective and measurable, indexable, browsable, searchable 'it.'"

58. Snricek, 2017: 39, 48.

59. In Young-Bruehl, 2006: 28.

60. Snricek, 2017: 39; Zuboff, 2019.

61. https://www.wired.com/insights/2014/07/data-new-oil-digital-economy/, accessed: 21 December 2017.

62. Peluso, 1993: 200.

63. Nelson, 2003: 67.

64. Wilson, 2016; Dinerstein et al., 2017.

65. Sandbrook, Fisher, et al. 2013; Bennet et al., 2017.

66. Sandbrook, Fisher, et al., 2013.

67. Peluso, 2012: 83.

68. Papacharissi, 2002: 18; Schulte, 2013.

69. Gillespie (2014: 169) argues that "a sociological analysis must not conceive of algorithms as abstract, technical achievements, but must unpack the warm human and institutional choices that lie behind these cold mechanisms."

CHAPTER 4. CONSERVATION 2.0

1. Interview senior social media officer, US Conservation organization, 5 June 2013.

2. Importantly, this distinction between offline and online is not to say that the latter is not real. The online or the virtual is often dichotomized in opposition to the real (Arora, 2012), whereby the real is the same as material. Clearly, as pointed out by Farman (2012: 22), this is a false opposition, "for, if it were an accurate opposition, then that which is virtual would also be considered 'not real.'"

3. While this distinction is crucial it is not meant to imply that lines between online and offline have not become blurred. New media, particularly through mobile devices, as well as "ubiquitous computing," have impacted dramatically and will continue to impact how online conservation informs offline conservation and vice versa (Gabrys, 2016). Ubiquitous computing, or "ubicomp," refers to the so-called third era of computing where "computational devices would be small and powerful enough to be worn, carried, or embedded in the world around us—in doors and tables, the fabric of cloths and buildings, and the objects of everyday life" (Dourish and Bell, 2011: 2). To a large degree, this is already happening yet the vision for the third era of computing, originally articulated by computer scientist Mark Weiser, goes much further. As Dourish and Bell point out, Weiser believed that technology would recede "into the background of our lives" and rationally, logically, and orderly anticipate and work alongside human actions (1–2). In reality, as argued by Dourish and Bell (2011: 92), ubicomp and the way it is developing are messy, "highly present, visible and branded."

4. Clearly, the organizations I refer to here are not just the familiar conservation organizations. They also include new internet-based organizations and virtual communities working for conservation, among others. These, however, do not concern me in this chapter, though I will come back to them in the following chapters as they are an important part of conservation as an industry or sector, as explained in chapter 1.

5. In this chapter, there is an implicit assumption that is important to make explicit—namely, that the gap in internet access combined with the history of

mainstream conservation means that still a lot of activists online are in the Global North, not in the Global South. This is also where most of the money for conservation is made and distributed, and hence why I focused my interviews mostly on Northern organizations, though some are, as stated, from South Africa. Moreover, I have also used some excerpts from later interviews done in the course of other projects on conservation, during which I still often kept asking about social media.

6. Despite my attempts to block trackers through programs such as Ghostery.

7. Interview senior community manager, Unites States, 16 April 2013.

8. Interview online marketing and social media advisor, The Netherlands, 28 September 2012.

9. Interview online marketing and social media advisor, The Netherlands, 28 September 2012.

10. Interview new media staff officer, The Netherlands, 3 October 2012.

11. Interview new media staff officers, the Netherlands, 17 October 2012.

12. https://uk.reputationdefender.com/, accessed 22 May 2017.

13. Interview senior communications advisor, The Netherlands, 8 June 2012.

14. Interview online marketing and social media advisor, The Netherlands, 28 September 2012.

15. Interview digital marketing specialist, United States, 15 April 2013.

16. Interview new media staff officer, The Netherlands, 3 October 2012.

17. Interview senior community manager, United States, 16 April 2013.

18. Interview manager media and stakeholder relations, South Africa, 11 February 2013.

19. Interview staff member, communications department, The Netherlands, 16 July 2012.

20. Interview new media staff officers, the Netherlands, 17 October 2012.

21. Interview manager media and stakeholder relations, manager social media affairs, and senior manager e-business, South Africa, 11 February 2013.

22. Interview senior community manager, United States, 16 April 2013.

23. Interview senior communications manager, The Netherlands, 20 June 2012.

24. http://theamazonismyfriend.wearejust.com/#/the-problem, accessed 8 August 2014.

25. http://theamazonismyfriend.wearejust.com/#/terms-of-use, accessed 8 August 2014.

26. http://www.theguardian.com/environment/2012/may/25/brazil-amazon -rainforest-law, accessed 26 May 2012.

27. Interview senior conservationist, Medan, Indonesia, 28 January 2018.

28. Interview new media staff officers, the Netherlands, 17 October 2012.

29. Interview online marketing and social media advisor, The Netherlands, 28 September 2012.

30. Interview senior communications manager, The Netherlands, 20 June 2012.

31. For another example, see Checker (2017). She shows how activist citizens coordinated their actions on social media to sound their displeasure with post-disaster relief management in New York State, including how they had

neglected the conservation of coast lines that protect their houses and properties. As Pickerill (2003) shows, online environmental activism has been around
since the early days of the Internet.

32. Sandbrook, Adams, et al., 2013.

33. Hawkins and Silver, 2017: 117.

34. Tinnell, 2011; personal communication, Dr. Brett Matulis, November 2013.

35. https://twitter.com/vbadpanda, accessed 4 January 2017.

36. Interview new media staff officer, The Netherlands, 3 October 2012.

37. Ibid.

38. This takes place in a larger discussion of animal welfare versus conservation, whereby the former focuses more on individual animals and the latter
more on species, as the focus for protection. Yet, as Ursula Heise (2016: 132)
argues, it is instructive that, "in their disagreements and critiques" each perspective "ultimately obeys cultural orientations that are rooted in different perspectives on modernization understood as a grand-scale process of domestication."

39. I use the word *appear* deliberately here, as outside of public appearances,
discontent with the neoliberal model is brewing in the conservation world. See
Büscher and Fletcher (2020).

40. Interview strategic communications manager, South Africa, 25 February
2013.

41. https://netnaturalist.com/about/, accessed 19 January 2018.

42. https://netnaturalist.com/2015/05/06/trail-guide-for-facebook/, accessed
14 February 2020.

43. https://netnaturalist.com/2011/10/17/exploring-the-social-media-ecosystem/,
accessed 19 January 2018.

44. Wajman, 2015: 25.

45. Ibid.

46. Büscher and Igoe, 2013: 290; Igoe, 2010; 2013.

47. Interview digital marketing specialist, United States, 15 April 2013.

48. While Twitter and Facebook can provide space to give organizations
direct feedback, even criticize or at attack organizations (as regularly happens),
many other social media possibilities do not necessarily provide this space. At
least not directly, as Facebook and Twitter are still almost always integrated
with and referred to in other social media applications and tools.

49. Büscher, 2016.

50. See my website, www.brambuscher.com, to view a still of the video that
illustrates this.

51. https://play.google.com/store/apps/details?id=za.co.flintsky.rhinoraid&
hl=en, accessed 30 December 2014.

52. Interview staff members WWF South Africa, 3 January 2014.

53. Ibid.

54. https://www.mygreenworld.org/mobile-game-application/, accessed
12 September 2020.

55. https://www.internetofelephants.com/custom-project/#conservation
-challenges, accessed 28 February 2018.

56. https://www.internetofelephants.com/custom-project/#new-page-4,
accessed 1 March 2018.

57. https://www.internetofelephants.com/custom-project/#new-page-5, accessed 1 March 2018.

58. http://tailsupapp.com/, accessed 1 March 2018.

59. https://tech.co/tailsup-app-launches-raise-awareness-animal-extinction -2015-03, accessed 1 March 2018.

60. Ibid.

61. Sandbrook et al., 2015: 122. See also Adams, 2019.

62. Fletcher, 2017: 153.

63. Stinson, 2017: 186.

64. This, according to Gerlitz and Helmond, has turned into what they call the "Like economy." They argue: "In order to extend its data mining and become the central hub of social linking, Facebook is reversely dependent on the dynamics of decentralization. . . . Simply because the platform can expand some of its key features into the entire web and integrate ever more objects into the social graph, it can recentralise and monetise the created connections and data flows, as they all direct back to Facebook. The dynamics of de- and re-centralisation are not only interconnected, they form a prerequisite for the Like economy. They enable Facebook to maximise its data mining activities while at the same time keeping control over the key entities of exchange—data, connections, traffic and . . . user affects" (Gerlitz and Helmond, 2013: 8).

65. This is worked out in more detail in Büscher, 2016.

CHAPTER 5. ELEPHANT 2.0

1. See my website, www.brambuscher.com, for print screens of the web-pages referred to here.

2. http://inventorspot.com/articles/twitters_100000_twelephants_can_aid _100000_elephants_35231, accessed 8 March 2018.

3. Ibid.

4. Ibid.

5. From 2010 to 2015 I followed Pifworld and the elephant corridor project online, regularly making print screens, and taking down notes as to the development of the website and the project. I also did interviews with people behind the organization and went to the site of the elephant corridor between Botswana and Zambia four times to conduct local interviews and do participatory observation. In the reference to websites online, I noted the original dates when I downloaded print screens to show the development of the project and the Pifworld website over time. Some of these links, therefore, are no longer active.

6. See, among others, Quarles van Ufford, 1988; Lewis et al., 2003; Mosse, 2004; Li, 2007; DeMotts and Hoon, 2012; Milne and Adams, 2012; Kepe, 2014.

7. See http://www.socialbrite.org/cause-organizations/ for a good overview, accessed 24 January 2015. See also Igoe, 2013.

8. http://www.1procentclub.nl/about, accessed 17 August 2012.

9. See http://www.myggsa.co.za/, http://www.givengain.com/. Doing good, obviously, goes beyond platforms: subscribing to @TwitterGood allows one to

stay abreast of the "forces of good in the Twitter community," https://twitter.com/twittergood. All sites accessed 28 March 2013.

10. http://www.pifworld.com/#/aboutpifworld, accessed 11 May 2010. Like any web 2.0 application you can customize your own prosumption of doing good. For example, one is encouraged to "Pimp your Profile by uploading your photo and giving your motivation to play it forward."

11. Ibid.

12. http://www.pifworld.com/aboutpifworld. Last viewed 9 October 2012.

13. Interview Pifworld executive, 6 June 2012, Amsterdam, the Netherlands.

14. https://www.pifworld.com/en/about/individual, accessed 24 January 2015.

15. Goldman and Papson, 2011: 176.

16. Castells, 2000; Boltanski and Chiapello, 2007; Fisher, 2010; Goldman and Papson, 2011.

17. See Van Dijck, 2013, chapter 2.

18. http://www.kavangozambezi.org/about-us, accessed 25 January 2015.

19. https://www.pifworld.com/en/projects/TheElephantCorridor/61#/about, accessed 25 January 2015.

20. http://www.dutchcowboys.nl/online/19891, accessed 24 January 2015.

21. http://www.gafawildlife.org/2010/06/30/nelson-mandela-dreams-of-elephant-corridors/, accessed 25 January 2015.

22. See my website, www.brambuscher.com.

23. https://www.pifworld.com/en/projects/TheElephantCorridor/61/blog/1106, accessed 25 January 2015.

24. http://925.nl/archief/2010/06/17/richard-branson-twittert-voor-nederlandse-chari-entrepreneur/, accessed 25 January 2015.

25. http://www.peaceparks.org/story.php?pid=1&mid=2, accessed 25 January 2015.

26. Ramutsindela, 2007; Büscher, 2013.

27. http://www.pifworld.com/#/players/peace/854, accessed 11 May 2010.

28. https://www.pifworld.com/en/people/loudon/155#/recentActivity, accessed 25 January 2015.

29. Interview senior civil servant, Ministry of Environment, Wildlife and Tourism of Botswana, 22 January 2013, Gaborone, Botswana.

30. Interview director local NGO, 24 July 2013, Kasane, Botswana.

31. Interview three staff officers KAZA secretariat, 23 July 2013, Kasane, Botswana.

32. DeMotts and Hoon, 2012: 848.

33. Interviews and informal communication, local community trusts and conservation agencies, southern Zambia, February 2015.

34. Metcalfe and Kepe, 2008: 114.

35. Ibid. 110.

36. Interviews and informal communication, local community trusts and conservation agencies, southern Zambia, February 2015.

37. Interview staff officer Ministry of Environment and Tourism, 12 March 2014, Katima Mulilo, Namibia.

38. Researcher at Namibia Nature Foundation (NNF) in an informal interview with Lieneke Eloff de Visser on 13 April 2014 at Katima Mulilo. I am grateful to Lieneke Eloff de Visser for allowing me to reproduce part of her interview.

39. A dynamic highly familiar to development interventions more generally, see Quarles van Ufford and Kumar Giri, 2003.

40. See also: https://www.dailymaverick.co.za/article/2014-01-09-southern -african-elephant-corridors-blocked-by-poachers/, accessed 8 March 2018.

41. Ramutsindela, 2007; Spierenburg and Wels, 2010; Büscher, 2013.

42. Prudham, 2009. Naomi Klein (2014: 251–252) shows that Branson's climate initiatives not only "failed to yield results" but has made matters worse for the climate: "Branson set out to harness the profit motive to solve the climate crisis—but the temptation to profit from practices worsening the crisis proved too great to resist. Again and again, the demands of building a successful empire trumped the climate imperative—whether that meant lobbying against needed regulation, or putting more planes in the air, or pitching oil companies on using his pet miracle technologies to extract more oil."

43. http://www.pifworld.com/#/projects/TheElephantCorridor/61, accessed 7 February 2015.

44. Büscher, 2011: 84; see also Fletcher et al., 2014.

45. Duffy 2014; Büscher and Ramutsindela, 2016.

46. Observation at the World Parks Congress, 10–21 November, 2014. The new government in 2018 abolished this shoot-to-kill policy.

47. From working and doing participatory observation in Botswana between 2005 and 2015, it was clear that the Botswana state became less patient with critical views and indeed more authoritarian in terms of protecting its carefully crafted reputation of Africa's peaceful and stable country and a safe, luxurious tourism destination (see Botswana Tourism videos on https://www.youtube .com/user/botswanatourism). I myself experienced this in 2014 when I was intimidated while doing an interview with a director of the Botswana Ministry of Environment and Parks after asking him about the poaching of elephants. See also Büscher and Ramutsindela, 2016.

48. See my website, www.brambuscher.com, for the accompanying figure.

49. Interview Pifworld executive, 6 June 2012, Amsterdam, the Netherlands. I did consider putting some of my early findings online, but ultimately decided against it, as I did not want to influence but rather observe the unfolding of dynamics without my interference.

50. Mosse, 2004: 663; cf. Quarles van Ufford, 1988; Lewis and Mosse, 2006.

51. Ferguson, 1994; Lewis and Mosse, 2006.

52. Van Dijck, 2013.

53. Andrejevic, 2013: 117.

54. https://www.pifworld.com/en/faq, accessed 15 April 2015.

55. Cf. Farrell, 2015.

56. Andrejevic, 2013: 13.

57. https://www.onepercentclub.com/en/, accessed 15 April 2015.

58. Prudham, 2009.

59. Arendt, 1968: 145.

60. Goldman and Papson, 2011: 38.

61. https://www.pifworld.com/en/organization, accessed 15 April 2015.

62. Gillespie, 2010.

63. Baumann, 2000.

64. This was Pifworld's slogan in 2015. https://www.pifworld.com/en, accessed, 16 April 2015.

65. Which arguably takes Arjun Appadurai's (1996) tension between 'the imagination' as a 'collective social fact' and the 'plurality of imagined worlds' to yet another level.

CHAPTER 6. KRUGER 2.0

1. https://www.sanparks.org/parks/kruger/, accessed 30 January 2019.

2. See: https://www.google.com/streetview/#discover-south-africa/kruger-national-park and http://www.dailymail.co.uk/travel/travel_news/article-3483902/See-South-Africa-lion-Google-Street-View-takes-stunning-SAFARI-Kruger-National-Park.html, accessed 16 March 2018. According to the *Daily Mail* article, "The virtual service now allows internet users to have a 360-degree adventure in Kruger National Park witnessing elephants, lions, and leopards in their natural habitat."

3. This has been a central trope in the history of conservation, and hence at the center of political ecology criticism for a long time. See Adams (2004) and Brockington (2002) for overviews.

4. The central tenets of fortress conservation thinking have been well rehearsed, and I will not delve into these in this chapter. According to Adams (2004: 112–114), they "typically involve a series of ideas about people and parks," namely, that people do not have a place in nature, that they "threaten park ecosystems" and species, and hence that conservation areas must be "defended" against (local) people, by force and coercion if necessary. Equally well rehearsed have been the critiques against the model from social justice, community-based or developmental points of view as well as its resurgence in the "back-to-the-barriers" literature (Dressler et al. 2010; Hutton et al. 2005). But no matter how well rehearsed, the idea and practice of the fortress seems to have lost little of its appeal. Critical researchers find that fortress thinking persists in the governance of protected areas (Harris, 2014; Kepe, 2014). For many conservation managers "the power of the fortress conservation narrative, its emotive appeal and the hard certainties it offers" (Brockington, 2002: 127) may well be why they continue to adhere to the model in practice (Holmes, 2013).

5. Interview Kruger National Park Staff Officer, 6 February 2014, Skukuza, South Africa.

6. https://www.sanparks.org/assets/docs/general/annual-report-2017.pdf, accessed 30 January 2019, p. 55.

7. Carruthers, 1995; Dlamini, 2020.

8. Carruthers, 1989, 1995.

9. Carruthers, 1995: 62.

10. Carruthers, 1989; Hughes 2010.

11. Carruthers, 1995, 65.

12. Cf. Neumann, 1998.

13. Bunn, 2003: 207–8.

14. Carruthers, 1995: 67–88.

15. Butler and Richardson, 2014; Carruthers, 1995: 88; Maguranyanga, 2009. Butler and Richardson (2014: 17) conducted a survey in the famous Soweto township of Johannesburg and concluded that "it is clear that national parks are still viewed as white leisure spaces in South Africa despite considerable political and organisational changes since 1994."

16. Dressler and Büscher, 2008; Ramutsindela and Shabangu, 2013; Tapela and Omara-Ojungu, 1999.

17. SANParks, 2006: 8.

18. Duffy et al. 2013. In 2013 over six hundred rhinos were poached in the KNP; 2014 figures exceeded eight hundred. Since then, numbers have gone down, though for 2018 were still close to four hundred. See https://africageographic.com/blog/dea-announces-2018-rhino-elephant-poaching-stats/, accessed 30 January 2019.

19. Personal communication, Kruger National Park staff, 4 February 2014, Phalaborwa, South Africa.

20. Interview Kruger National Park Staff Officer, 6 February 2014, Skukuza, South Africa; Lunstrum 2014.

21. Massé, 2019. See, for example, http://www.huffingtonpost.com/natalie-lapides/the-rhino-war-zone_b_3666132.html, or http://www.nytimes.com/2014/08/01/opinion/south-africa-fights-the-poachers.html?_r=0, last accessed 17 October 2014.

22. The influence of traditional media on park access and control, however, is an understudied phenomenon.

23. See my website, www.brambuscher.com, to view the banner.

24. https://www.youtube.com/watch?v=LU8DDYz68kM, last accessed 30 January 2019.

25. http://www.theguardian.com/travel/2013/jul/12/kruger-national-park-best-animal-videos, last accessed 19 October 2014.

26. Blewitt 2010, 60–61.

27. Rijsdijk, 2010: 369.

28. Massé, 2019.

29. Butler and Richardson, 2014.

30. Bourdieu, 1984: 6.

31. Ibid.: 470–471

32. Ibid.: chapter two.

33. Andrejevic, 2013: 48–49.

34. Kamphof, 2013.

35. http://www.africam.com/wildlife/about_us, last accessed 22 October 2014.

36. Interview, director Africam, 24 January 2014, Johannesburg, South Africa.

37. Ibid.

38. Ibid.

39. Interview Game Reserve Owner, 14 February 2014, Hoedspruit, South Africa.

40. Ibid.

41. See for example this weblog of a self-proclaimed "Africam addict": http://mavimet.com/about/, last accessed 22 October 2014.

42. Candea, 2010.

43. Groups are dedicated Facebook spaces that can be "secret," closed, or "open (public)," representing degrees of control over who can view and participate; https://www.facebook.com/about/groups, last accessed 23 October 2014. During my research, I became a member of the most active and biggest conservation Facebook groups dedicated to KNP and South African conservation issues. For over a year I followed them very regularly (almost daily) and took regular notes and print screens.

44. Interview, SANParks media and communication staff, 11 February 2013, Pretoria, South Africa.

45. Ibid.

46. https://www.facebook.com/groups/kruger.sanparks/, last accessed 16 March 2018.

47. Interview SANParks staff, Pretoria, 11 February 2013.

48. https://www.facebook.com/groups/krugerparkearth/, last accessed 16 March 2018.

49. https://www.facebook.com/notes/kruger-national-park-best-place-on -earth/rhino-poaching-and-reporting-kruger-national-park-best-place-on-earth /10150535406090978, last accessed 31 January 2014.

50. https://www.facebook.com/groups/krugerappreciationsociety/, last accessed 16 March 2018. The announcement for this Facebook Group starts with the following sentences, again corroborating the two themes highlighted in this section: "This group has been created for fellow Kruger lovers to share their experiences and memories. PLEASE DON'T POST THE LOCATIONS OR INFO ABOUT KRUGER'S RHINOS! This is an APPRECIATION Society so it would be appreciated if we could keep discussions positive!" (Capital letters in original). The group was archived on 21 September 2017.

51. Butler and Richardson 2014.

52. Ibid.

53. Interview, SANParks staff, 24 February 2014, Pretoria, South Africa.

54. http://www.sanparks.org/forums/index.php?style=2, last accessed 22 July 2020.

55. Participatory observation Facebook groups, SANParks forums, interviews with key moderators.

56. Forum moderator interview, 5 May 2014, Somerset West, South Africa.

57. Former Forum moderator interview, 4 December 2013, Dordrecht, the Netherlands.

58. http://www.sanparksvolunteers.org/, last accessed 28 October 2014.

59. See: http://www.sanparks.org/forums/viewtopic.php?f=23&t=41143&sid =4doe1a158f787ae65183ebd95b696437, and http://www.sanparksvolunteers .org/virtual-region, last accessed 28 October 2014.

60. Former Forum moderator interview, 23 November 2013, The Hague, the Netherlands.

61. Forum moderator interview, 5 May 2014, Somerset West, South Africa.

62. Former Forum moderator interview, 4 December 2013, Dordrecht, the Netherlands.

63. http://www.sanparks.org/forums/viewtopic.php?style=2&f=70&t=76971, last accessed 31 January 2014. Spelling mistakes in original.

64. Ibid.

65. Former Forum moderator interview, 4 December 2013, Dordrecht, the Netherlands.

66. Forum moderator interview, 5 May 2014, Somerset West, South Africa.

67. http://mg.co.za/article/2011-07-01-kruger-row-becomes-racist-game, last accessed 29 October 2014.

68. Forum moderator interview, 5 May 2014, Somerset West, South Africa.

69. Bunn, 2003: 212.

70. Former Forum moderator interview, 4 December 2013, Dordrecht, the Netherlands.

71. See https://www.facebook.com/pages/Against-Hotel-Development-in-Kruger-Park/212487065493829, last accessed 29 October 2014.

72. I have been following Latest Sightings since it began in 2011 on Facebook and www.latestsightings.com and since early 2014 joined a Latest Sightings Whatsapp group, which I have been observing daily since.

73. http://edition.cnn.com/2012/12/31/tech/web/kruger-latest-sightings-nadav-ossendryver/, accessed 29 October 2014.

74. http://www.entrepreneurmag.co.za/advice/success-stories/upstarts/african-enterprise-we-interview-nadav-of-latest-sightings/, accessed 29 October 2014.

75. Including the Young Jewish Entrepreneurial Award 2014 (http://www.sajr.co.za/news-and-articles/2014/08/24/absa-achievers-2014-the-live-blog), the Nelson Mandela Young Leadership Award 2014 (http://www.latestsightings.com/nadav-ossendryver-founder-latest-sightings-honoured-with-nelson-mandela-young-leadership-2014-award/), and others; accessed 29 October 2014.

76. http://www.latestsightings.com/about-nadav-ossendryver/, accessed 29 October 2014.

77. Nadav Ossedryver interview, Gareth's Guests, 15 October 2014 http://iono.fm/e/106482?utm_content=buffer42f61&utm, accessed 10 December 2014.

78. https://www.latestsightings.com/about-us, accessed 16 March 2018.

79. Ibid.

80. Though this is something that is hard to verify, and KNP management actually noted that they do not see much bigger congestions. Interview Kruger National Park management staff, Skukuza, 6 February 2014.

81. Andrejevic, 2013: 48–50.

82. Neumann, 1998: 24.

83. TV interview with Nadav Ossendryver on *Tonight with Bruce Whitfield*, https://www.youtube.com/watch?v=oxCImBeJmkA&list=PL

_K2CjlrV2nC2Q7ydqOf_u1FYNpt6L-cN&index=1, last accessed 29 October 2014.

84. Evidence of this is based on my membership of and following Latest Sightings Facebook, Twitter, and Whatsapp groups almost since their inception. See also next chapter.

85. TV interview with Nadav Ossendryver on *Tonight with Bruce Whitfield*.

86. https://www.latestsightings.com/film-earn, accessed 16 March 2018.

87. Ibid.

88. Interview Kruger National Park management staff, Skukuza, 6 February 2014.

89. Igoe, 2010: 391.

90. While I have not done systematic research on new media use in local communities around the Kruger, in many interactions and discussions I did notice that for many local people the park seems to play a very small role in their online engagements and they were more interested in leisure, community, and other types of online engagement. Further research would be useful to corroborate these observations, but they seem to be in line with Payal Arora's (2019) findings about "digital life beyond the West."

91. One major exception, among others, is a radio discussion on "Do you care about Rhino," by DJ Eusebius McKaiser on 19 February 2014, that was heavily discussed on Facebook, https://www.facebook.com/groups/OSCAP/permalink/604600976297262/?stream_ref=2#_=_, last accessed 10 November 2014.

92. Maguranyanga, 2009: 183.

93. This does not mean that no contexts are taken into account. One is highlighted often, also in Latest Sightings: the rhino-poaching crisis. Yet this context further strengthens Fortress Kruger, though ironically new media enable certain individuals to gain access to Kruger precisely by calling for the reinforcement of its fortress properties. New media focused on the rhino poaching crisis, therefore, are breathing new life into the idea of Kruger as a "modernist form of symbolically enclaved space" (seemingly) separate from the "destructive forces" of global capitalism (Bunn, 2003). More on this in the next chapter.

94. This conclusion challenges recent posthumanist political ecology conceptualizations of conservation boundaries. According to Juanita Sundberg (2011: 322): "a posthumanist political ecology refuses to treat nonhuman nature as the thing over which humans struggle and instead builds on and enacts a relational approach in which all bodies are participants in constituting the world." Sundberg is right that "all bodies are participants in constituting the world." But they do not participate equally. In her account—and yet others, see Barua (2017)— there is a slippage between nonhuman agency and nonhuman *political* agency. Following Swyngedouw and Ernston (2018), I hold that making distinctions between forms of agency is critical, as this allows us to see that in the Kruger case, nonhuman nature is precisely "the thing over which humans struggle" in the online sphere, with disturbing political consequences. And since there is not a single animal in Kruger active on social media out of their own account, their bodies only feature as representations-without-context over which claims are made over a contested conservation space.

Does this mean that animal and other nonhuman bodies are without consequences when examining online politics? No. Their acting within the park has a major impact on human visitors (and vice versa) and the latter's ability to represent the former. But when methodological attention only focuses on "the relations and practices" that bring emergent associations into being on an everyday level (i.e., on the continuous and never-ending process of micro-socioecological change—Sundberg, 2011: 322), we lose sight of the macro structural, historical trends that are mutually constituted by but also transcend these everyday relations and practices. In other words, when the focus is only (or mainly) on the shifting sands of everyday change and when all (human and nonhuman) agencies are regarded as politically equal, we lose sight over how nonhuman nature can precisely be the thing over which (different groups of) humans struggle. The more-than-humans in the Kruger do not care whether it is black or white humans using their representations in particular truth discourses. But white humans do buy into and distinguish themselves more in relation to the fortress truth regime that the park was built on than black humans. The *political* consequences of these distinctions, as shown, come to matter in very real ways.

CHAPTER 7. RHINO 2.0

1. https://www.environment.gov.za/mediarelease/update_on_rhino_poaching, accessed 16 January 2014.

2. See, for example, Dr. William Fowlds, a well-known South African veterinarian, who argued that "Rhino poaching is beyond a crisis now; it is simply out of control." http://activateonline.co.za/rhinos-suffering-in-silence/, accessed 4 April 2014.

3. Including the revival of some long-standing and controversial debates such as those around the legalization of rhino horn trade (see Biggs et al., 2013).

4. Scull, 2009.

5. See http://www.merriam-webster.com/dictionary/hysteria and http://www.oxforddictionaries.com/definition/english/hysteria. Last viewed: 7 April 2014.

6. Lunstrum, 2014; Büscher and Ramutsindela, 2016.

7. Among others: Carruthers, 1995; Neumann, 1998; Brockington, 2002; Igoe, 2004; Brooks, 2005.

8. Brooks, 2005: 236.

9. Moore, 2005: 13.

10. Hughes, 2010: 25.

11. Hughes, 2010: 137. Hughes has been criticized for generalizing white experiences in Zimbabwe and not recognizing (enough) the diversity of white positionalities (Hartnack, 2014). This critique is important and undoubtedly applies to some of the statements about whites in this chapter.

12. Steyn, 2001.

13. Humphreys and Smith (2014: 796) argue that "for many whites the management and conservation of wildlife, with its closely linked tourism industry, forms an iconic article of self-definition."

14. Brooks et al., 2011; Butler and Richardson, 2015; Maguranyanga, 2009.

15. Steyn and Foster, 2008; Kepe, 2009.

16. Wajcman, 2009: 128–129.

17. In this regard, one could wonder whether the obsessive focus in climate change debates on "adaptation" relates to this very point. Rather than thinking about the possibility of changing the capitalist system responsible for climate change, we almost seem anxious to see who the strongest, most adapted humans will be by virtue of their surviving climate disasters (see Klein, 2014).

18. Žižek, 2011: 82–83.

19. Cf. Seekings, 2008.

20. Bunn, 2003.

21. Hartnack, 2014.

22. Key informant interview, 5 May 2014, Somerset West, South Africa.

23. Rogerson, 2004.

24. Büscher and Ramutsindela, 2016.

25. Lunstrum, 2014.

26. Neumann, 2004: 818.

27. Karatzogianni and Kuntsman, 2012. See also work on emotional and affective geographies, which have explored the relations between emotion and space more broadly: Brown and Pickerill (2009), Clough (2012).

28. Steyn and Foster, 2008; Kuntsman, 2012; Hannan, 2018.

29. http://wwf.panda.org/what_we_do/endangered_species/rhinoceros/?src=footer, accessed 18 March 2018.

30. http://www.awf.org/wildlife-conservation/rhinoceros, accessed, 27 December 2014.

31. http://www.savetherhino.org/rhino_info/threats_to_rhino/poaching_for_rhino_horn, accessed 18 March 2018.

32. Duffy et al., 2013: 5.

33. Milliken and Shaw, 2012.

34. Rademeyer, 2012.

35. http://www.iam4rhinos.com/, accessed 27 December 2014.

36. http://www.timeslive.co.za/scitech/2013/09/19/world-rhino-day-aims-to-take-twitter-by-storm-with-iam4rhinos, accessed 27 December 2014.

37. See my website, www.brambuscher.com, to view the image.

38. Interview staff members WWF South Africa, 3 January 2014, Cape Town, South Africa.

39. Lovink, 2011: 2.

40. See: https://www.facebook.com/groups/OSCAP/ and http://www.oscap.co.za/, accessed 18 March 2018.

41. http://www.oscap.co.za/rhino-conference-2014, accessed 18 March 2018.

42. Interview, OSCAP facilitator, 18 February 2014, Pretoria, South Africa.

43. As corroborated, for example, by members ensuring the facilitator that she speaks "on behalf of" the members, or the facilitator apologizing for not being online when she is away for a day or two.

44. http://fightforrhinos.com/about/ and http://www.helpingrhinos.org/, accessed 27 December 2014.

45. http://www.earthtouchnews.com/conservation/endangered/gaming-for-good-online-game-runescape-is-raising-awareness-for-rhinos, accessed 27 December 2014.

46. See my website, www.brambuscher.com, to view the figure.

47. See https://www.youtube.com/watch?v=GpaEWIQOURA, http://www .thandisfundraiser.com/ and https://www.facebook.com/ThandisFundRaiser, accessed 28 December 2014.

48. Interview SANParks staff, Pretoria, 11 February 2013.

49. Heise, 2016.

50. Lorimer and Whatmore, 2009.

51. http://www.unitedforwildlife.org/#!/about, accessed 28 December 2014.

52. See https://twitter.com/hashtag/whosesideareyouon and https://www .facebook.com/hashtag/whosesideareyouon, accessed: 17 July 2014.

53. http://www.unitedforwildlife.org/#!/home, accessed: 17 July 2014.

54. http://rockingforrhinos.org.dedi196.cpt3.host-h.net/, accessed 28 December 2014.

55. See my website, www.brambuscher.com, to see the figure.

56. See http://www.timeslive.co.za/lifestyle/2011/10/02/wildlife-war-zone -hero, accessed 28 December 2014.

57. http://www.iapf.org/en/getinvolved/green-army, accessed 28 December 2014.

58. http://www.animalplanet.com/tv-shows/battleground-rhino-wars/, accessed 28 December 2014.

59. Interview, 28 March 2014, Orpen, South Africa.

60. http://www.telegraph.co.uk/culture/tvandradio/tv-and-radio-reviews /10274799/Poaching-Wars-with-Tom-Hardy-ITV-review.html, accessed 29 December 2014.

61. http://therhinoorphanage.co.za/.

62. See https://www.facebook.com/TheRhinoOrphanage, accessed 29 December 2014.

63. See for the story: http://www.kariega.co.za/about-us/help-save-our-rhino -project, accessed 29 December 2014.

64. http://www.thandisfundraiser.com/, http://therhinorun.com/, accessed 29 December 2014.

65. Observation at the South African Veterinary Association meeting, 6 March 2014, Stone Cradle, Centurion, Pretoria.

66. See https://www.youtube.com/playlist?list=PLAwvZrI4xN6LDyhFPRA 6sJOut9jOgiuCx, accessed 29 December 2014.

67. http://www.iucn.org/news_homepage/news_by_date/?17186/Hail-the -heroes-who-tread-the-thin-green-line, http://www.thingreenline.org.au/, accessed 29 December 2014.

68. https://www.unitedforwildlife.org/, accessed 31 January 2019.

69. https://www.facebook.com/groups/OSCAP/, accessed 25 December 2014.

70. http://thesilentheroes.org/about-silent-heroes/, accessed 31 January 2019.

71. Foucault, 2008a: 131.

72. Duffy, 2014: 819.

73. Lunstrum, 2014: 817.

74. Humphreys and Smith, 2014: 795.

75. Büscher and Ramutsindela, 2016.

76. Cf. Lunstrum, 2014.

77. All comments are copied literally as they appeared on various Facebook group pages, and rendered anonymous.

78. See my website, www.brambuscher.com, to see these figures.

79. Agamben, 1998.

80. Büscher and Ramutsindela, 2016.

81. See, for example, this short documentary made by Earth Touch insider: http://www.earthtouchnews.com/videos/earth-touch-insider/can-social-media -help-conservation/, accessed 30 December 2014.

82. Interviews, OSCAP facilitator, 18 February 2014, Pretoria, South Africa; Key informant interview, 5 May 2014, Somerset West, South Africa.

83. https://www.facebook.com/groups/OSCAP/announcements/, accessed 31 January 2019.

84. http://www.rhinorescueproject.com/, accessed 30 December 2014.

85. See Demmers, 2014.

86. Kepe, 2009.

87. See Unterhalter, 2000, for a discussion in relation to the struggle against apartheid.

88. As was visible, for example, in a much-shared figure at the time where the South African flag and the symbols of the presidency of the Republic of South Africa were dripping with blood, combined with the text "the blood of our rhino is on your hands."

89. Cf. Hughes, 2010.

90. This sense came out vividly in discussions on South Africa's white gun culture during the trial around Oscar Pistorius, the famous athlete who shot dead his girlfriend in his own house because he thought he was being burgled; http://edition.cnn.com/2013/02/23/world/africa/south-africa-gun-violence/, accessed 31 December 2014.

91. Wajcman, 2009; Žižek, 2011.

92. Humphreys and Smith, 2014: 801.

93. Burnett, 2018.

94. Ahmed, 2004: 45–46, in Kuntsman, 2012: 7.

95. Kuntsman, 2012: 7.

96. Ceballos et al., 2017.

97. See Büscher and Fletcher, 2018.

98. https://news.mongabay.com/2017/10/attacks-on-militarized-conservation -are-naive-commentary/, accessed 12 October 2017.

99. Ibid. The argument that "otherwise there is nothing left" is a key theme in the neo-protectionist literature. See, especially, Oates (1999).

100. Mogomotsi and Madigele, 2017: 57.

101. Crawford, 2009: 29.

CONCLUSION: SPEAKING TRUTH TO POWER

1. See Mbaria and Ogada, 2017.

2. Harvey, 1996: 2.

3. Braidotti, 2013: 27, 166, 172.

4. Cf. Braidotti, 2013: 27.

5. Foucault, 1980: 133.

6. See https://www.conservation.org/Pages/default.aspx and https://www.youtube.com/watch?v=h6bTR0Y45Rw&feature=youtu.be, accessed 24 March 2018.

7. See Iyengar and Massey (2018), who do point at structural changes in the media environment as the most important element in understanding why scientific communication is different and difficult in the post-truth age. However, they then still resort to individualistic explanations where "unscrupulous actors with ulterior motives" are the main problem, rather than combining this with attention to structural power dynamics.

8. Srnicek, 2017: 63.

9. Andrejevic, 2013: 140.

10. Rouvroy, 2013.

11. This is a generic statement that is meant to distinguish modes of connections through the internet and modern media technologies from other modes of connection before these.

12. Van Dyck, 2013.

13. Pettman, 2017: 19.

14. See Laclau and Mouffe, 1985.

15. Proctor, 2001.

16. Arendt, 1994: 307.

17. Lee, 2015.

18. To be clear, I am not arguing that truth wars are not sometimes necessary and certainly not that they can be avoided. There is a major tension between truth tensions and truth wars and this is not easily overcome.

19. Hence, in Mouffe's own terms, I believe that the differences are agonistic, which may lead to productive tensions, and not antagonistic, which often lead to destructive tensions. More problematic are the larger critiques of Arendt's ideas about the social (cf. Brown, 2019: 46–50), which I acknowledge but believe are also based on a rather limited reading of Arendt outside of context.

20. Mouffe, 2005: 20–21.

21. Arendt, 1994: 314.

22. Zuboff, 2019: chapters 12 and 13.

23. Although Arendt would argue that books could never actually achieve this, as understanding is unending. As she argues: "Many well-meaning people want to cut this process short in order to educate others and elevate public opinion. They think that books can be weapons and that one can fight with words. But weapons and fighting belong in the realm of violence, and violence, as distinguished from power, is mute; violence begins where speech ends. Words used for the purpose of fighting lose their quality of speech; they become clichés. The extent to which clichés have crept into our everyday language and discussions may well indicate the degree to which we not only have deprived ourselves of the faculty of speech, but are ready to use more effective means of violence than bad books (And only bad books can be good weapons) with which to settle our arguments. The results of all such attempts is indoctrination" (Arendt, 1994: 308).

24. Büscher and Fletcher, 2020.

25. Merrifield, 2011.

26. Nealon, 2008: 110.

27. Foucault, in Nealon, 208: 111.

28. See Vigh and Sausdal, 2014; West, 2016.

29. Smith, 2010.

30. Arendt, 1994: 307–308.

31. Cf. Bridle, 2018. Likewise, I also do not see how the hyped blockchain technologies will fundamentally change the workings of platform power. Besides the enormous energy demands of distributed ledger systems (at least for now), they seem to not be as impervious as often stated; they seem to thrive on, and so stimulate, rather absolute ideas about property rights and do not do away with or threaten many (current and other) intermediary structures, including current big tech companies (Werbach, 2018: 57, 67, 79). Moreover, one of the core value propositions of blockchain technologies, according to Werbach (2018: 80), is what he refers to as "shared truth," where "everyone can have a copy of the master ledger, but no participant can claim its own ledger is the final word." This, in my conceptualization, is not truth but "fact": something that is solid outside of context, history, and positionality. Indeed, part of blockchain development seems precisely to limit or even erase the influence of context, history, and positionality on online transactions and activities, something that will, I venture, always lead to unintended consequences and new conflicts, particularly if the technology continues to develop in a hyper-capitalist political economy.

32. Gillespie, 2014. Blockchain possibilities are often mentioned in this context, but, as mentioned in the previous note, I do not yet see how they will fundamentally challenge or change platform capitalism.

33. Büscher and Fletcher, 2020.

34. See https://www.monbiot.com/2019/04/30/the-problem-is-capitalism/; https://www.irishtimes.com/life-and-style/people/why-is-greta-thunberg-so-triggering-for-certain-men-1.4002264. In a speech to the UN on 23 September 2019, Thunberg did scold world leaders and adults that all they "can talk about is money and fairytales of eternal economic growth," https://www.youtube.com/watch?v=KAJsdgTPJpU, accessed 23 September 2019. Having said this, there are clearly major problems in making "nature" the basis for solving the environmental crises we are in, as this book as shown in detail. One might expect Thunberg and Monbiot to be fully aware of this, though the video does not communicate this explicitly.

35. https://www.youtube.com/watch?v=-QoxUXo2zEY, last viewed: 23 September 2019.

36. Foucault, 2008: 356.

Bibliography

Adams, William, M. *Against Extinction. The Story of Conservation*. London: Earthscan, 2004.

———. "Geographies of Conservation II: Technology, Surveillance and Conservation by Algorithm." *Progress in Human Geography* 43 (2019): 337–350.

Agamben, Giorgio. *Homo sacer. Sovereign Power and Bare Life*. Stanford, CA: Stanford University Press, 1998.

Ahmed Sara. *The Cultural Politics of Emotions*. Edinburgh: Edinburgh University Press, 2004.

Andrejevic, Mark. *Infoglut: How Too Much Information Is Changing the Way We Think and Know*. London: Routledge, 2013.

Angermuller, Johannes. "Truth after Post-truth: For a Strong Programme in Discourse Studies." *Palgrave Communications* 4, no. 30 (2018): 1–8.

Appadurai, Arjun. *Modernity at Large: Cultural Dimensions of Globalization*. Minneapolis: University of Minnesota Press, 1996.

Arendt, Hannah. *The Origins of Totalitarianism*. Orlando: Harcourt, 1968.

———. *Essays in Understanding 1930–1954*. New York: Schocken Books, 1994.

Arora, Payal. "Typology of Web 2.0 Spheres: Understanding the Cultural Dimension of Social Media Spaces." *Current Sociology* 60, no. 5 (2012): 599–618.

———. *The Next Billion Users: Digital Life beyond the West*. Cambridge, MA: Harvard University Press, 2019.

Arsel, Murat, and Bram Büscher. "Nature™ Inc: Changes and Continuities in Neoliberal Conservation and Environmental Markets." *Development and Change* 43, no. 1 (2012): 53–78.

Arts, Koen, René van der Wal, and William M. Adams. "Digital Technology and the Conservation of Nature." *Ambio* 44, no. 4 (2015): 661–673.

Arvidsson, Adam. *Brands: Meaning and Value in Media Culture*. London: Routledge, 2006.

Bagust, Phil. "'Screen Natures': Special Effects and Edutainment in 'New' Hybrid Wildlife Documentary." *Continuum: Journal of Media & Cultural Studies* 22, no. 2 (2008): 213–226.

Bakker, Karen, and Gavin Bridge. "Material Worlds? Resource Geographies and the 'Matter of Nature.'" *Progress in Human Geography* 30, no. 1 (2006): 5–27.

Bakker, Karen, and Max Ritts. "Smart Earth: A Meta-review and Implications for Environmental Governance." *Global Environmental Change* 52 (2018): 201–211.

Barassi, Veronica, and Emiliano Treré. "Does Web 3.0 Come after Web 2.0? Deconstructing Theoretical Assumptions through Practice." *New Media & Society* 14 no. 8 (2012): 1269–1285.

Barua, Maan. "Nonhuman Labour, Encounter Value, Spectacular Accumulation: The Geographies of a Lively Commodity." *Transactions of the Institute of British Geographers* 42 (2017): 274–288.

Baumann, Zygmunt. *Liquid Modernity*. Cambridge: Polity Press, 2000.

Beinart, William, and Lotte Hughes. *Environment and Empire*. Oxford: Oxford University Press, 2007.

Beinart, William, and Katie McKeown. "Wildlife Media and Representations of Africa, 1950s to the 1970s." *Environmental History* 14, no. 3 (2009): 429–542.

Bennett, Nathan, Robin Roth, Sarah Klain, Kai Chan, Patrick Christie, Douglas Clark, Georgina Cullman, Deborah Curran, Trevor Durbin, Graham Epstein, et al. "Conservation Social Science: Understanding and Integrating Human Dimensions to Improve Conservation." *Biological Conservation* 205 (2017): 93–108.

Berger-Tal, Oded, and José Lahoz-Monfort. "Conservation Technology: The Next Generation." *Conservation Letters* 11, no. 6 (2018): e12458.

Biersack, Aletta. "Reimagining Political Ecology: Culture/Power/History/Nature." In *Reimagining Political Ecology*, edited by Aletta Biersack and James Greenberg, 3–42. Durham, NC: Duke University Press, 2006.

Biggs, Duan, Franck Courchamp, Rowan Martin, and Hugh Possingham. "Legal Trade of Africa's Rhino Horns." *Science* 339, no. 6123 (2013): 1038–1039.

Blewitt, Jon. *Media, Ecology and Conservation: Using the Media to Protect the World's Wildlife and Ecosystems*. Dartington, UK: Green Books, 2010.

Boltanski, Luc, and Eve Chiapello. *The New Spirit of Capitalism*. London: Verso, 2005.

Bottici, Chiara. "Imaginal Politics." *Thesis Eleven* 106, no. 1 (2011): 56–72.

Bourdieu, Pierre. *Distinction: A Social Critique of the Judgement of Taste*. Cambridge, MA: Harvard University Press, 1984.

Bousé, Derek. *Wildlife Films*. Philadelphia: University of Pennsylvania Press, 2000.

Boyd, Danah, and Kate Crawford. "Critical Questions for Big Data: Provocations for a Cultural, Technological, and Scholarly Phenomenon." *Information, Communication & Society* 15, no. 5 (2012): 662–679.

Braidotti, Rosi. *The Posthuman.* Cambridge: Polity Press, 2013.

Brashares, Justin, Briana Abrahms, Kathryn Fiorella, Christopher Golden, Cheryl Hojnowski, Ryan Marsh, Douglas McCauley, Tristan Nuñez, Katherine Seto, and Lauren Withey. "Wildlife Decline and Social Conflict." *Science* 345, no. 6195 (2014): 376–378.

Bridle, James. *New Dark Age: Technology and the End of the Future.* London: Verso, 2018.

Brockington, Dan. *Fortress Conservation: The Preservation of the Mkomazi Game Reserve, Tanzania.* Oxford: James Currey, 2002.

———. "Powerful Environmentalisms: Conservation, Celebrity and Capitalism." *Media Culture Society* 30, no. 4 (2008): 551–568.

———. *Celebrity and the Environment.* London: Pluto Press, 2009.

Brooks, Shirley. "Images of 'Wild Africa': Nature Tourism and the (Re)Creation of Hluhluwe Game Reserve, 1930–1945." *Journal of Historical Geography* 31, no. 2 (2005): 220–240.

Brooks, Shirley, Marja Spierenburg, Lot van Brakel, Annemarie Kolk, and Khethabakhe LuKhozi. "Creating a Commodified Wilderness: Tourism, Private Game Farming, and 'Third Nature' Landscapes in KwaZulu-Natal." *Tijdschrift voor Sociale en Economische Geografie* 102, no. 3 (2011): 260–274

Brown, Gavin, and Jenny Pickerill. "Space for Emotion in the Spaces of Activism." *Emotion, Space and Society* 2, no. 1 (2009): 24–35.

Brown, Wendy. *In the Ruins of Neoliberalism: The Rise of Antidemocratic Politics in the West.* New York: Columbia University Press, 2019.

Bryant, Raymond, ed. *The International Handbook of Political Ecology.* Cheltenham: Edward Elgar, 2015.

Bunn, David. "An Unnatural State: Tourism, Water and Wildlife Photography in the Early Kruger National Park." In *Social History and African Environments*, edited by William Beinart and Joann McGregor, 199–220. Oxford: James Currey, 2003.

Burnett, Scott. *Giving Back the Land: Whiteness and Belonging in Contemporary South Africa.* PhD dissertation, University of the Witswatersrand. Johannesburg, 2018.

Büscher, Bram. The Neoliberalization of Nature in Africa. In *New Topographies of Power? Africa Negotiating an Emerging Multi-polar World*, edited by Ton Dietz, Kjell Havnevik, Mayke Kaag, & Terje Ostigard, 84–109. Leiden: Brill, 2011.

———. *Transforming the Frontier: Peace Parks and the Politics of Neoliberal Conservation in Southern Africa.* Durham, NC: Duke University Press, 2013.

———. "Nature on the Move: The Value and Circulation of Liquid Nature and the Emergence of Fictitious Conservation." In *Nature™ Inc: New Frontiers of Environmental Conservation in the Neoliberal Age*, edited by Bram Büscher, Wolfram Dressler, and Robert Fletcher, 183–204. Tucson: University of Arizona Press, 2014.

———. "Nature 2.0: Exploring and Theorizing the Links between New Media and Nature Conservation." *New Media and Society* 18, no. 5 (2016): 726–743.

Büscher, Bram, Wolfram Dressler, and Robert Fletcher, eds. *Nature™ Inc: New Frontiers of Environmental Conservation in the Neoliberal Age*. Tucson: University of Arizona Press, 2014.

Büscher, Bram, and Robert Fletcher. "Accumulation by Conservation." *New Political Economy* 20, no. 2 (2015): 273–298.

———. Under Pressure: Conceptualising Political Ecologies of Green Wars. *Conservation and Society* 16, no. 2 (2018): 105–113.

———. *The Conservation Revolution: Radical Ideas for Saving Nature beyond the Capitalocene*. London: Verso, 2020.

Büscher, Bram, and Jim Igoe. "'Prosuming' Conservation? Web 2.0, Nature and the Intensification of Value-Producing Labour in Late Capitalism." *Journal of Consumer Culture* 13, no. 3 (2013): 283–305.

Büscher, Bram, and Maano Ramutsindela. "Green Violence: Rhino Poaching and the War to Save Southern Africa's Peace Parks." *African Affairs* 115, no. 458 (2016): 1–22.

Butler, G., and S. Richardson. 2015. "Barriers to Visiting South Africa's National Parks in the Post-apartheid Era: Black South African Perspectives from Soweto" *Journal of Sustainable Tourism* 23(1): 146–166

Candea, Matei. "'I fell in love with Carlos the meerkat': Engagement and Detachment in Human–Animal Relations." *American Ethnologist* 37, no. 2 (2010): 241–258.

Carolan, Michael. "Society, Biology, and Ecology: Bringing Nature Back into Sociology's Disciplinary Narrative through Critical Realism." *Organization & Environment* 18 (2005): 393–421.

———. "The Problems with Patents: A Less Than Optimistic Reading of the Future." *Development and Change* 40, no. 2 (2009): 361–388.

Carruthers, Jane. "Creating a National Park, 1910 to 1926." *Journal of Southern African Studies* 15, no 2 (1989): 188–216.

———. The *Kruger National Park. A Social and Political History*. Pietermaritzburg: University of Natal Press, 1995.

Castells, Manuel. *The Rise of the Network Society*. Malden, MA: Blackwell, 2000.

Castree, Noel. "Commodifying What Nature?" *Progress in Human Geography* 27, no. 3 (2003): 273–297.

———. *Making Sense of Nature*. London: Routledge, 2014.

Castree, Noel, and Bruce Braun, eds. *Social Nature: Theory, Practice and Politics*. Oxford: Blackwell, 2001.

Cavanagh, Connor. "Political Ecologies of Biopower: Diversity, Debates, and New Frontiers of Inquiry." *Journal of Political Ecology* 25 (2018): 402–425.

CBD. *Global Biodiversity Outlook 4*. Montreal: CBD Secretariat, 2014.

Ceballos, Gerardo, Paul Ehrlich, and Rodolfo Dirzo. "Biological Annihilation via the Ongoing Sixth Mass Extinction Signaled by Vertebrate Population Losses and Declines." *PNAS* 114, no. 30 (2017): E6089–E6096.

Checker, Melissa. "Stop FEMA Now: Social Media, Activism and the Sacrificed Citizen." *Geoforum* 79 (2017): 124–133.

Chris, Cynthia. *Watching Wildlife*. Minneapolis: University of Minnesota Press, 2006.

Clough, Nathan. "Emotion at the Center of Radical Politics: On the Affective Structures of Rebellion and Control." *Antipode* 44, no 5 (2012): 1667–1686.

Cooper, Melissa. *Life as Surplus: Biotechnology and Capitalism in the Neoliberal Era.* Seattle: University of Washington Press, 2008.

Corson, C., K. I. MacDonald, and B. Neimark. "Grabbing Green." Special issue. *Human Geography*, 6, no. 1 (2013).

Coté, Mark, and Jennifer Pybus. "Learning to Immaterial Labour 2.0: MySpace and Social Networks." *Ephemera* 7, no. 1 (2007): 88–106.

Crawford, K. "Emergency Environmentalism: On Fear, Lifestyle Politics and Subjectivity." *Angelaki. Journal of the Theoretical Humanities* 14, no. 2 (2009): 29–35.

Cronon, William. "The Trouble with Wilderness." In *Uncommon Ground*, edited by William Cronon, 69–90. New York: W.W. Norton, 1995.

Dean, Jodi. "Communicative Capitalism: Circulation and the Foreclosure of Politics." *Cultural Politics* 1, no. 1 (2005): 51–74.

———. *Blog Theory. Feedback and Capture in the Circuits of Drive.* London: Polity Press, 2010.

Debord, Guy. *Society of the Spectacle.* London: Rebel Press, 1967.

Demmers, Jolle. "Neoliberal Discourses on Violence: Monstrosity and Rape in Borderland Wars." In *Gender, Globalisation and Violence: Postcolonial Conflict Zones*, edited by Sandra Ponzanesi, 27–44. London: Routledge, 2014.

DeMotts, Rachel, and Parak Hoon. "Whose Elephants? Conserving, Compensating, and Competing in Northern Botswana." *Society & Natural Resources* 25, no. 9 (2012): 837–851.

Descola, Philippe, and Gisli Pálsson. "Introduction." In *Nature and Society. Anthropological Perspectives*, edited by Philippe Descola and Gisli Pálsson, 1–21. London: Routledge, 2016.

Deuze, Mark. *Mediawork.* Cambridge: Polity Press, 2007.

Dinerstein, Eric, David Olson, Anup Joshi, Carly Vynne, Neil Burgess, Eric Wikramanayake, Nathan Hahn, Suzanne Palminteri, Prashant Hedao, Reed Noss, et al. "An Ecoregion-Based Approach to Protecting Half the Terrestrial Realm." *BioScience* 67, no. 6 (2017): 534–545.

Dlamini, Jacob. *Safari Nation: A Social History of the Kruger National Park.* Athens: Ohio University Press.

Dourish, Paul, and Genevieve Bell. *Divining a Digital Future: Mess and Mythology in Ubiquitous Computing.* Cambridge, MA: MIT Press, 2011.

Dressler, Wolfram, and Bram Büscher. "Market Triumphalism and the So-Called CBNRM 'Crisis' at the South African Section of the Great Limpopo Transfrontier Park." *Geoforum* 39, no. 1 (2008): 452–465.

Dressler, Wolfram, Bram Büscher, Michael Schoon, Dan Brockington, Tania Hayes, Christian Kull, James McCarthy, and Krishna Streshta. "From Hope to Crisis and Back? A Critical History of the Global CBNRM Narrative." *Environmental Conservation* 37, no. 1 (2010): 5–15.

Duffy, Rosaleen. "Waging a War to Save Biodiversity: The Rise of Militarized Conservation." *International Affairs* 90, no. 4 (2014): 819–834.

Duffy, Rosaleen, Richard Emslie, and Michael Knight. *Rhino Poaching: How Do We Respond?* London: Evidence on Demand, 2013.

Elliot, Nils Lindahl. *Mediating Nature*. London: Routledge, 2006.

Extinction Rebellion. 2019. *This Is Not a Drill. An Extinction Rebellion Handbook*. London: Penguin.

Farman, Jason. *Mobile Interface Theory: Embodied Space and Locative Media*. London: Routledge, 2012.

Farrell, Nathan. "'Conscience Capitalism' and the Neoliberalisation of the Non-Profit Sector." *New Political Economy* 20, no. 2 (2015): 254–272.

Ferguson, James. *The Anti-Politics Machine: "Development," Depoliticization and Bureaucratic Power in Lesotho*. Minneapolis: University of Minnesota Press, 1994.

Fisher, Eran. *Media and New Capitalism in the Digital Age*. New York: Palgrave Macmillan, 2010.

Fletcher, Robert. "Orchestrating Consent: Post-politics and Intensification of Nature™ Inc. at the 2012 World Conservation Congress." *Conservation and Society* 12, no. 3 (2014): 329–342.

———. "Gaming Conservation: Nature 2.0 Confronts Nature-Deficit Disorder." *Geoforum* 79 (2017): 153–162.

Fletcher, Robert, Jan Breitling, and Valerie Puleo. "Barbarian Hordes: The Overpopulation Scapegoat in International Development Discourse." *Third World Quarterly* 35, no.7 (2014): 79–99.

Fletcher, Robert, and Bram Büscher. "The PES Conceit. Revisiting the Relationship between Payments for Environmental Services and Neoliberal Conservation." *Ecological Economics* 132 (2017): 224–231

Foucault, Michel. *Power/Knowledge: Selected Interviews and Other Writings 1972–1977*. New York: Vintage Books, 1980.

———. *The Courage of Truth. Lectures at the Collège de France 1983–1984*. New York: Picador, 2008.

Frankfurt, Harry. *On Bullshit*. Princeton, NJ: Princeton University Press, 2005.

———. *On Truth*. New York: Alfred A. Knopf, 2017.

Fraser, Caroline. "Tapping Social Media's Potential to Muster a Vast Green Army." *Environment360*, online magazine, Yale University, 2011.

Fujimura, Joan, and Christopher Holmes. "Staying the Course: On the Value of Social Studies of Science in Resistance to the "Post-Truth" Movement." *Sociological Forum* 34, no. S1 (2019): 1251–1263.

Gabrys, Jennifer. *Digital Rubbish. A Natural History of Electronics*. Ann Arbor: University of Michigan Press, 2013.

———. *Program Earth: Environmental Sensing Technology and the Making of a Computational Planet*. Minneapolis: University of Minnesota Press, 2016.

Gehl, Robert. "The Archive and the Processor: The Internal Logic of Web 2.0." *New Media & Society* 13, no. 8 (2011): 1228–1244.

Gerlitz, Carolin, and Anne Helmond. "The Like Economy: Social Buttons and the Data-Intensive Web." *New Media & Society* 15, no. 8 (2013): 1348–1365.

Gillespie, Tarleton. "The Politics of 'Platforms.'" *New Media & Society* 12, no. 3 (2010): 347–364.

———. "The Relevance of Algorithms." In *Media Technologies: Essays on Communication, Materiality, and Society*, edited by Tarleton Gillespie, Pablo Boczkowski, and Kirsten Foot, 167–194. Cambridge, MA: MIT Press, 2014.

Giraud, Eva Haifa. *What Comes after Entanglement? Activism, Anthropocentrism, and an Ethics of Exclusion.* Durham, NC: Duke University Press, 2019.

Giraud, Eva Haifa, and Sarah-Nicole Aghassi-Isfahani. "Post-Truths, Common Worlds, and Critical Politics: Critiquing Bruno Latour's Renewed Critique of Critique." *Cultural Politics* 16, no. 1 (2020).

Gitelman, Lisa. *Always Already New. Media, History and the Data of Culture.* Cambridge, MA: MIT Press, 2006.

Goldman, Mara. "Constructing Connectivity? Conservation Corridors and Conservation Politics in East African Rangelands." *Annals of the Association of American Geographers* 99, no. 2 (2009): 335–359.

Goldman Robert. "Contradictions in a Political Economy of Sign Value." *Current Perspectives in Social Theory* 14 (1994): 183–211.

Goldman, Robert, and Stephen Papson. *Landscapes of Capital.* Cambridge: Polity Press, 2011.

Goodman, Michael, Jo Littler, Dan Brockington, and Maxwell Boykoff. "Spectacular Environmentalisms: Media, Knowledge and the Framing of Ecological Politics." *Environmental Communication* 10, no. 6 (2016): 677–688.

Green, Leslie, ed. *Contested Ecologies: Dialogues in the South on Nature and Knowledge.* Pretoria: HSRC Press, 2013.

Han, Byung-Chul. *The Transparency Society.* Stanford, CA: Stanford University Press, 2015.

———. *Psycho-Politics: Neoliberalism and New Technologies of Power.* London: Verso, 2017.

Hannan, Jason. "Trolling Ourselves to Death? Social Media and Post-truth Politics." *European Journal of Communication* 33, no. 2 (2018): 214–226.

Haraway, Donna. *Primate Visions: Gender, Race, and Nature in the World of Modern Science.* London: Routledge, 1989.

Harris, Peter. "Fortress, Safe Haven or Home? The Chagos MPA in Political Context." *Marine Policy* 46 (2014): 19–21.

Hartnack, Andrew. "Whiteness and Shades of Grey: Erasure, Amnesia and the Ethnography of Zimbabwe's Whites." *Journal of Contemporary African Studies* 33, no. 2 (2014): 285–299.

Harvey, David. *Justice, Nature and the Geography of Difference.* Cambridge: Blackwell, 1996.

———. *Spaces of Global Capitalism: Towards a Theory of Uneven Geographical Development.* London: Verso, 2006.

———. *The Enigma of Capital and the Crises of Capitalism.* Oxford: Oxford University Press, 2010.

———. 2014. *Seventeen Contradictions and the End of Capitalism.* London: Profile Books.

Hawken, Paul. *Blessed Unrest: How the Largest Social Movement in History Is Restoring Grace, Justice, and Beauty to the World.* London: Penguin, 2007.

Hawkins, Roberta, and Jennifer Silver. "From Selfie to #Sealfie: Nature 2.0 and the Digital Cultural Politics of an Internationally Contested Resource." *Geoforum* 79 (2017): 114–123.

Heise, Ursula. *Imagining Extinction: The Cultural Meanings of Endangered Species.* Chicago: University of Chicago Press, 2016.

Hillis, Ken. *Digital Sensations: Space, Identity, and Embodiment in Virtual Reality*. Minneapolis: University of Minnesota Press, 1999.

Holmes, George. "Exploring the Relationship between Local Support and the Success of Protected Areas." *Conservation and Society* 13, no. 1 (2013): 72–82.

Horkheimer, Max, and Theodor Adorno. *Dialectic of Enlightenment. Philosophical Fragments*. Stanford, CA: Stanford University Press, 2002.

Hughes, David. *Whiteness in Zimbabwe: Race, Landscape, and the Problem of Belonging*. New York: Palgrave, 2010.

Humphreys, Jaspar, and Michael Smith. 2014. "The 'Rhinofication' of South African Security." *International Affairs* 90, no. 4 (2014): 795–818.

Hutton, Jon, William M. Adams, and James C. Murombedzi. "Back to the Barriers? Changing Narratives in Biodiversity Conservation." *Forum for Development Studies* 32, no. 2 (2005): 341–370.

Igoe, Jim. *Conservation and Globalization: A Study of National Parks and Indigenous Communities from East Africa to South Dakota*. Riverside, CA: Wadsworth, 2004.

———. "The Spectacle of Nature in the Global Economy of Appearances: Anthropological Engagements with the Spectacular Mediations of Transnational Conservation." *Critique of Anthropology* 30, no. 4 (2010): 375–397.

———. "Consume, Connect, Conserve: Consumer Spectacle and the Technical Mediation of Neoliberal Conservation's Aesthetic of Redemption and Repair." *Human Geography* 6, no. 1 (2013): 16–28.

———. *The Nature of Spectacle: On Images, Money, and Conserving Capitalism*. Tucson: University of Arizona Press, 2017.

IPBES (Intergovernmental Science-Policy Platform on Biodiversity and Ecosystem Services). *Global Assessment Report on Biodiversity and Ecosystem Services*. Bonn: IPBES, 2019.

Iyengar, Shanto, and Douglas Massey. "Scientific Communication in a Post-Truth Society." *PNAS* 116, no.16 (2019): 7656–7661.

Jasanoff, Sheila, ed. *States of Knowledge: The Co-production of Science and Social Order*. London: Routledge, 2006.

Jasanoff, Sheila, and Hilton Simmet. "No Funeral Bells: Public Reason in a 'Post-truth' Age." *Social Studies of Science* 47, no. 5 (2017): 751–770.

Jeffries, Michael. "BBC Natural History versus Science Paradigms." *Science as Culture* 12, no. 4 (2003): 527–545.

Kamphof, Ike. "Linking Animal and Human Places: The Potential of Webcams for Species Companionship." *Animal Studies Journal* 2, no. 1 (2013): 82–102.

Kang, Jaeho. *Walter Benjamin and the Media*. Cambridge: Polity Press, 2014.

Karatzogianni, Athina, and Adi Kuntsman. *Digital Cultures and the Politics of Emotion. Feelings, Affect and Technological Change*. Basingstoke, UK: Palgrave, 2012.

Kepe, Thembela. "Shaped by Race: Why "Race" Still Matters in the Challenges Facing Biodiversity Conservation in Africa." *Local Environment* 14, no. 9 (2009): 871–878.

———. "Globalization, Science, and the Making of an Environmental Discourse on the Wild Coast, South Africa." *Environment and Planning A* 46, no. 9 (2014): 2143–2159.

Keyes, Ralph. *The Post-Truth Era: Dishonesty and Deception in Contemporary Life*. New York: St. Martin's Press, 2004.

Kitchin, Rob. "Big Data, New Epistemologies and Paradigm Shifts." *Big Data & Society* April–June (2014): 1–12.

Klein, Naomi. *This Changes Everything: Capitalism vs. the Climate*. London: Allen Lane, 2014.

Kolbert, Elizabeth. *The Sixth Extinction: An Unnatural History*. London: Bloomsbury, 2014.

Kuntsman, Adi. "Introduction: Affective Fabrics of Digital Cultures." In *Digital Cultures and the Politics of Emotion. Feelings, Affect and Technological Change*, edited by Athina Karatzogianni and Adi Kuntsman, 1–20. Basingstoke, UK: Palgrave, 2012.

Laclau, Ernesto, and Chantal Mouffe. *Hegemony and Socialist Strategy: Towards a Radical Democratic Politics*. London: Verso, 1985.

Langley, Paul, and Andrew Leyshon. "Platform Capitalism: The Intermediation and Capitalisation of Digital Economic Circulation." *Finance and Society* 3, no. 1 (2016): 11–31.

Latour, Bruno. *The Pasteurization of France*. Cambridge, MA: Harvard University Press, 1988.

———. *Reassembling the Social. An Introduction to Actor-Network-Theory*. Oxford: Oxford University Press, 2005.

Lee, Peter. *Truth Wars: The Politics of Climate Change, Military Intervention and Financial Crisis*. New York: Palgrave Macmillan, 2015.

Lejano, Raul, Mrill Ingram, and Helen Ingram. *The Power of Narrative in Environmental Networks*. Cambridge, MA: MIT Press, 2013.

Lepore, Jill. *These Truths. A History of the United States*. New York: W.W. Norton & Company, 2018.

Levitt, James. *Conservation in the Internet Age*. Washington, DC: Island Press, 2002.

Lewis, David, Anthony Bebbington, Simon Batterbury, Alpa Shah, Elizabeth Olson, M. Shameem Siddiqi, and Sandra Duvall. "Practice, Power and Meaning: Frameworks for Studying Organizational Culture in Multi-Agency Rural Development Projects." *Journal of International Development* 15, no. 5 (2003): 541–557.

Lewis, David, and David Mosse. *Development Brokers and Translators: The Ethnography of Aid Agencies*. Bloomfield, CT: Kumarian Press, 2006.

Li, Tania. *The Will to Improve. Governmentality, Development, and the Practice of Politics*. Durham, NC: Duke University Press, 2007.

Locke, Harvey. "Green Postmodernism and the Attempted Highjacking of Conservation." In *Keeping the Wild: Against the Domestication of Earth*, edited by George Wuerthner, Eileen Crist and Tom Butler, 146–161. New York: Island Press, 2014.

Loftus, Alex. *Everyday Environmentalism: Creating an Urban Political Ecology*. Minneapolis: University of Minnesota Press, 2012.

Lorimer, Jamie. *Wildlife in the Anthropocene: Conservation after Nature*. Minneapolis: University of Minnesota Press, 2015.

Lorimer Jamie, and Sarah Whatmore. "After the 'King of Beasts': Samuel Baker and the Embodied Historical Geographies of Elephant Hunting in Mid-Nineteenth-Century Ceylon." *Journal of Historical Geography* 35, no. 4 (2009): 668–689.

Louw, Pat. "Nature Documentaries: Eco-tainment? The Case of MM&M (Mad Mike and Mark)." *Current Writing* 18, no. 1 (2006): 146–162.

Lovink, Geert. *Networks without a Cause: A Critique of Social Media*. Cambridge: Polity Press, 2011.

Lunstrum, Elizabeth. "Green Militarization: Anti-Poaching Efforts and the Spatial Contours of Kruger National Park." *Annals of the American Association of Geographers* 104, no. 4 (2014): 816–832.

Maguranyanga, Brian. "'Our Battles Also Changed': Transformation and Black Empowerment in South African National Parks, 1991–2008." PhD thesis, University of Michigan, 2009.

Malm, Andreas. *The Progress of This Storm: Society and Nature in a Warming World*. London: Verso, 2018.

Marazzi, Christian. *Capital and Affects: The Politics of the Language Economy*. Los Angeles: Semiotext(e), 2011.

Marres, Noortje. "Why We Can't Have Our Facts Back." *Engaging Science, Technology, and Society* 4 (2018): 423–443.

Marris, Emma. *Rambunctious Garden: Saving Nature in a Post-Wild World*. New York: Bloomsbury, 2011.

Marvier, Michelle, Peter Kareiva, and Robert Lalasz. "Conservation in the Anthropocene: beyond Solitude and Fragility." *Breakthrough Journal* 2 (2011): http://thebreakthrough.org/index.php/journal/past-issues/issue-2/conservation-in-the-anthropocene/.

Marx, Karl. *Capital. Volume I*. London: Penguin Books, 1976.

Massé, Francis. "Anti-poaching's Politics of (In)visibility: Representing Nature and Conservation amidst a Poaching Crisis." *Geoforum* 98 (2019): 1–14.

Massumi, Brian. *99 Theses on the Revaluation of Value: A Postcapitalist Manifesto*. Minneapolis: University of Minnesota Press, 2018.

Mbaria, John, and Mordecai Ogada. *The Big Conservation Lie: The Untold Story of Wildlife Conservation in Kenya*. Auburn, WA: Lens&Pens, 2017.

McAfee, Kathleen. "Selling Nature to Save It? Biodiversity and Green Developmentalism." *Society and Space* 17, no. 2 (1999): 203–219.

McKibben, Bill. "A Bad Day for the Environment, with Many More to Come." *New Yorker*, 18 August, 2017. Online: https://www.newyorker.com/news/news-desk/a-bad-day-for-the-environment-with-many-more-to-come.

McLuhan, Marshall. *Understanding Media: The Extensions of Man*. Cambridge, MA: MIT Press, 1964.

Meadows, Donella, Dennis Meadows, Jørgen Randers, and William Behrens III. *The Limits to Growth*. New York: Universe Books, 1972.

Medina, José, and David Wood, eds. *Truth: Engagements across Philosophical Traditions*. Oxford: Blackwell, 2005.

Merchant, Carolyn. *The Death of Nature: Women, Ecology and the Scientific Revolution.* New York: HarperOne, 1983.

Merrifield, Andy. *Magical Marxism: Subversive Politics and the Imagination.* London: Pluto, 2011.

Metcalfe, Simon, and Thembela Kepe. "'Your Elephant on Our Land': The Struggle to Manage Wildlife Mobility on Zambian Communal Land in the Kavango-Zambezi Transfrontier Conservation Area." *Journal of Environment & Development* 17, no. 2 (2008): 99–117.

Miller, Brian, Michael Soulé, and John Terborgh. "'New Conservation' or Surrender to Development?" *Animal Conservation* 17, no. 6 (2014): 509–515.

Milliken, Tom, and Jo Shaw. *The South Africa–Viet Nam Rhino Horn Trade Nexus: A Deadly Combination of Institutional Lapses, Corrupt Wildlife Industry Professionals and Asian Crime Syndicates.* Johannesburg: Traffic, 2012.

Milne, Sarah, and William Adams. "Market Masquerades: The Politics of Community-Level Payments for Environmental Services in Cambodia." *Development and Change* 43, no. 1 (2012): 133–158.

Mitman, Gregg. *Reel Nature: America's Romance with Wildlife on Film.* Seattle: University of Washington Press, 1999.

Mogomotsi, Goemeone, and Patricia Madigele. "Live by the Gun, Die by the Gun. Botswana's 'Shoot-to-Kill' Policy as an Anti-poaching Strategy." *South Africa Crime Quarterly* 60 (2017): 51–59.

Moore, Donald. *Suffering for Territory. Race, Place, and Power in Zimbabwe.* Durham, NC: Duke University Press, 2005.

Moore, Jason W. *Capitalism in the Web of Life: Ecology and the Accumulation of Capital.* London: Verso, 2015.

Mosse, David. "Is Good Policy Unimplementable? Reflections on the Ethnography of Aid Policy and Practice." *Development and Change* 35, no. 4 (2004): 639–671.

Mouffe, Chantal. *On the Political.* London: Routledge, 2005.

Muradian, Roldan, Mariana Walter, and Joan Martinez-Allier. "Hegemonic Transitions and Global Shifts in Social Metabolism: Implications for Resource-Rich Countries. Introduction to the Special Section." *Global Environmental Change* 22, no. 3 (2012): 559–567.

Nealon, Jeffrey. *Foucault beyond Foucault: Power and Its Intensification since 1984.* Stanford, CA: Stanford University Press, 2008.

Nelson, Robert. "Environmental Colonialism: 'Saving Africa from Africans.'" *The Independent Review* 8, no. 1 (2003): 65–86.

Neumann, Roderick. *Imposing Wilderness: Struggles over Livelihoods and Nature Preservation in Africa.* Berkeley: University of California Press, 1998.

———. "Moral and Discursive Geographies in the War for Biodiversity in Africa." *Political Geography* 23, no. 7 (2004): 813–837.

———. *Making Political Ecology.* London: Hodder Arnold, 2005.

Newbold, Tim, Lawrence Hudson, Andrew Arnell, Sara Contu, Adriana De Palma, Simon Ferrier, Samantha Hill, Andrew Hoskins, Igor Lysenko, Helen Phillips, et al. "Has Land Use Pushed Terrestrial Biodiversity beyond the

Planetary Boundary? A Global Assessment." *Science* 353, no. 6296 (2016): 288–291.

Nitzan, Jonathan, and Shimshon Bichler. *Capital as Power: A Study of Order and Creorder*. London: Routledge, 2009.

Noss, Reed, Andrew Dobson, Robert Baldwin, Paul Beier, Cory Davis, Dominick Dellasala, John Francis, Harvey Locke, Katarzyna Nowak, Roel Lopez, et al. "Bolder Thinking for Conservation." *Conservation Biology* 26, no. 1 (2012): 1–4.

Nustad, Knut. *Creating Africas. Struggles over Nature, Conservation and Land*. London: Hurst & Company, 2015.

Oates, John F. *Myth and Reality in the Rain Forest: How Conservation Strategies Are Failing in West Africa*. Berkeley: University of California Press, 1999.

Oreskes, Naomi. *Why Trust Science?* Princeton, NJ: Princeton University Press, 2019.

Oreskes, Naomi, and Eric Conway. *Merchants of Doubt: How a Handful of Scientists Obscured the Truth of Issues from Tobacco Smoke to Global Warming*. New York: Bloomsbury, 2010.

Ostrom, Elinor. *Governing the Commons: The Evolution of Institutions for Collective Action*. Cambridge: Cambridge University Press, 1990.

Palliser, Anna, and Giles Dodson. "Avoiding Post-truth Environmental Conflict in New Zealand: Communicating Uncertainties in Endangered Species Science." *Journal of Science Communication* 18, no. 4 (2019): A05.

Papacharissi, Zizi. "The Virtual Sphere: The Internet as a Public Sphere." *New Media & Society* 4, no. 1 (2002): 9–27.

———. *A Private Sphere: Democracy in the Digital Age*. Cambridge: Polity, 2010.

Pasquale, Franck. *The Black Box Society: The Secret Algorithms That Control Money and Information*. Cambridge, MA: Harvard University Press, 2014.

Peluso, Nancy. "Coercing Conservation? The Politics of State Resource Control." *Global Environmental Change* 3, no. 2 (1993): 199–218.

———. "What's Nature Got to Do with It? A Situated Historical Perspective on Socio-natural Commodities." *Development and Change* 43, no. 1 (2012): 79–104.

Perrault, Tom, Gavin Bridge, and James McCarthy, eds. *The Routledge Handbook of Political Ecology*. London: Routledge, 2015.

Pettman, Dominic. *Infinite Distraction*. Cambridge: Polity, 2017.

Pickerill, Jenny. *Cyberprotest: Environmental Activism Online*. Manchester: Manchester University Press, 2003.

Player, Ian. *The White Rhino Saga*. Johannesburg: Jonathan Ball, 2013.

Poovey, Mary. *A History of the Modern Fact: Problems of Knowledge in the Sciences of Wealth and Society*. Chicago: Chicago University Press, 1998.

Poster, Mark. *What's the Matter with the Internet?* Minneapolis: University of Minnesota Press, 2001.

Proctor, James. "Solid Rock and Shifting Sands: The Moral Paradox of Saving a Socially Constructed Nature." In *Social Nature: Theory, Practice and Politics*, edited by Noel Castree and Bruce Braun, 225–239. Oxford: Blackwell, 2001.

Prudham, Scott. "Pimping Climate Change: Richard Branson, Global Warming, and the Performance of Green Capitalism." *Environment and Planning A* 41 (2009): 1594–1613.

Purdy, Jedediah. *After Nature: A Politics for the Anthropocene.* Cambridge, MA: Harvard University Press, 2015.

Quarles van Ufford, Philip. "The Hidden Crisis in Development: Development Bureaucracies in between Intentions and Outcomes." In *The Hidden Crisis in Development: Development Bureaucracies*, edited by Philip Quarles van Ufford, Dirk Kruijt, and Theodore Downing, 9–38. Amsterdam: VU University Press, 1988.

Quarles van Ufford, Philip, and Anta Kumar Giri, eds. *A Moral Critique of Development: In Search of Global Responsibilities.* London: Routledge, 2003.

Rademeyer, Julian. *Killing for Profit: Exposing the Illegal Rhino Horn Trade.* Cape Town: Zebra Press, 2012.

Ramutsindela, Maano. *Transfrontier Conservation in Africa: At the Confluence of Capital, Politics and Nature.* Wallingford: CABI, 2007.

Ramutsindela, Maano, and Medupi Shabangu. "Conditioned by Neoliberalism: A Reassessment of Land Claim Resolutions in the Kruger National Park." *Journal of Contemporary African Studies* 31, no. 3 (2013): 441–456.

Rijsdijk, Ian-Malcolm. "Between a Croc and a Herd Place: Battle at Kruger and Nature Interpretation." *Communicatio* 36, no. 3 (2010): 359–370.

Ritzer, George, and Nathan Jurgenson. "Production, Consumption, Prosumption: The Nature of Capitalism in the Age of the Digital 'Prosumer.'" *Journal of Consumer Culture* 10, no. 3 (2010): 13–36.

Robertson, Morgan. "The Nature That Capital Can See: Science, State, and Market in the Commodification of Ecosystem Services." *Society and Space*, 24, no. 3 (2006): 367–387.

Rogerson, Chris. "Transforming the South African Tourism Industry: The Emerging Black-Owned Bed and Breakfast Economy." *GeoJournal* 60 (2004): 273–281.

Rouvroy, Antoinette. "Algorithmic Governmentality and the End(s) of Critique." Presentation at *Society of the Query* #2, 13 November 2013.

Rouvroy, Antoinette, and Bernard Stiegler. "The Digital Regime of Truth: From the Algorithmic Governmentality to a New Rule of Law." *La Deleuziana—Online Journal of Philosophy* 3 (2016): 6–29.

Sadowski, Jathan. "When Data Is Capital: Datafication, Accumulation, and Extraction." *Big Data & Society* 6, no. 1 (2019): 1–12.

Sandbrook, Chris, William Adams, Bram Büscher, and Bhaskar Vira. "Social Research and Biodiversity Conservation." *Conservation Biology* 27, no. 6 (2013): 1487–1490.

Sandbrook, Chris, Janet Fisher, and Bhaskar Vira. "What Do Conservationists Think about Markets?" *Geoforum* 50 (2013): 232–240.

Sandbrook, Chris, William Adams, and Bruno Monteferri. "Digital Games and Biodiversity Conservation." *Conservation Letters* 8, no. 2 (2015): 118–124.

SANParks. *Coordinated Policy Framework Governing Park Management Plans.* Pretoria: SANParks, 2006.

Schulte, Stephanie Ricker. *Cached: Decoding the Internet in Global Popular Culture*. New York: New York University Press, 2013.

Schurman, Rachel, and Dennis Kelso. *Engineering Trouble: Biotechnology and Its Discontents*. Berkeley: University of California Press, 2003.

Scott, Karen. "Popularizing Science and Nature Programming: The Role of 'Spectacle' in Contemporary Wildlife Documentary." *Journal of Popular Film and Television* 31, no. 1 (2003): 29–35.

Scull, Andrew. *Hysteria: The Biography*. Oxford: Oxford University Press, 2009.

Seekings, Jeremy. "The Continuing Salience of Race: Discrimination and Diversity in South Africa." *Journal of Contemporary African Studies* 26, no. 1 (2008): 1–25.

Shapin, Steven. *A Social History of Truth: Civility and Science in Seventeenth-Century England*. Chicago: Chicago University Press, 1994.

Sismondo, Sergio. "Post-Truth?" *Social Studies of Science* 47, no. 1 (2017): 3–6.

Smith, Neil. "The Revolutionary Imperative." *Antipode* 41, no. S1 (2010): 50–65.

Soulé, Michael. "The "New Conservation." *Conservation Biology* 27, no. 5 (2014): 895–897.

Soulé, Michael, and Gary Lease, eds. *Reinventing Nature. Responses to Postmodern Deconstruction*. Washington, DC: Island Press, 1995.

Spierenburg, Marja, and Harry Wells. "Conservative Philanthropists, Royalty and Business Elites in Nature Conservation in Southern Africa." *Antipode* 42, no. 3 (2010): 647–70.

Srnicek, Nick. *Platform Capitalism*. Cambridge: Polity Press, 2017.

Steyn, Melissa. *Whiteness Just Isn't What It Used to Be: White Identity in a Changing South Africa* Albany: State University of New York Press, 2001.

Steyn, Melissa, and Don Foster. "Repertoires for Talking White: Resistant Whiteness in Post-Apartheid South Africa." *Ethnic and Racial Studies* 31, no. 1 (2008): 25–51.

Stinson, James. "Re-creating Wilderness 2.0: Or Getting Back to Work in a Virtual Nature." *Geoforum* 79 (2017): 174–187.

Sullivan, Sian. "Banking Nature? The Spectacular Financialisation of Environmental Conservation." *Antipode* 45, no. 1 (2013): 198–217.

———. "The Natural Capital Myth; or Will Accounting Save the World? Preliminary Thoughts on Nature, Finance and Values." LCSV Working Paper Series no 3. Manchester: LCSV, 2014.

———. "Beyond the Money Shot; or How Framing Nature Matters? Locating Green at Wildscreen." *Environmental Communication* 10, no. 6 (2016): 749–762.

———. "Towards a Metaphysics of the Soul and a Participatory Aesthetics of Life: Mobilising Foucault, Affect and Animism for Caring Practices of Existence." *New Formations* 95 (2019): 5–21.

Sundberg, Juanita. "Diabolic Caminos in the Desert and Cat Fights on the Río: A Posthumanist Political Ecology of Boundary Enforcement in the United States–Mexico Borderlands." *Annals of the Association of American Geographers* 101, no. 2 (2011): 318–36.

Sutherland, William, and Claire Wordley. "Evidence Complacency Hampers Conservation." *Nature Ecology and Evolution* 1 (2017): 1215–1216.

Svarstad, Hanne, Tor Benjaminsen, and Ragnhild Overå. "Power Theories in Political Ecology." *Journal of Political Ecology* 25 (2018): 350–363.

Swyngedouw, Erik, and Henrik Ernston. "Interrupting the Anthropo-obScene: Immuno-biopolitics and Depoliticizing Ontologies in the Anthropocene." *Theory, Culture & Society* 35, no. 6 (2018): 3–30.

Tapela, Barbara, and P. Omara-Ojungu. "Towards Bridging the Gap between Wildlife Conservation and Rural Development in Post-Apartheid South Africa: The Case of the Makuleke Community and the Kruger National Park." *South African Geographical Journal* 81, no. 3 (2012): 148–155.

Thomas, Chris. *Inheritors of the Earth. How Nature Is Thriving in the Age of Extinction*. London: Allen Lane.

Tinnell, John. "Scripting Just Sustainability: Through Green Listing towards Eco-Blogging." *Environmental Education* 5, no. 2 (2011): 228–242.

Turner, Graham. *Is Global Collapse Imminent?* MSSI Research Paper No. 4, Melbourne Sustainable Society Institute, The University of Melbourne, 2014.

Turnhout, Esther. "The Politics of Environmental Knowledge." *Conservation and Society* 16, no. 3 (2018): 363–371.

Turnhout, Esther, Katja Neves, and Elisa de Lijster. "'Measurementality' in Biodiversity Governance: Knowledge, Transparency, and the Intergovernmental Science–Policy Platform on Biodiversity and Ecosystem Services (IPBES)." *Environment and Planning A* 46, no. 3 (2014): 581–597.

UNEP. *UNEP Yearbook: Emerging Issues in our Global Environment 2014*. Nairobi: UNEP, 2014.

Unterhalter, Elaine. "The Work of the Nation: Heroic Masculinity in South African Autobiographical Writing of the Anti-apartheid Struggle." *European Journal of Development Research* 12, no. 2 (2000): 157–178.

Van Dijck, José. *The Culture of Connectivity: A Critical History of Social Media*. Oxford: Oxford University Press, 2013.

Vigh, Henrik, and David Sausdal. "From Essence Back to Existence: Anthropology beyond the Ontological Turn." *Anthropological Theory* 14, no. 1 (2014): 49–73.

Waisbord, Silvio. "The Elective Affinity between Post-Truth Communication and Populist Politics." *Communication Research and Practice* 4, no. 1 (2018): 17–34.

Wajcman, Gérard. "The Animals That Treat Us Badly." *Lacanian Ink* 33 (2009): 126–145.

Wajcman, Judy. *Pressed for Time: The Acceleration of Life in Digital Capitalism*. Chicago: Chicago University Press, 2015.

Wapner, Paul. *Living through the End of Nature: The Future of American Environmentalism*. Cambridge, MA: MIT Press, 2010.

Ward, Steven. *Reconfiguring Truth. Postmodernism, Science Studies, and the Search for a New Model of Knowledge*. Lanham, MD: Rowman & Littlefield, 1996.

Watson, James, Danielle Shanahan, Moreno Di Marco, James Allan, William Laurance, Eric Sanderson, Brendan MacKey, and Oscar Venter. "Catastrophic

Declines in Wilderness Areas Undermine Global Environment Targets." *Current Biology* 26, no. 21 (2016): 2929–2934.

Weeks, Priscilla. "Cyber-Activism: World Wildlife Fund's Campaign to Save the Tiger." *Culture & Agriculture* 21, no. 3 (1999): 19–30.

Werbach, Kevin. *The Blockchain and the New Architecture of Trust.* Cambridge, MA: MIT Press, 2018.

West, Paige. *Dispossession and the Environment. Rhetoric and Inequality in Papua New Guinea.* New York: Columbia University Press, 2016.

White, Damian, and Chris Wilbert. "Introduction: Inhabiting Technonatural Time/Spaces." In *Technonatures: Environments, Technologies, Spaces, and Places in the Twenty-First Century,* edited by Damian White and Chris Wilbert, 1–32. Waterloo, ON: Wilfried Laurier University Press, 2009.

Wilson, Edward. *Half-Earth: Our Planet's Fight for Life.* London: Liferight Publishing, 2016.

WWF. *Living Planet Report 2016.* Gland, Switzerland: WWF, 2016.

Young-Bruehl, Elisabeth. *Why Arendt Matters.* New Haven, CT: Yale University Press, 2006.

Žižek, Slavoj. *Living in the End Times.* London: Verso, 2011.

Zuboff, Shoshana. *The Age of Surveillance Capitalism: The Fight for a Human Future at the New Frontier of Power.* London: Profile Books, 2019.

Index

access and control, politics of: Facebook
    groups and, 128–29; of Kruger National
    Park, 124, 130, 131, 136, 138, 141,
    143, 144; through new/old media, 125,
    128–29; webcams and, 131–32
accountability, 88–89
actor-network theory, 14–15
Adams, William, 204n4
Adorno, Theodor, 66
Africam, 131–32
African Wildlife Foundation, 152
agency, 42, 119, 186n12, 188n50, 190n38;
    false sense of, 102; non-human, 51,
    208n94
Aghassi-Isfahani, Sarah-Nicole, 16, 185n22
Ahmed, Sarah, 164–65
Aikona (Against Interference in Kruger Our
    Nature Asset), 137
algorithms, 19, 178, 179, 194n26, 198n69;
    data and knowledge, 30–31, 63–65, 83;
    Facebook's, 66, 69, 95; Google's, 69, 85;
    truth and, 7, 16, 65–66, 67, 74, 170–71;
    web tracking, 47–48; YouTube's, 145
Amazon (online platform), 25, 26, 68, 77
Amazon (rainforest), 89, 90, 91
ampyourimpact.com, 97
Andrejevic, Mark, 48, 51, 64, 71, 118, 130,
    141, 194n26
animal societies, 150
anti-sealing campaigns, 92–93
Appadurai, Arjun, 204n65

apps, environmental, 100–102
Arendt, Hannah, 10, 28, 76, 174–75,
    213n19; on books as weapons, 213n23;
    on knowledge and understanding,
    22–23, 30, 31, 173, 178; on public life,
    118–19; on truth and power, 187n38
Arsel, Murat, 67
Arvidsson, Adam, 187n45
Association of Zoos and Aquariums (AZA),
    101
Attenborough, Sir David, 45, 191n56
audiences: distractions, 52–53; Dutch, 111;
    fragmentation and nichification of, 48,
    75, 141, 144; global, 100–101; reaching
    or targeting, 43, 54, 55, 57–58, 61, 98,
    103, 152; television, 45–46
AVAAZ, 89

Bagust, Phil, 44
Barnett, Cynthia, 3
BBC Natural History Unit, 43, 45
Beinart, William, 43, 191n44
Bell, Genevieve, 198n3
Benjamin, Walter, 126
biases, 83, 104
Bichler, Shimshon, 197n50
biodiversity, 38, 39, 45, 91, 184n14,
    184n16; commodification of, 78; con-
    servation, 113, 151, 159, 179
biological annihilation, 4, 165, 184n14
bird watching, 94

blockchain technologies, 214nn31,32
blogs, 95, 96, 106, 154; eco-blogging, 93
Bos, Gerard, 39–40
Botswana, 105–6, 110, 112–15, 116, 166,
    201n5, 203n47
Bottici, Chiara, 193n10
Bourdieu, Pierre, 129–30
Bousé, Derek, 44–45, 52, 193n85
Boyd, Danah, 195n27
Branson, Richard, 111, 115, 203n42
Brazilian Friend Finder, 90, 91
Brazilians, 89–90
Brexit, 2, 14
Brigida, Daniella, 95, 96
British empire, 191n44
Brooks, Shirley, 149
Brown, Wendy, 185n27
Butler, G., 134, 205n15

capital: accounted, 195n28; accumulation,
    38, 179, 188n48; definition of, 74; emo-
    tions as, 164; flows or circulation, 107,
    109, 120, 197n50; power and, 7, 25, 31,
    74, 175–76, 180, 197n50; surplus value
    for, 194n11; white South African, 149,
    151. See also natural capital
capitalism, 6, 67, 146, 179, 188n61,
    195n34; communicative, 72, 73; data
    and, 68, 76; the environment under, 74,
    180; global, 25, 26, 122, 127, 188n48,
    208n93; idea of equivalence and, 66,
    195n28; power of, 192n61; sharing
    nature and, 38, 189n15; surveillance,
    6, 187n47, 197n57; uneven geographi-
    cal development of, 25, 38, 77. See also
    platform capitalism
care2.com, 97
Carolan, Michael, 19–20, 42, 186n24,
    191n39
Carruthers, Jane, 125–26, 127
Castree, Noel, 42, 186n24
celebrities, 44, 93, 152, 155–56, 191n56
Chobe National Park, 105, 111, 114
Chris, Cynthia, 43
civic behavior, 54
climate change, 2, 14, 24, 38, 180, 184n14,
    196n44; adaptation and, 210n17; Bran-
    son and, 115, 203n42; climoji symbols
    for, 193n2
#ClimateTruth, 1, 7, 26
Cockle, Adrian, 57–58
cocreation, 47, 54, 61, 69, 128, 141;
    conservation organizations and, 91–92,
    96, 103; of nature, 24, 48–51, 101, 123;

platform, 7, 26, 75, 76, 85, 117, 118;
    politics of, 83, 92, 96, 103, 172; social
    media and, 63, 103; web 2.0 and, 49,
    50, 72, 196n34
colonialism, 43, 115, 191n44
commodities, 30, 164, 195n34; custom-
    izable, 48, 49, 130, 141; images as,
    193n10; nature as, 39, 56, 67
commons, 115, 122, 178, 185n22
commonsense, 29, 40, 175, 177–78, 179,
    181; understanding, 20, 22, 23
community-based programs, 127
concealment of connections, 91, 96
connectivity vs. community, 54, 171, 213n11
conservation: "algorithmization" of, 119;
    boundaries, 144, 208n94; funding flows,
    107; games or apps, 36, 81, 97–98,
    99fig., 100–102, 154; hegemonic strug-
    gles and, 176, 179, 180; intensification
    of development interventions, 116–21;
    mediation and, 42, 46; messages, 62–63,
    91; militarization of, 115, 151, 156–57,
    159; narratives, 92, 178, 204n4; natural
    capital and, 39, 56, 180; platform
    capitalism and, 69–70, 77–78, 82, 123,
    144–45, 172; politics, 82, 90, 93, 102,
    146, 173, 179; privatizing nature and,
    40–41; race and control dynamics,
    148–51, 163–64; of species, 94, 200n38;
    state intervention, 113; of truth, 168–69,
    179; zeal and urgency of, 77, 176. See
    also conservation organizations; fortress
    conservation
conservation 2.0, 77, 82, 90, 102, 103;
    politics of cocreation and, 83, 92; term
    usage, 69–70
conservationevidence.com, 3–4
Conservation International, 2–3, 22, 170;
    wildlife trafficking and, 1, 2fig.
conservation organizations: challenges and
    criticism of, 92–93, 100; daily praxis,
    8–9, 81; digital natureglut and, 47–49,
    96; Global North/South, 199n5; neo-
    liberal vision, 93, 94; sharing truths
    about nature, 1–2, 83, 92, 96; sup-
    porters, 43, 45, 48–49, 50–51, 55, 62,
    95; use of social media, 57–60, 62–63,
    83–91, 94–96, 102–3
consumption, 48, 49, 130, 141; of narratives,
    53, 54; sign, 195n34
control, losing/taking: new media and emo-
    tions and, 147–48, 162–63; race and,
    148–51, 163–64. See also access and
    control, politics of

COVID-19 pandemic, 184n14
Cox, Chris, 197n51
Crawford, Kate, 166, 195n27
critical theory, 13, 19, 177, 188n61
Cronon, William, 41
crowdsourcing, 105, 107, 108, 110, 120
culture-jamming, 93
customization, 54, 69, 75, 76; of commodity subjects, 48, 49, 130, 141; to individual preferences, 55, 123

data, 6, 24, 83, 197n57; Big Data, 185n23, 185n28, 195n27; capitalism and, 68, 170; commodification of, 7, 31; knowledge and algorithms, 30–31, 63–65; in Marxian terms, 30; post-truth and, 76; social media, 86
Dean, Jodi, 72, 73
death of nature, 65, 67
Debord, Guy, 61
Department of Environmental Affairs (DEA), South African, 128, 146
DeSmog UK, 196n44
Deuze, Mark, 187n45
development cooperation, 108, 117
digital economy, 73, 76
digital natureglut, 25, 50, 72, 83, 91, 122, 179; conservation organizations and, 54–55, 60, 62, 96, 101, 102, 103; term usage, 24, 47–49
Dimas, Stavros, 38
dispossession, 148–49, 164, 173, 188n61
distinction, politics of, 143–44, 145, 169, 209n94; Latest Sightings and, 140–41; new media and, 124–25, 129–30
documentaries. See films
Dodson, Giles, 16
"doing good" online, 69, 107–10, 201n9; contradictions of, 121–22; intensification and politics of, 117–21
donors/donations, 59–60, 100, 105–6, 165; Peace Parks Foundations, 111, 115
double alienation, 55
Dourish, Paul, 198n3
Duffy, Rosaleen, 158–59

ecogamer.org, 100
ecological crisis. See environmental crisis
ecological search engines, 97
"Economics of Ecosystems and Biodiversity, The" (TEEB), 38–39
ecosearch.org, 97
ecosia.org, 97
elephant 2.0, 120–21

elephants, 27, 184n14, 187n45; "liquid" idea of, 120–21; Pifworld corridor project, 105–7, 110–13, 115–16, 172, 201n5; poaching, 114, 115, 161; post-truth action, 121–22
emotions: attachment, 44, 94; reactions to rhino-poaching crisis, 146–48, 151, 154–63; role of social media, 164–65; sentiment, 141; of webcam viewers, 131–32
#EndangeredEmoji, 57–58, 58fig., 62
endangered species, 57–58, 62, 77, 155
environmental crisis, 4, 14, 18, 24, 27, 77; alleviating, 171, 214n34; post-truth conundrum of, 167, 176; responsibility for, 6, 7; sharing truths and natures and, 8, 38, 180
environmental indicators, 1–2, 183n2, 184n16
environmentalism, 42, 76, 77, 83, 166, 176, 177; challenges to, 2–3; natural capital and, 73; origins of, 43; technonatural forms of, 51. See also conservation; spectacular environmentalism
environmentalists, 56, 81, 95, 180; everyday praxis of, 27–28; post-truth and, 37, 166; truth about nature and, 3–4, 20, 21, 22, 38, 146, 167, 174; use of online platforms, 7, 25, 29, 35–36. See also conservation organizations
environmental politics, 72, 166, 191n56; platform capitalism and, 6, 9, 10, 16, 27, 29; truth tensions and, 13, 18, 26; web 2.0 and, 25, 49
equivalence and difference, 66–67, 195n28
evidence-based action, 4, 184n12, 184n21
exchange value, 30
extinction: rhino, 41, 148, 154, 166; sixth, 3, 6, 165, 184n14; species, 36, 57, 155
Extinction Rebellion, 3, 9

Facebook, 1, 35, 52, 74, 84, 120, 196n36, 200n48; antipolitical positionality, 194n23; anti-rhino poaching groups, 128, 133–35, 153–54, 157, 158, 159–62; average time spent on, 64, 194n18; Cambridge Analytica scandal, 196n38; capitalism and, 26; decentralization dependency, 201n64; free speech and, 75, 197n51; frequency of posting, 95–96; games, 97–98, 101; internet.org initiative, 197n54; intimacy and, 94; like/dislike button, 66, 103, 201n64; for meaningful engagement, 86–87, 91; for political action, 90 fact: algorithms and, 64, 65; alternative *vs.* actual, 2, 3; compared to truth, 20–21, 23, 214n31; construction of, 50; experimental, 16; power and, 187n38; sharing, 1–2, 7, 37

#FactsOfWildlife, 1, 4, 7, 20, 26, 50, 96

Farman, Jason, 187n45, 198n2

films, 90, 150, 156–57, 193n85; mediation of nature and, 52–53, 191n52; YouTube wildlife, 52–53, 128–29

Fletcher, Robert, 102, 176

fortress conservation: central tenets of, 204n4; dispossession and, 149; Kruger National Park as, 124–25, 126–31, 132, 134–35, 208n93; Latest Sightings and, 141, 142–43, 144; SANParks Forums and, 137–38, 144

Foster, Don, 151

Foucault, Michel, 10, 20, 28, 176; on truth and power, 17–18, 70, 103, 167, 168–69

Fowlds, William, 153, 154, 157, 209n2

Frankfurt, Harry, 5, 20, 21, 75, 167, 170

Fraser, Caroline, 36

Friedman, Thomas, 65

Fujimura, Joan, 15

game reserves, 114, 126, 132; Hluhluwe, 149; Kariega, 154, 157

gamesfornature.org, 100

games/game apps: conservation, 81, 97–98, 99*fig.*, 100–102, 154; on molleindustria.org, 93

Gerlitz, Carolin, 201n64

Ghostery, 47, 199n6

Gillespie, Tarleton, 198n69

Giraud, Eva Haifa, 16, 185n22, 186n23

Gitelman, Lisa, 41–43

givengain.com, 69, 108

global community, 100, 101, 103

Goldman, Robert, 119, 195n34

Goodman, Michael, 46, 192n61

Google, 26, 74, 75, 98; Kruger National Park on, 123, 204n2; search results, 85, 95–96; tracking, 47; ubiquity of, 68–69, 196n35

Gough, Mark, 73–74

governance systems, 113, 131, 132, 143

Greater Good South Africa, 108

"green militarization," 125, 133, 166, 184n14; rhino poaching and, 124, 127, 147, 151, 159

Greenpeace, 89–90

Gros, Frédéric, 18

Han, Byung-Chul, 6, 185n23, 185n28, 196n36

Hardy, Tom, 156–57

Harry, Prince, 155

Harvey, David, 25, 28, 197n50

Hawken, Paul, 36

Hawkins, Roberta, 92–93

hegemony: challenging, 8, 29, 30–31, 174, 177, 179; power and truth, 18, 19, 169, 180–81; struggles of, 175–76, 180

Heise, Ursula, 184n16, 200n38

Helmond, Anne, 201n64

heroism, 147, 155–58, 163

hierarchies, 137, 143, 144; of fortress conservation, 125, 129, 130

Hillis, Ken, 192n76

Holmes, Christopher, 15

Horkheimer, Max, 66

Hughes, David, 149, 209n11

Hughes, Lotte, 191n44

human nature, 6, 24, 41

Humphreys, Jaspar, 159, 164, 209n13

hysteria: definition, 147, 154, 155; politics of, 100, 147–48, 162–65, 172; truth discourses and, 165–66

#IAm4Rhinos, 152

Igoe, Jim, 51, 61, 96

images: consuming mediated, 51, 71, 118; fortress conservation, 141; of Kruger National Park, 126, 127; of nature, 61, 62, 191n44, 193n10

individualization, 7, 50, 53–54

infoglut, 48, 91, 100. *See also* digital natureglut

infrastructures, 68, 75, 76, 93

International Anti-Poaching Foundation, 156

International Cooperation 2.0, 108, 117

International Union for Conservation of Nature (IUCN), 39

internet access, 128, 197n54, 198n5

Internet of Elephants, 100–101

intimacy, creating, 94

IPM (interaction per mile), 86

Iyengar, Shanto, 213n7

Jasanoff, Sheila, 26

Jeffries, Michael, 45

Kafue National Park, 105, 111, 114

Kang, Jaeho, 54

Kavango Zambezi Transfrontier Conservation Area (KAZA TFCA), 110, 112–14

Kepe, Thembela, 113, 163

Klein, Naomi, 36, 54, 203n42

knowledge: claims, 15; construction of, 29, 31, 177, 179; data and algorithms and,

Index | 235

30–31, 63–65, 74, 96, 170–71; facts and, 20; meaningful, 23; of nature, 20, 21; scientific, 16, 22, 173; shifting forms of, 13; sociology of, 14, 16; and understanding, 22–23, 173, 177–78
Kotze, Dex, 35–36, 54
Kruger, Paul, 125
Kruger 2.0, 127–28, 145
Kruger National Park (KNP): annual braai, 136; Facebook group, 132–35, 206n43, 206n50; Google Street View of, 123, 204n2; "green militarization" in, 159; history and representations of, 125–27, 130, 143–44, 208n94; Latest Sightings service, 138–43, 144, 145; local communities, 143, 144, 208n90; material natures in, 173; new media and politics of distinction, 128–31, 140–41, 143–44; rhino-poaching crisis, 127, 150–51, 205n18, 208n93; sharing truths and natures of, 28, 123–25; social order and, 137–38, 141; tourists, 62–63, 125, 129; white belonging and control, 149–51
Kuntsman, Adi, 164–65

land tenure, 113–14
#LastSelfie campaign, 58, 59fig., 60, 62, 95, 96, 103
Latestsightings.com, 139–43, 144–45, 208n93
Latour, Bruno, 5, 17, 167, 185n22, 186n14; actor-network theory, 14–15
ledger systems, 214n31
Lee, Peter, 15
Levitt, James N., 92
lies/liars, 17, 66, 70–71, 75–76
Like economy, 201n64
Limits to Growth (1972), 184n14
Lovink, Geert, 153, 194n16
Lunstrum, Elizabeth, 159

Mabunda, David, 137
Madigele, Patricia, 166
Maguranyanga, Brian, 144
#MakeEarthGreatAgain, 82
Malm, Andreas, 186n23
Mandela, Nelson, 110–11, 116
Mander, Damien, 156
Marazzi, Christian, 186n25
Marris, Noortje, 16
Marx, Karl, 10, 19, 26, 28, 30
Massey, Douglas, 213n7
MAVA Foundation, 106
McCann, Niall, 166
McKeown, Katie, 43

meaningful/meaningless engagement, 21, 22–23, 86–87, 175–76, 180, 213n23
media: definition, 41–43; older and new, 46–47, 56, 192n63; types, 44, 52. See also new media platforms; social media
mediation: of information, 75, 197n52; of Kruger National Park, 125–29; of nature, 41–46, 55, 67, 191n39; of relationships, 61, 62, 96, 142, 143; technological, 119
Merchant, Carolyn, 67
Metcalfe, Simon, 113
Mitman, Gregg, 43, 55–56
Mogomotsi, Goemeone, 166
Monbiot, George, 180, 214n34
Montaigne, 70–71
Moore, Donald, 149
Moore, Jason, 25
Mosse, David, 116–17
Mouffe, Chantal, 29, 174–75, 176, 188n52, 213n19
My Conservation Park (game), 98, 101, 103
My Green World, 100, 101, 103

Namibia Nature Foundation (NNF), 114
Namibian Caprivi Strip, 105, 111, 114
narratives, 44–45, 52–54, 56, 71; of speaking truth to power, 178–79, 181
natural capital, 38, 66, 173, 180, 195n28; concepts and language of, 39–40, 73–74, 175; truth regime on, 56, 70, 73
Natural Capital Coalition, 39, 73
nature (general): colonial, 191n44; commodification of, 39, 56, 67; definitions of, 19–20, 24, 42, 186nn24,25, 191n39; getting back to, 41; images of, 61, 62, 191n44, 193n10; local connections to, 91; material, 51, 173; mediation of, 41–46, 55, 126, 191n39; offline, 49, 51, 67, 82, 107, 173; online, 24, 47–49, 51, 55, 115, 118; ownership and privatizing, 37–38, 40–41, 189n10; power and truth relations, 19–22, 73; social construction of, 21; value of, 39, 66, 73–74. See also sharing nature
nature 2.0, 46, 55, 60, 68, 78, 129, 192n76; cocreated, 24, 50–51, 118; elephant 2.0 and, 121; initiatives, 106; intensification dynamics and, 117, 118, 119; Kruger's, 142; main categories of, 97; natures in, 51–52; saving offline natures and, 82, 173; use of, 25, 28; worldwide web of, 83, 97, 107
Nature Conservancy, 7, 47, 49, 50, 93, 192n72

natureglut. *See* digital natureglut
Nature Needs Half, 3, 9, 165
#NatureNow, 180
Nealon, Jeffrey, 176
Nelson, Robert, 77
neoliberalism, 93, 94, 177, 185n27, 200n39
Netherlands, 86, 91, 111
netizens, 24, 49–50, 108, 117–18, 133
networks, 69, 109; power of, 15, 17, 36, 191n53
Neumann, Roderick, 151
new materialism, 186n12, 186n23
new media platforms: algorithms and data processing, 63–65, 76, 119; cocreation of, 49–51, 75–76, 141; content screening, 188n57; for doing good, 69, 107–10; for effecting offline change, 89–92; environmental actors and, 7–8, 9, 29, 35–36, 188n1; everyday praxis and, 27–28; forms of distinctions and, 129–30, 169; global capitalism and, 26, 188n48; hysteria and, 147–48, 162–63; Kruger National Park and, 123–25, 128–29, 143–44; narratives and, 52–54; natural capital and, 74; network effects of, 69; politics, 72, 75, 107, 117, 120, 121–22; power of, 8, 9, 18, 36–37, 77, 171; for sharing truths and nature, 6, 7, 23, 24–25, 28, 37, 60, 171; sign values, 68, 195n34; spectacular environmentalisms and, 46–47, 56, 61. *See also* platform capitalism; social media
new media studies, 187n45, 189n1
Nitzan, Jonathan, 197n50
nudge.nl, 97

offline/online dynamics: disconnect in, 116; distinction, 70, 81, 82, 83, 187n45, 198nn2,3; effecting change and, 89–91, 102; of elephant conservation, 106–7, 121; of rhino-poaching crisis, 148, 159, 165; sharing or saving nature, 25, 28, 67, 98, 147, 173; truths, 107, 121
1% Club, 108, 117, 118
online discussions: echo chambers and, 153, 194n16; monitoring, 86, 162; on rhino-poaching crisis, 133, 154, 160–62; SANParks Forums for, 135–38
ontology, 42, 65, 185n12, 185n22, 186n23; society and, 188n52; of wilderness, 102
Oosterbaan, Gregg, 101
Oreskes, Naomi, 16
Ossendryver, Nadav, 138–40, 139*fig.*, 141–42

Ostrom, Elinor, 189n15
Outraged South African Citizens Against Poaching (OSCAP), 128, 133, 153, 154, 158, 162, 210n43

Palliser, Anna, 16
pangolins, 1, 2*fig.*
Papacharissi, Zizi, 46, 54
Papson, Stephen, 119
Pasquale, Frank, 197n52
Pay It Forward (film), 119
Peace Parks Foundation (PPF), 110–11, 112, 114–15
Peluso, Nancy, 77
petitions, 89–90
Pettman, Dominic, 30–31, 52, 187n45
Pickerill, Jenny, 200n31
Pifworld, 69, 202n10; elephant corridor project, 105–7, 110–13, 115–16, 122, 201n5; idea behind, 108–9; intensification dynamics, 117–19; public relations and marketing, 120
Pistorius, Oscar, 212n90
platform capitalism: conservation and, 69–70, 77–78, 82, 123, 144–45, 172; environmental politics and, 9, 10, 16, 37; hegemonic power and, 8, 175–76; political economy and, 7, 26–27, 61, 66, 67, 78, 109, 122; politics of hysteria and, 148, 166; post-capitalist platforms and, 179–81; post-truth and power under, 26, 30–31, 60, 70–72, 75–76, 107, 121, 148, 169–70, 174; rise and power of, 68–70, 72–74, 145, 170; sharing of truths and natures and, 56, 96, 171; term usage, 6, 25–26, 187n47
Player, Ian, 62, 63
poachers, 98, 114, 115, 153, 156; death of, 151, 159–62, 165. *See also* rhino-poaching crisis
Poaching Wars with Tom Hardy, The (film), 156–57
political action, 54, 89–91, 199n31
political ecology, 19, 24, 107, 204n3; media studies and, 187n45; posthumanist, 208n94; of truth, 10, 16–17, 169
political economy, 37, 93, 148, 185n22; apartheid, 126, 127; capitalist, 25, 56, 61, 66, 67, 73, 178, 214n31; cocreation and, 51; of colonialism, 43; everyday praxis and, 9, 19, 28; of Kruger National Park, 143–44; mediation of nature and, 46, 55; of platform capitalism, 7, 26, 78, 82, 122, 144, 171; power and, 6,

16, 26–27, 73, 74, 130, 173, 188n52;
of sign values, 68; of South Africa,
151, 164
political shifts, 195n28
politics and "the political," 174–75, 188n52
Poovey, Mary, 20
positionality, 21, 23, 64, 149, 194n23,
214n31
post-capitalist platforms, 8, 10, 179–81
post-truth: contemporary discourses,
16–17; conundrum, 3, 15, 37, 167, 176;
countering, 3, 4, 6, 22, 23, 37, 166, 171;
emergence of, 7, 14, 25; meaninglessness
and stupidity and, 175; politics, 5–6,
9, 10, 16, 72; as power under platform
capitalism, 6, 26, 30–31, 60, 70–72,
75–76, 107, 121, 148, 169–70; shared
reality and, 171, 178; sharing truths and
natures and, 19, 23
power: capitalist, 21, 25, 31, 40, 66, 67;
confronting and transcending, 169,
174, 176; factual truth and, 187n38;
Foucault on truth and, 17–18, 70, 103,
167, 168–69; nature and truth relations,
19–22, 38–40, 72; of networks, 15, 17,
36, 191n53; of new media technologies,
36–37; platform, 8, 9, 77, 171, 214n31;
political economy and, 6, 16, 26–27, 73,
74, 130, 173, 188n52; post-truth as an
expression of, 6, 7, 26, 30–31, 70–72,
107, 148, 169–70; structural, 9, 19,
26–27, 28, 52, 169, 173, 213n7; truth
claims and, 13, 15, 23, 31, 184n21. See
also speaking truth to power
praxis, everyday, 30, 104, 117; conservation
organizations and, 8–9, 81; political
economy and, 9, 19, 23, 173; of saving
nature, 78, 158, 172; shifting politics of,
27–28, 168
private ownership, 37, 40–41
Proctor, James, 21–22
profitability, 7, 64, 75, 76, 145, 148
prosumption, 49–50, 54, 118, 196n34,
202n10. See also cocreation

racialization, 100, 169, 209n94; community
and, 141–42; control and belonging
dynamics, 148–52, 163–64; park
management and, 144; rhino-poaching
crisis and, 157, 159, 163; SANParks
Forums and, 136–38; sharing Kruger
natures and, 123–24, 126–27, 145
rainforests, 89–90
Ramutsindela, Maano, 159

rangers, 91, 135–36, 157–58, 161
realization labor, 196n34
representations, 42, 45, 51; of Kruger
National Park, 126–27, 128, 129, 130,
143–44; symbolic, 64, 170
Reputation Defender, 85
resource extraction, 24, 184n14
rhino 2.0, 165
rhino horn trade, 146, 152, 153, 164
Rhino Orphanage, 157
rhino-poaching crisis: heroism and violence
of, 147–48, 155–62; in Kruger National
Park, 28, 62–63, 127, 128, 150–51,
205n18; politics of hysteria, 100, 147,
162–65; private ownership and, 40–41;
public outcry, 146–47; race and control
aspects, 150–51, 163–64; social media
campaigns and online platforms for, 98,
99fig., 128, 133–35, 152–54
Rhino Raid (game), 98, 99fig., 103, 154
Rhino Rescue Project, 162–63
Richardson, S., 134, 205n15
Rijsdijk, Ian-Malcolm, 129
Rocking for Rhinos, 156, 163
Rousseff, Dilma, 90
Rouvroy, Antoinette, 30, 64–65
RuneScape (game), 154
Rupert, Anton, 111

Sandbrook, Chris, 102
Save Our Rhino, 128, 154
saving nature: everyday praxis of, 78, 172;
offline, 28, 30, 82, 98, 173, 187n45;
online, 7, 9, 29, 47, 65, 121, 152–54,
158, 179; under platform capitalism, 37,
52, 77; sharing and, 38, 148
science: disbelief in, 2–3, 22, 170; facts and,
50; material nature and, 173; natural
history and, 45, 56; and truths, 3–4, 55,
70, 82; wars, 15
science and technology studies (STS), 14,
15–16, 26, 185n12
search for truth, 10, 28, 104, 187n35,
188n61; continuous need to, 13, 22, 31,
104, 168; truth tensions and, 168–69
second nature, 50
Sekute Community Development Trust, 114
#Selfie campaign, 92–93
Shapin, Steven, 21, 70–71, 103
shared realities, 2, 25, 30, 181; creating, 28,
54; truth and post-truth, 23, 76, 119,
171, 175
sharing nature: capitalist power and, 38–40,
73–74; of cocreated natures, 101, 123;

sharing nature (*continued*)
conservation organizations and, 83, 103;
contradictions of, 40–41, 55, 67, 77; of
Kruger natures, 123–25, 129, 130, 143;
meaning and examples, 37–38, 55, 56;
offline, 25, 67; online, 47–48, 49, 60, 65,
67, 92, 104, 121–22, 148; and truths,
19, 24–25, 37, 55, 72–73, 96, 172, 174,
180; web searches and, 47–48
sign values, 62, 68, 69, 195n34
Silent Heroes Foundation, 158
Silver, Jennifer, 92–93
Simalaha Community Conservancy, 113–14
Simmet, Hilton, 26
Smith, Michael, 159, 164, 209n13
Smith, Neil, 177
Snapchat, 35, 58–59
social media: algorithms, 16, 64; capitalism and, 26; changing trends, 94–96;
conservation campaigns, 35–36, 57–60,
189n6, 193n2; creativity and originality of, 92, 96, 103; for effecting change,
89–92, 199n31; rhino-poaching crisis
and, 62–63, 128, 133–35, 146–47,
152–54, 164–65; rise and professionalization of, 83–87, 132; for sharing
truths and nature, 16, 23–24, 27–28, 37,
60, 65. *See also* Facebook; new media
platforms; Twitter
social order, 21, 71, 142; fortress conservation and, 125, 130, 141; in Kruger
National Park, 137–38, 143–44; SAN-
Parks Forums and, 138
social reality, 14–15, 30
social theory, 18, 168, 185n12
sociology of knowledge, 14, 16
socio-natural relations, 51, 77–78
South Africa, 111, 138, 145, 168, 172;
apartheid, 124, 126–27, 150, 163;
national parks, 127, 149; race and
control dynamics, 149, 151, 163–64;
rhino-poaching crisis, 146–48, 152–54,
157, 212n88; Soweto township, 134,
205n15; white gun culture, 212n90. *See
also* Kruger National Park (KNP)
South African National Parks (SANParks),
127, 129, 154–55, 165; Facebook group,
132–35; forums, 131, 135–38, 140, 144
speaking truth to power, 26, 31, 71, 72,
188n52; challenging hegemony and, 29,
30, 174, 177; confronting capitalism
and, 179; rekindling the art of, 8, 10,
18–19, 168, 169, 176; understanding
and, 177–78, 181

spectacular environmentalism, 53, 63, 96,
107, 122; de-politicization and, 192n61;
idea of, 46–47; intensification of, 47, 56,
61, 76; Kruger National Park as, 141, 142
Srnicek, Nick, 6, 25, 73, 75; on data and
capitalism, 68, 76, 170; on data and
knowledge, 63, 76
Steyn, Melissa, 151
Stinson, James, 102
storytelling. *See* narratives
structural change, 10, 122, 169, 170, 213n7
stupidity, 175
subject-objects, 119–20, 121
Sukhdev, Pavan, 39
Sullivan, Sian, 195n28
Sundberg, Juanita, 208n94
surveillance, 185n23; capitalism, 6, 187n47,
197n57
Svarstad, Hanne, 19
Swyngedouw, Erik, 29, 208n94

Tails Up!, 101
technonatures, 51–52, 78
TEEB ("The Economics of Ecosystems and
Biodiversity"), 38–39
television programs, 45
Thin Green Line Foundation, 158
Thunberg, Greta, 180, 214n34
Tinnell, John, 93
totalitarianism, 175, 178
tourism: Kruger National Park, 62–63, 125,
129, 140, 143; SANParks, 134; South
Africa, 149, 151, 164, 209n13
Tracebuzz, 85–86
true and false statements, 18, 20, 70–71, 75
Trump, Donald, 2, 26, 70, 194n23
truth (general): "about nature" concept, 3,
4–5, 9, 38–39, 69, 92–94, 124, 173–76;
commonsense, 20, 179; compared to
facts, 20–21, 23; construction of, 71; context and history and, 172–73; disinterest
in, 50; divergent, 107; finding, 21, 22;
Foucault on, 17–18, 70, 103, 158, 167,
168–69; indifference to, 5, 167; kernels,
180–81; knowledge and, 30, 64, 65, 76,
96, 170–71, 175; offline *vs.* online, 107,
121; political ecology and, 10, 16–17,
169; power and nature relations, 19–22;
profitability and, 7; wars, 13, 14, 15, 18,
31, 174, 213n18. *See also* post-truth;
search for truth; speaking truth to power
truth claims, 10, 13, 14, 31, 180, 184n21;
deconstructing, 5, 71, 168; knowledge
claims and, 15

truth discourses, 170, 176, 178, 180; hero
vs. villain, 155–56, 158, 159, 165;
Kruger National Park, 148, 209n94;
politics of hysteria and, 165–66
truth tensions: metaphysics of, 5, 10, 13–14,
168, 179; politics of, 26, 31, 173–74,
176; power of, 17–19; searching for the
truth and, 168–69; term usage, 22, 28;
truth wars and, 14, 15, 18, 174, 213n18
Twitter, 1, 31, 35, 75, 85, 90, 120, 200n48;
capitalism and, 26; compared to Facebook, 91; creative hashtags, 92–93; factchecking, 194n23; frequency of posting,
95–96; The Panda Bare, 93; rhino-
poaching crisis on, 152–53; Twelephants
campaign, 106; @TwitterGood, 201n9;
WWF followers, 59, 60, 62, 86

ubiquitous computing, 198n3
understanding: commonsense, 20, 29, 175;
environmental politics and, 10, 16;
holistic, 177, 187n35; journey toward,
29, 31, 175–76, 177, 180; knowledge
and, 22–23, 30, 173; meaningful, 21, 22;
of reality, 171; truth and, 15, 17, 18, 23,
56, 169, 177–78, 181
uneven geographical development, 25, 38, 77
United For Wildlife, 155–56, 158
universality, 21

Van Dijck, José, 54, 117
violence, 147, 151, 155, 158–63, 166,
213n23. See also "green militarization"
Virtual Ecotourism, 189n6
virtual reality, 97, 192n76
Visser, Lieneke Eloff de, 114

Wajcman, Gérard, 150
Wajcman, Judy, 64, 95
Ward, Steven, 14–15
web 2.0, 24, 25, 51, 97, 119, 192n76,
194n11; cocreation or prosumption and,
49, 50, 72, 118, 196n34; conservation
organizations and, 198n4; development
cooperation causes, 108, 117; political

action and, 54; virtual-material interactions, 125
webcams, 97, 100, 131–32, 143
web tracking, 47–48, 85–86, 199n6
Weeks, Priscilla, 45
Weiser, Mark, 198n3
Werbach, Kevin, 214n31
West, Paige, 184n19, 188n61
What Works in Conservation 2017, 3–4
white belonging, 149–51, 163–64
Whitfield, Bruce, 141–42
#WhoseSideAreYouOn, 155, 163, 190n32
wilderness: African, 126, 138, 149–50;
estates, 149; experience, 126; recreation,
102
WilderQuest, 189n6
wildlife: cams, 131–32, 143; charities, 155;
crime, 1, 24, 184n14, 190n32; damage,
113; films, 43–44, 52–53, 128–29,
191n52, 193n85; management, 149n13,
159; parks, 106, 108, 110, 129; protection, 156–58, 166; sightings, 138–42;
trafficking, 1, 2fig.
William, Prince, 41, 155, 190n32
Wilmore, Sean, 158
Wired magazine, 76
World Conservation Congress (Hawaii), 39
World Parks Congress (2014), 36, 115
World Wide Fund for Nature (WWF): anti-
rhino poaching campaign, 98, 152–53,
154; #EndangeredEmoji campaign,
57–58, 58fig., 62; #LastSelfie campaign,
58–60, 59fig., 62, 95, 96, 103; supporters and followers, 86, 91

YouTube, 52–53; "Battle at Kruger" video,
128–29; Latest Sightings channel, 138,
139fig., 145

Zambia, 105–6, 110, 111–15, 201n5
Zimbabwe, 149, 209n11
Žižek, Slavoj, 150
Zuboff, Shoshana, 6, 187n47, 196n35,
197n57
Zuckerberg, Mark, 194n23

Founded in 1893,
UNIVERSITY OF CALIFORNIA PRESS
publishes bold, progressive books and journals
on topics in the arts, humanities, social sciences,
and natural sciences—with a focus on social
justice issues—that inspire thought and action
among readers worldwide.

The UC PRESS FOUNDATION
raises funds to uphold the press's vital role
as an independent, nonprofit publisher, and
receives philanthropic support from a wide
range of individuals and institutions—and from
committed readers like you. To learn more, visit
ucpress.edu/supportus.